AGAINST THE GRAIN: A 1950s MEMOIR

E.A. MARKHAM

AGAINST THE GRAIN

A 1950s MEMOIR

PEEPAL TREE

First published in Great Britain in 2008
Peepal Tree Press Ltd
17 King's Avenue
Leeds LS6 1QS
UK

ISBN13: 9781845230258

Peepal Tree gratefully acknowledges Arts Council support

CONTENTS

ACKNOWLEDGEMENTS

Grateful thanks to members of the family, to Norman and Julie who have checked early versions of this text and corrected inaccuracies, and to Joe and Gwen (niece) who have provided additional information.

Thanks to Peter Fraser, who also read the text and made (improving) suggestions of a literary kind; and to Jeremy Poynting and Hannah Bannister of Peepal Tree for their continued editorial support.

A more generalized form of recognition should go to (Sir) Howard Fergus whose books on Montserrat, including his own Memoir, *Road from Long Ground* – triggered lots of memories.

Acknowledgements are due to *Ambit* magazine where part of 'Death in the House' first appeared under the title of 'Horace, a Wonder of the World', and to *Wasafiri* for first publishing 'Making Ladies Belts in Great Portland Street' and 'Talent Spotting at the Finsbury Park Empire'. A fuller version of 'Oswald Mosley at the Front Door' appeared as 'The Mosley Connection' in the short story collection, *Meet Me in Mozambique* (Tindal Street Press, 2005).

PREFACE: A TALE OF THREE HOUSES

The second was the house on Bevington Road, Ladbroke Grove. It was an unlucky house in a quiet street in West London, and it still makes me uneasy to write about it. Semi-detached because the street had suffered war-damage and a new primary school had been set down on one side. The house to which it was attached, the one on the corner of Goldbourne Road, the main street with chemist, small shops, etc. – an old church of some kind – was occupied by a declared fascist.

My mother acquired the house some months after we arrived in this country in 1956. (We being my mother, my sister and myself: both my elder brothers had already been here for a couple of years.) My mother had vowed never to live in a house in England that wasn't her own, and had managed it within a shortish time of her coming over. It wasn't just pride at work there, reflecting her status 'at home', it was also fear of the NO COLOURED signs that we had long read about in the West Indies, and had witnessed, from time to time, in London. (Having said that, the months of rented accommodation in Maida Vale (the Harrow Road end) and Goldney Road (next to a bomb site but where the English family in the next flat invited us to come in and watch the television) seemed fairly painless: we got ourselves into all sorts of mental tangles in deciding what programmes – what *sorts* of programme it was politic to express a desire to see. I seem to remember that it turned out to be the news, mainly.)

Our next-door neighbour at Bevington Road – the one off-Ladbroke Grove – was Geoffrey Hamm, Oswald Mosley's 'right hand man'. But before we come to Geoffrey Hamm, there was the problem with our builders. The house was bought from a man called Jimmy Forde, and had a structural fault. A couple of Irish brothers were engaged to deal with the repairs and that took a long time. There was a dangerous crack down the front of the building and it was propped up with huge wooden strut. It proved to be an unlucky house.

The third house, not a family house, was in Shepherds Bush. It was in Elsham Road, the back entrance onto the busy Holland Road. By then (well into the '60s, after university) I was with people who felt sophisticated enough to identify with the more down-market Shepherds Bush, and not hanker for Holland Park status. (Up there you occasionally ran into people you saw on the television, emerging from Holland Park underground – Anthony Howard, Tony Benn …) The house was owned by John Elsom, the theatre critic and Sally Mays, the concert pianist; and sheltered an assortment of people on the edge of the arts. I had a room upstairs, and wrote to the sound of the piano drifting up from two floors below.

Elsham Road was a sort of arts laboratory where the making of music, poetry and drama defined your claim to interest. John Elsom once confided to me, 'It doesn't matter if you can't pay the rent, if you're writing well.' After that, it was important to demonstrate that one *was* writing well. There was a sort of competition for, if not excellence, at least *newness* at Elsham Road. John wrote non-naturalistic plays and taught a course on theatre at the City Literary Institute; and led the play-writing group of which I was a member. There were performances at various Further Education venues, where some of us taught, and in the open-plan, living-dining-kitchen space downstairs that housed Sally's grand piano. The music from Sally and her group, The Mouth of Hermes – atonal stuff from John Cage and Stockhausen and Ichiyanagi and Morton Feldman – challenged us, writers, not to be conventional.

The first house was, of course, in Montserrat in the Eastern Caribbean, then as now, a British colony, then as now, proud of its Britishness. This particular house, the family home in Harris' (pronounced Harrises) on the east of the island, was where I grew up, effectively alone with my grandmother, until I was eleven, when I went to the Grammar School in Plymouth, the capital, and became more part of the household of which my mother was head.

The house in Harris' – all twelve rooms of it – though long gone, is the one none of us has been able to shake off, completely. For some it was a symbol of status and good living. Others are simply nostalgic for the rituals of the time, which the house symbolized: the baking of bread and cakes on a Saturday, being the social centre of village life, having the animal pound on the other side of the back yard, leading to frequent 'auctions' of animals that the owners failed to recover. These auctions were presided over by my grandmother and we, children, were sometimes allowed to participate. Significantly – we weren't allowed to forget this – the house was important because the original structure was erected after 1834, the year of the abolition of slavery, so that my grandmother's mother would be born in a house uncontaminated by slavery.[1] The house was added to in my time – and I never thought, as a lad of, say, eight, when effectively sharing it with my grandmother who was eighty, that it was too large for us.

Much of my life since has been to lay claim to, or to try to make sense of these three houses.

Notes

1. This was somewhat fanciful. It was one of my grandmother's stories to me. The house was built later, sometime in the 1860s. But it must have made emotional sense, for the family, subsequently, in England, spent a fortune trying to preserve this 'family home' which had remained empty since our departure, in 1956.

PART ONE

OVER THERE

CHAPTER ONE
GOING EAST WITH OBEAHMAN, 1997

I was going east, and apparently no one went east. Too dangerous. I was fed-up with being cossetted; so I was quite psyched up to be going into the danger zone, against the advice of everyone. The man who promised to take me was called 'Obeahman'. I liked that. And we were to set out at five o'clock in the morning. Nice.

I was up and dressed before light. (I was staying alone, in a villa of a friend of a friend, and enjoyed the sensation of being on the edge of the safe zone, at Salem.) I was an hour early. I went into the kitchen and made a cup of tea, relieved that the huge cockroach that had lodged itself under the draining tray had now vanished. So it was easier making a cup of tea now than it had been in the middle of the night. (One cockroach unnerving a man my age!) I was still a bit concerned where the cockroach might have got to, prompting me to rinse the cup with extra care. This was foolish: I put it down to years of living in England making me unfit for a robust life. (Several members of the family, not only my mother, admit to being queasy about insect and 'yard' life in the house.)

I was still slightly disorientated from the visit to Teacher Morgan the day before: I had gone up to the Sunshine Home, just down from the relocated university centre, a splendid building put up by the Red Cross. I couldn't share the confidence of a new building. The volcanic mountain was still on the move, two-thirds of the island out of bounds and everyone was being driven north, forced into a narrower and narrower strip of what was traditionally considered one of the less fashionable parts of Montserrat: how could they have the confidence to erect a building like that in this climate of instability! It put me in mind of the bright, new library that had been built in the capital, Plymouth, when I last visited – certainly the most attractive public building on the island. Then the volcano had struck and the library, like the rest of the capital, had had to be abandoned. The library was now invisible under tons of ash: it had never been officially opened.

So, I was still thinking about yesterday's visit to Teacher Morgan:

As I walked down the wide gallery running along the front of the building, looking down on the new government development at Brades, I'd felt stupidly out of place. The residents were lined up along the wall in what seemed to be a lot of wheelchairs, some looking vaguely out towards the sea. I was glad that Teacher Morgan wasn't among them; I wanted him to be more alert, not part of the set. With him there I couldn't have risked the careful Good Afternoons and Howdys and nods, or even the few words I managed to say to the woman I thought I recognized. But at least the place had nothing of the fug or staleness that one was tempted to associate with these institutions. It was a relief when I was shown into Teacher Morgan's (private) room to find that I was still in the presence of my old teacher, at 89, razor-sharp, as they say, and with total recall.

Still early at the villa, waiting for Obeahman. I had some cheese and biscuits, crackers – lodged secure in the fridge – and went back into the bedroom and decided to change my clothes, into something less touristy, more fitting for the trip, much of which would be wading in ash or scrambling through bush. I picked up the book I'd been reading last night; Ian McEwan's *Amsterdam*. An easy read; but how could something so riddled with cliché have won the Booker? I'll review it for the students back home; *mark* it for the students.

At twenty-to-six, Obeahman turned up in his open-back truck. This was it. This had echoes of Haiti and Graham Greene. Hemingway. I refused to be disappointed by the appearance of Obeahman. He was small and fit-looking and brisk of movement with an open, easy manner. The vehicle was a bit battered and unkempt, which at least fed my fantasy of adventure. Yesterday I had 'done' Plymouth. You couldn't get into the capital, couldn't get further than Look Out where you could see the surreal effect of the volcano, the pyroclastic flow towards Gages burying everything in its wake. And again, that way towards Plymouth, not quite burying everything, the odd roofs or upper storeys of buildings on high ground, sticking out. Also one or two industrial structures; a gas tower, etc.

Apparently, the devastation had now stimulated 'adventure tourism' (someone had called it Official Whoredom), tourists from Antigua doing it in a day, lunch thrown in, and returning to Antigua the same evening. So hotels were now going up to accommodate the 'disaster tourists'. What shocked me yesterday was the *depth* of the ash. My last time here a couple of years ago, Plymouth had been evacuated and I had gone in there to find the eeriness of a ghost-town, Utrillo-like, beautiful in a way. This time as I looked down from the height of what used to be called Lovers' Lane, looking down at the unfamiliar landmarks, it was impossible to get my bearings: where were we in relation to places I knew? Where was George Street, and Aunt Amy's house: would it be on this line? No one knew what was under the ash. Some houses had been blown away, demolished by huge rocks, hot rock coming down from the mountain; others were simply buried. I was told that most of the houses hadn't been cleared of things. Not that there wasn't warning, but people who had been rehoused in the safe zone in the north, still lived in hope and left the bulk of their belongings at home. And of course, many, many families were abroad, having already been evacuated. People were saying that, in time, the town would be given over to agriculture. Pol Pot. Cambodia. The rebirth of history.

Obeahman checked out my trousers and shoes. The guide was wearing jeans and walking boots, but he didn't pull rank. He confirmed that my Doc Martens were OK. His bustling get-on-with-it manner didn't grate.

'We drive into Trants,' he said. 'Then we have to walk. We walk across, then we go up Stowe's Hill, and we in Harris'.'

I told him I knew the area well, that my grandmother used to have a house in Harris'. I had spent part of my childhood there; that when I had visited two years ago it didn't look good. Even then.

'So, it's all a mess, eh?'

'Yes... What you mean?'

'Harris'.'

'Harris'? Nothing wrong with Harris', man. I have a little house up there.'

'I see.'

'Up there green and nice.'

'But I thought...'

'And is only Harris' church there, down that side there, down the ghaut that mash up. But Harris' just the same.'

'I see.'

'But the houses up there all right and everything. You only want them to turn on the electricity. And the water. That's all you need; the electricity and the water. And then for them to open up the road.'

'But no one lives up there.'

'No, but it have plenty of mango and that.'

'Heartbreaking. My brother was thinking of building a little house up there.'

'Yes man. People were just building houses and thing. Things like that. And houses were easy to build there because you have... you already have all the infrastructure already.'

'Precisely.'

'Everything there.'

We were settling into it; this was going to be easy.

'So how come you call yourself, "Obeahman"?

He laughed: 'Just a gimmick, you know.'

'I like it. Like it.'

A few minutes along the road Obeahman started pumping the brake pedal of his vehicle. No brakes. (Frontier country.) He wasn't worried but he was responsible enough to indicate that he knew he had no brakes and that as a professional driver/guide he ought to be concerned. 'It wasn't like this last night,' he said with some interest. And what's more he had given away his last can of brake fluid.

He pulled up on a steep incline, pumping the pedal.

'Out of brake fluid, you know.'

'Problem.'

'Didn't realize that till I was coming here this morning.'

'Ah.'

'I had a can, you know; I did give it to a fellow who run out and...'

'And it's a bit early to...'

'Garage don't open till half-past seven.'

'Ah.'

'Though, maybe it have at the other place. At...'

I didn't catch the name of the other place. And I was strangely not panicked. In circumstances like this I would usually counsel myself not to panic, not to give the appearance of panicking. But I *was* curiously relaxed, parked on this steepish hill in a vehicle without brakes. With Obeahman who was now out there doing something under the bonnet. At Obeahman's invitation I half-slipped into the driver's seat and pumped the brake-pedal. There was absolutely no resistance there, and Obeahman said something about not bothering to bleed the carburettor but instead trying to see if this other place, which was Seventh Day Adventist, would let him have brake-fluid on a Saturday. Either way we would make the trip east. Safely.

I couldn't help wondering how people managed to stick to their pre-volcano arrangements; church today and no business, sort of thing. Everyone walking round in spotless, freshly-ironed, designer clothes (not yet, of course, give it a couple of hours, though no one actually *walked* anywhere): I had had an invitation to a 'do' at the Government House – relocated, like most public buildings – and a friend who would be attending found it necessary to make the most complicated arrangements to get himself a haircut for the occasion. Would the people of Kosovo understand this type of fastidiousness?

But back to the present. Good news. Good omens. Obeahman returned from the Seventh Day Adventist place with a can of brake fluid. (I made a mental note to be less impatient with religious fundamentalists in the islands.)

The place was Brades. Just before we set off a young man came up with a message for Obeahman. I thought he looked African. He *was* African, a carpenter, like Obeahman. The young African had a workshop further along the road. I knew of another African carpenter to whom I'd been introduced last time round. With a workshop at Richmond Hill, on the outskirts of Plymouth. Couldn't remember the fellow's name. Then I remembered.

'Felix. The African who used to be at Richmond Hill. Making furniture.'

'Yes.'

'Is this young boy, sort of...'

'Isaac.'

'Isaac. Is he related to Felix? Are they family?'

'No no. But they come from the same place. Africa.'

'Ah!'

'But is Felix send for him.'

'Oh, I see.'

'But they fall out, and he go by heself now.'

Naturally, that's not what I wanted to hear. 'They fall out. The only two Africans on the island.'

Obeahman laughed; maybe because he was expected to.

'That's a shame.' And I was uncomfortably aware of listening to the sound of my own voice.

'When they come here they couldn't talk English, you know.'

'Ah, so it's Montserrat who taught them English!'

'Right. Although they come from Africa, the two of them talk two different language.'

It was my turn to see Obeahman's joke.

'But I wonder how they got to know about Montserrat?' Changing the mood I asked Obeahman if he was really a carpenter.

'Yes man. I make me dressing-table myself.' And he went on to talk a bit about his carpentry, his skill at joinery.

It was a very relaxed ride (even though the seat-belts didn't work) despite having to negotiate the infamous Fugarty Hill – feared from childhood – round the extensive Blakes estates, heading for what, in the old days, would be the northern way to the airport.

There was a flock of sheep in the distance, on a hill, the other side of the road from the beach, which now came into view.

'You've got someone's sheep up there.'

'Yes, they fencing them back up. They was scattered all over the

19

place and they fencing them back, so they could breed back. One man down there had hundreds of sheep. When the sheep them come out you can't see the road. I tell you people tief plenty. But we lost a lot of animals. Man like me now lose all that I have. My house still in Harris' but I can't live in it. So I have to say I lose it.'

'Yeah.'

'So, over the years, you know, you see the place being built up, gradually, and then *bang*.'

'I don't know how…'

'It was just coming. People was just coming back to build houses. And you see what happen now. People was building modern houses. No more old time house. Tile and bathroom in the house, and all that.'

'Doesn't bear thinking about.' I mentioned again that my brother, too, had planned to build a house in Harris'.

Soon – we were parallel with the coast now, on low ground – we came to a gate blocking off the road, and we prepared to get out of the car. Before that Obeahman decided to turn the car around, facing the way we had come.

'So we can get out fast. If anything happen. If the mountain erupt you can't outrun the mountain. When that come you don't have time to turn the car round. That's why I always point the right way.'

I commended his good sense, thinking that this was still a classic picture-postcard setting: I hadn't remembered this bit of the island looking so perfect. Extravagantly green. Fruit everywhere. On the trees. Fruit on the ground. Emerald sea. Lots and lots of new beach, laid down by the volcano.

The walk, on flat, level ground, seemed rather pleasant: what was all the fuss about? But immediately I was disorientated. It opened up into a wide valley the like of which Montserrat never had. Sand. Desert.

'So where are we?'

'This is Trant's Ghaut.'

'And what's that in front of us?'

'In front? Up there where it have the… Up there used to be Farms village.'

'Where? Where the sand is?'

'Farms village.'

'What, under the sand?'

'Sand cover the whole of Farms village.'

But… not even the highest house showing? (At least with Plymouth there was *evidence* of prior habitation.)

'Bury the whole village, sah. There's no such thing as Farms village any more.'

'But this is ridiculous.' (Wasn't there anything built on higher ground?) 'The whole village?'

'Not even the... Bugby Harris had a house at the top there. It was a high, high hill. The bridge was about 300 or 400 feet below. And it come down and cover the house; you can't see the house. A big house is covered there. Covered with the ash. That's all that left back. All here was house that it cover.'

'So, that's Farms.'

'And because the flow was supposed to be light, that why they don't want people to come in. In case it open up.' He was laughing. 'In case you fall through.'

'Yes, though it's been rained on for, what, two years?'

'We taking a big risk here. Because if anything was to happen now, we dead.'

We shared the joke.

'Yes man. And my policy is; you're not going to live for ever.'

'Well, you got to go somehow.'

'Even the Bible say so.'

'Better this... Better this than to go in some boring... hotel room. In America or... y'know, someone coming in with a gun to shoot you.' The sight of a straggle of houses on the far hill was confusing me. 'And those houses at the top of the hill?'

'That's Harris'.'

'Oh, I didn't know that Harris'... I didn't know Harris' had spread that far.'

'But you can't get into Harris'. Have to walk.'

'Over the mountain.'

'That's the only way up. To Harris'.'

'Well... No wonder they were saying no one went into Harris'.'

'People go into Harris'. Me used to go in there, what, two times a week. And take people sometimes. That's why me so fit. You have to fit to go into Harris'.'

We were still walking through the sand valley, avoiding the bits of pyroclastic flow which looked as if it hadn't been impacted; and avoiding the gullies (the highs and lows) to conserve energy.

'It looks pretty safe.'

'It had plenty rain. This last year. Half year. The sand solid. Except when the rain trying to cut a new ghaut. Me come up here all the time; it safe.' There was reference to Spanish Point and one or two other place names that I recalled from childhood, but had forgotten.

Out of deference to me Obeahman chose the gentler of the two paths (Path? What path?) up the mountain. I concealed my disappointment in being protected from the steeper path: I would show Obeahman.

And, for a time, I actually went ahead of him to prove that a man over fifty was not one to let the side down.

But half an hour into the climb the old shortness of breath, the gasping (no pain in the legs, but...) heaviness caused me to slow down.

Obeahman was tactful and discreet, which spurred me to greater effort. But it wouldn't do. It wouldn't do to have a heart attack on this mountain to prove some sort of point. So I came clean, admitted to being beaten and proposed a short rest.

Obeahman of course praised my stamina and fitness: for a man of my age I was doing magnificently. But Obeahman didn't deny that he, himself, usually took the steeper path when he did his run, unaccompanied, to Harris'.

I didn't rise to the bait, but took time to compose myself. And yes, through all this I could still get a whiff of – that combination of grass and fruit. Flowers, maybe – that distinctive smell of childhood. I mentioned this to Obeahman.

'You don't get that no place else,' he said. He sounded genuine.

I got up but still wasn't rested; I noticed some berries on the trees, ripe and black, that must have accounted for the smell.

'I know these,' I plucked a couple. 'I love these, I can't remember the name.'

'Berries, man. Berries.'

'Yeah, I know they're...'

'There's two of them. One is birch. And one is berry.' We were sampling them. 'This is berry. They sweet.'

'Ummm. Lovely. I remember this, man.'

'When we was small we used to look for them.'

'Um. Same here.'

'But I remember. We didn't use to get berries. What we used to get was birch; same as them.'

'I see.'

'All we used to get is birch.'

'Lovely. I remember them.'

'Tired?'

So it was time to move on.

'No, no man. I always puff and blow. I'm fine. Fine.'

So we resumed the climb sooner than I would have liked; and we set off, not yet on the home straits, for Harris'.

Further up the hill in the middle of the track we came across the spillage of office equipment. Printing materials. Lots and lots of tiny vials of something called Scribbles Fashion-writer. (A fleeing artist!) All colours. (I broke cover and scribbled this down.)

We were now able to look down the way we had come. Past Bugby

Hole and Trants to the old airport on the right; and match stories. When the first abandoned houses reappeared at the top of the hill I felt a huge sense of achievement. To celebrate, Obeahman picked a couple of mangoes from one of the laden trees on the lower side of the track, and we had breakfast.

Obeahman kept up the commentary: this house belonged to the children of Mr. so and so who had gone to Canada. This one... was Brother Jim's. No, it was Brother Galloway's, he used to do carpentry. He didn't live here but a branch of the family used to live on this side of the hill. I didn't remember these people. Obeahman was two decades, at least, younger than me: our map of Harris' didn't match. I was more concerned in trying to remember the names of plants that had eluded me. Then:

'Mrs. Shoy used to live up that hill.'

'What, up there?'

(The Shoys were friends of the family, the surviving members not seen in, perhaps, thirty years. I remember the blaze lighting up the night sky, when I was a child.)

'The house burned down.'

'I don't think I know...'

'Before your time, man; before your time... Then the Lee's used to live further back – past the little Seventh Day Adventist church.'

He knew the Lee's house. It was standing till... not so long ago.

And we started the descent into Harris' village. There was Mr. Jeffers' house; Mr. Jeffers had died in St. Croix. The place was like a botanical gardens gone mad, the growth everywhere as if in defiance of the volcano, the sand, ash, which was totally absent from this area. Breadfruit and pawpaws in profusion. Custard apple (but no sugar-apple) and avocados everywhere. Even pigeon peas. Yes, a Garden of Eden abandoned. And this brought forth a homily from Obeahman. Specifically, it was a breadfruit tree on its side, damaged, virtually split in two, but straining to recover, bearing fruit.

'If the tree doesn't leave its root, why should you leave your root?' he demanded, making me feel guilty. (For living abroad?) I resolved not to be guilty. Then we came across the black mango tree, laden. Obeahman picked a ripe one for me.

'Why do they call it black mango?'

'Well, that's what they call it.'

The black mango was yellow, and very sweet.

'Originally, they say it come down from Windy Hill.'

I recognized it as one of the types of mango we used to have in my grandmother's yard. But Obeahman's interest had moved on: this was a new house that someone had built at the same time that he had built his; the man was insured. The insurance had paid out. Those were the early days when the insurance people paid out. The man paid off the bank and still got $21,000 left over for himself.

So some people were lucky.

'If I did borrow money when I was building mine, I would have got the same deal.'

'But I take it you didn't.'

'But I believe in God, right. In this life a man cannot own anything. Because God tell you you can *occupy*. Until He come. If a man could dead, tell me if he could own anything!'

'Precisely.' I wasn't sure where this was leading.

'You cannot own nothing. As long as you could dead, you can't own anything.'

I didn't want to disagree; Obeahman was on a roll.

'If you could lost you life, you could lose everything else you have. You can *occupy* it for a certain time. If you read the Bible and know these things, you know nothing belongs to you. *Occupy until I come.* Anything you got and can lose um, can't be yours. Since you can lose you life, what else you can't lose!'

We were at the bottom of the hill now. What astonished me – it shouldn't, but it always did – was to discover how close together things were, the half-hour walk of childhood reduced to a couple of hundred yards. There was Hammy White's house. (Hammy was the curbside preacher who had predicted the hurricane and then – 'Fire and Brimstone' – the volcano.) The new house next to Hammy's, oddly-shaped for a country house, as if it had to fit into a tight corner, had had to be abandoned even before the owner moved in.

Through the village now, main street, on the right a church, one of the Christian Mission places that the Catholics and Methodists disapproved of because of the 'rowdiness' of the singing and clapping. And chanting. And then the space, a few yards along, where our own little Bethesda church used to be. Nothing left on that side of the road. On the other side, too, the little rum shops had long vanished. The rum shops and Mr. Lee's bread-shop. But on that side, still recognizable as a house, was where the Obeahwoman had lived.

Obeahman. Obeahwoman!

'Obeahwoman. Surely, you don't believe that.'

''Harris' had a lot of obeahwoman. Obeahman.'

'Come on.'

He was laughing.

'But surely, that was only ... old time talk. Old people talk.'

'No, man.'

'How come: what did they do? Obeah people?'

'They did a lot of things. You had a lot of sore foot and big foot in Harris'. Lots of people have sore foot and big foot. Sore foot, you know, that never heal.' He was having the time of his life.

I had my own childhood memory of being bathed in tin baths with herbs and readings from De Lawrence, the mystery healer. 'So, that's the main thing. To give you sorefoot.'

'Anything, man. Make you pappyshow. Anything.'

I conceded that I knew about bathing in tin baths, with herbs.

'Yes, man.'

'Because they said people were working obeah against us.' (It had crossed my mind if my slower-than-average pace of reading might not have come about by someone trying to interfere with my education.)

'They mash you up, man. Yeah, man.'

'But if sorefoot is the best they can do...'

'And it can't get better. And big foot, too.'

'Of course, nowadays we know better, we know how that sort of thing...'

'When people put something pon you, you get big foot, too.' The laughter was contagious; I surrendered myself to it.

'So, she's in Canada now. The Obeahwoman.'

'No, man, she dead long time. Her daughter in Canada.'

We were at the crossroads where shops used to be on both sides of the still-large space, one large general goods store belonging to an uncle – a great-uncle, Cousin Reggie. The bit of main road from town to the east, further east than this, to Bethel and Long Ground gave out, apparently, down just past where the butcher used to be. Down the side road was the elementary school that I attended for a few years, taught by, among others, Teacher Morgan. This was the heart of Harris', the crossroads where, in the early '50s I attended my first political meeting. It was in the evening and not very light; and one great-uncle (Harold) was introducing the prospective candidate, another great-uncle (Reggie) to an audience of mainly labourers working for one or other brother.

I recalled the dramatic moment when Harold summoned Reggie to step forward and to stand in the light, rigged up for the occasion, so that people could see him more clearly. He then invited us to look on the (unsmiling) face of a man who, at aged fifteen, had volunteered to go off to fight in the First World War on Britain's behalf, ending up in places like Palestine. Well, what this brave man had done for Europe he would now do for the people of Montserrat. The argument seemed so conclusive to me – and the presentation so dramatic – that I couldn't work out for years why this great uncle had been defeated in the elections by a man who hadn't fought in any war.

We were outside the Anglican church now, which was a ruin. Everything on that lower side of the village was gone, nothing but sand, undulating acres of it stretching down to the ghaut, and all the way down the valley to the airport. So you had one half of Harris' (that we'd just gone through) returning to bush, the other half a desert. The church was a wreck, but the walls were standing, and Obeahman, the carpenter, thought it wouldn't be too big a problem to fix it up again. Its construction history was chiselled into the wall.

THIS STONE WAS LAID BY
MRS MP DUKES, JULY 20th. 1899
CW JOHNSON, RECTOR

And the record said it had been rebuilt three times: 1900, 1917 and 1939.

'All they need to do,' Obeahman said, 'is to put on the roof. And the windows... And door.' I suspected the structure might be weakened by the fire. But he was the expert. I was curiously not dismayed that Montserrat's new ruins, balancing the old plantation-type ones of sugar mills and planters' houses, would change the tone of how Montserrat's past was written up.

I couldn't get so close and not visit my grandmother's old house, further up the hill. Of course it had been abandoned, effectively, in the '50s. We took the suggestion of a path leading up from what was Teacher Morgan's house at the bottom of the hill opposite the water trough. What were they called, these little plants, these leaves that closed up when you touched them?

'Prickle tree.'

'Doesn't ring a bell, somehow. "Prickle tree". No.' There were more fruit trees in this area than I remembered.

'You hear about the man used to live in this house?' (This was on the left side of the path leading, eventually, to our house. The 'house' referred to was no more than a tiny concrete foundation. I had vague memories of someone living there; but that must have been before Obeahman's time.)

'No, so what about him?'

'His money burn down in there.'

I waited for the story.

'He had a tin full of money. In a bag; he hide it in the cupboard. A tin where he had over $4,000. And the house catch fire, and the money in the tin; and the man outside and he want to go back and grab the bag with the tin. But he can't get back in because of the fire. Otherwise he was a dead man. He just have to run and left the bag and go.'

'$4,000.'

'Over four thousand. Just trying to get to the bag, he would be a dead man. When he reached up there the heat faint him away. And he have to go into the cellar. And that's how he survive.'

It was too ludicrous to point out that there was no possibility of a cellar to this house; but I didn't discourage Obeahman.

'So I tell you, for a man to leave his money – if he just try to touch that bag, he'd be a dead man.'

'Well, it's your money or your life.'

'It would have kill you. If he had just try to touch the box he would have been a dead man.'

'I think I might have had a grab, you know.'

'Then you would a dead. Is either your life or your money. He would have been a dead man. I think he did the right thing.'

Looking behind us, having gained a few yards up the hill, we could see the sea again.

'I always forget, you know, that you can see the sea from everywhere. Here are we in the middle of Harris', and we can see the sea.'

'You want to go up Windy Hill? Then you can see the sea on both sides.'

'Where I live in the middle of Yorkshire I never see the sea.'

We couldn't get into my grandmother's place. It was the cluster of the guava trees that prevented us. Behind the guava I could imagine the grafted mango and the sugar-apple and the avocados; the coconuts, the breadfruit, and the variety of abandoned ground provisions, and I thought: waste waste waste.

It was good, in a way, not to have got to the house. Not that there was much emotional tug any more about the old place: after it had fallen into ruin in the '70s, one could begin distancing oneself from it; by the '80s it was reduced to a foundation, the approaches overgrown, preventing access. The difficulty was early on, fifteen or so years after we had abandoned it in 1956, to see the still-recognizable house, bits of roof sagging, upper storey listing, as a ship might when in trouble. Then, it was difficult, *that* had to be kept from my mother in London. Though, of course, she knew.

Like my mother, then, I could now still indulge in the memory of the house as it was when we lived there; a hub of village life – though set somewhat apart, on its hill – presided over by my grandmother. She was an Osborne, originally, and the Osbornes were distinguished and respected throughout the island. It was a large house, twelve rooms in the end, colonial in style with a stone base and timber on top, with an attic which attracted bats; and my brothers had to clean out the bat-droppings in the summer holidays, the smell hanging in the air for hours. No one doubted that my grandmother ran the show, even though she was confined to one room at the far end of the house, and had to be helped to visit other areas, or the yard at the bottom of the (fourteen) steps. My grandmother ("Mammie") had had an accident as a child, when the family buggy had run over her legs and she lost a kneecap as a result: she was twelve years old at the time, and managed to walk with a limp for many years before she was finally disabled. It was more or less accepted that this was the reason she travelled much less widely than most of her eight brothers and sisters (though she did visit St. Vincent and the Virgin Islands): it was hinted that this was why she didn't marry until well into middle age, to Mr. Lee (Grandfather), a gentle, caring man who had been married before. My mother, her only child, was born when my grandmother was aged forty-two.

Because my grandmother, as a young woman, stayed at home to look after her parents she had some claims to the family house, and bought out the shares of the other girls in the family, to whom the property was jointly left. All this happened well before I came along. As the youngest in the family I rely somewhat on the memories of my sister (five years my senior) and my brothers (seven and eight years, respectively). They remember when *they* lived in another house in the middle of the village, opposite the Anglican church, a property which, in my time, had been reduced to an imposing foundation which we used to walk round, daring one another to fall in. The demise of that house hadn't come about by 'hurricane', but because the upper (wooden) portions had been moved and set down on a new site a few hundred yards away. Part of the building became Uncle Mike's house (Uncle Mike's and Tan Tan's) the rest was converted to the small Methodist church, Bethesda, where we used to go to Sunday School. Apparently, just before the outbreak of the Second World War, my parents and the then three children came back from Aruba where my father had been working (so that I could be born British, in Montserrat, the story goes), and they headed up the hill to join my grandparents, selling the village house to Uncle Mike who had returned from America where he had been some sort of miner – either coal or gold miner, we weren't sure. What I remember is that he wore very sharp, heavy suits on a Sunday, or when he came visiting – though he, too, had a bad leg. I remember, too, Uncle Mike's and Tan Tan's dining room with its highly-polished floor and furniture, which made me a little self-conscious when I passed by and, occasionally, Tan Tan sat me down at the dining-room table, and persuaded me to eat something. (Tan Tan's brother, Uncle George, lived in his own house, just a few yards further on, away from the main road. They were from the Lee's, not the Osborne's branch of the family.) Uncle George was a bit of a mystery. As a young man, he had won the lottery in Cuba – where he had spent about seventeen years – and again in Haiti before the first World War (about £500 worth each time, we think) and, having resettled, grew increasingly dismissive of the ways of Montserrat and Montserratians.[1] There were some lively discussions in our back yard between brother and sister (Uncle George and Tan Tan) with my grandmother, looking down on it all from her room, imploring Uncle George not to be so 'ignorant'. When, on occasion, Uncle George's frustration spilled over into 'bad language', then my grandmother's strictures were correspondingly severe, drawing attention to his drinking habits (though, of course, avoiding using 'bad language' herself).

Having been born in that house and lived there more or less alone with my grandmother until I was eleven, I have, I suppose, a sort of proprietorial feeling about it.

For while my mother was away in town during the week, where

my sister and brothers were at school, I was being brought up by my grandmother – with only Nellie and Sarah for company. Nellie came in every day to do the washing and ironing and cooking, and Sarah – who was my age – ran errands, went to school, and slept in. I remember the evenings when I had to occupy myself in the drawing-room while Sarah gave my grandmother her bath, in her room next-door.

During the week the ritual didn't change much. Nellie would probably see to my washing my hands and feet and cleaning my teeth before she left for home; or if she didn't actually oversee this she would remind me of what was expected. When we had an extension made to the house at the back – I was about seven – three rooms added, one huge oblong one downstairs that was never used for anything much but storing lumber, an upstairs bathroom and WC, along with a new spare room and corridor extending the space in that direction from the drawing-room – I tended to do the evening washing of feet and cleaning of teeth upstairs rather than at the stopcock on the front lawn, and usually after Nellie had gone.

After Nellie left for home, Sarah would lock all the downstairs doors, the kitchen, breadroom and dining-room that were most in use during the day, and check that the other four doors downstairs – the coalroom under the verandah at the front of the house, the servants' room and the two spare-room doors at the back were secure. Upstairs, my grandmother's room overlooking the back yard, my mother's at the front and the drawing room – these last two leading onto the verandah – would be secured after making the ritual check that no thieves had got in and were hiding in any of the rooms. The only outside door we didn't bother much about was the one in the boys' room, overlooking the yard: i.e. that section between front and back yards. As this was on the upper floor with no outside access, it didn't pose a problem. (Incidentally, the 'boys' room was literally the room designated for us boys, not the loo; and was slept in when my brothers came home at weekends – and in the holidays.) I slept in my grandmother's room under a mosquito net, and Sarah slept on the floor just outside, her bedding put down in the passage between the drawing-room and the boys' room. The trap door, leading down to the dining room, was on the other side of the corridor, protected by a rail, and it was shut at night, lowered into place.

So, the house made secure, the lamps would be lit, a kerosene lamp for my grandmother, and one downstairs for Sarah to see her way as she heated water for my grandmother's bath, and also to make a hot drink for us. In the drawing-room, the lamp had a long, thin, elegant shade, and the kerosene was poured into the glass base through which you could see the wick. This was placed on the round table in the corner next to my mother's room, the other side from the piano: I would sit with my book and try to stay awake while Sarah assisted my grandmother with her bath next door. At the end, Sarah would empty the tin bath and I would sometimes be asked to help – if I wasn't too sleepy. When I got to my grandmother's room – now smelling of Canadian Healing Oil – I might be asked to read to her. If she was in a good mood she'd ask Sarah to make me not the usual drink of 'bush' tea (herbs plucked from the garden) but maybe cocoa or hot milk – with a piece of sweetbread from the cupboard thrown in. Then I would climb under the mosquito net into bed, a small bed set up each night next to my grandmother's. Oh, yes, first I would kneel down and say my prayers. (One thing Sarah was reminded of, nightly, before shutting up, was to check if the water tap at the trough in the front yard was properly turned off. 'Make sure the cock shut', my grandmother would warn.)

Sometimes, in the evenings, my grandmother would talk to me about her family, her eight brothers and sisters, who all seemed then – and now – to be remarkable people. There were her brothers Ned and Bird. They had both lived in New York. Uncle Ned was a doctor and Uncle Bird (Burdett), training to be a lawyer, had run into some sort of difficulty that we were never to know about and ended up in Boston doing something we never quite found out about. Apart from those two there was Uncle James who, as a Justice of the Peace in Montserrat, went to England twice, and witnessed some sort of disturbance on the street in London, which made him compare, favourably, the state of orderliness in Montserrat to that of London. Cousin Vivie, the daughter of one sister, worked for many years in America as a maid with a family who treated her well (I was never told about her having been a maid until much, much later; but we all liked her accent)[2]. Another sister was widowed but well taken care of in Plymouth: when we visited her, in her darkened room, she, too, seemed to sound and look not like family but like someone from 'abroad'. Yet another sister was so brilliant that, as a girl of fourteen, she played the organ in the Methodist church in Bethel, on a Sunday. These were all my grandmother's family, my mother's family, whom I must never forget. My father's family, the Markhams, came from further east, Bethel. Though we met them in the village and at church on Sunday – and, later, some came to live with us in the town – we were never encouraged to be curious about them. My paternal great-grandfather, Mr. Markham, came to Montserrat from Trinidad, as a policeman, married, and produced a son, Henry. When he was transferred to another island he left the family behind. During my growing up, my father was in Canada studying for the priesthood, having fought in Europe in the war.

But even then there was someone in the family more worthy of military praise. Cousin Reggie, my grandmother's nephew, had fought in World War I. The story is that his father, a lay-preacher, made an appeal in church after the sermon, for volunteers to go to war. And the first person who stepped forward was his young son, aged fifteen.

Cousin Reggie ended up in the Middle East, and was said to have had a good war. In later life he was one of the three Osborne brothers who controlled much of the business-activity in Montserrat. (He was a Freemason, dressed in heavy suits and a broad-brimmed hat and, in the '50s and '60s, attended 'Lodge' frequently, in England.[3]) My father was in the Canadian army, and was part of the section detailed to getting rid of the Germans occupying the port of Antwerp, in Belgium – Battle of Normandy, and all that; in 1944.

★ ★ ★

Recently, I met my brothers and sister in London for one of our periodic 'reunions' and we had occasion, among other things, to reminisce about the whole 'economy' of that house in Harris', presided over by my grandmother. (In England, my mother would summon the family when important decisions were to be made. This was usually in the East End after she moved from Kilburn to live with my sister and her husband; my brothers, who lived in London, tended to visit once a month. The ritual of 'coming together' continued even after my mother died.)

What sustained the 'house' was something larger than I imagined. It's all to be traced back to the Osborne family and to the legendary 'Uncle James'/'Cousin James', son of a millwright and estate manager, William Michael and Julia Gordon, the daughter of an Englishman. Just as James' father had catapulted himself out of slavery to become a plantation overseer (at Bethel), James attained both political and economic power. As a Justice of the Peace and member of the Montserrat 'Council', he supported, in 1914, a Council motion to donate £1,000 to the British for war relief [as] 'they wished Montserratians to bear "their humble share of the burden now imposed on the empire."' He was, of course, the father of Cousins Harold, Reggie and Michael (Gen). Apart from managing estates, being active in trade (including the legal trafficking of cattle between the islands) Cousin James built houses, houses houses – and substantial ones. The entire extended family benefited from this.

But, talking about the more particularized 'economy' of the house: as Grandfather had died in 1940, it really was my grandmother's domain as far as we were concerned. (Grandfather had been a tailor by trade; and for many years was the manager of Mulcares estate.) How did Mammie keep it going? We were never conscious of being short of money when we were growing up. My brothers pointed to the 'windfall' from the Will of Uncle Ned, the doctor in New York. (He had studied at the Mico, a college in Antigua, become a teacher, before working his way through to medical school in America, and was held up as a role model to us.) Uncle Ned was a bachelor, and left the bulk of his estate to his sisters; and even though they were (apparently) robbed by the lawyers, the sisters each ended up with about £900 which, in the 1940s, was a lot of money.

But really, the main 'economy' of the house rested on rents and on what the social historians call 'metayage', the practice of having people work bits of land and contributing part of the produce as payment. We had 'land' not only around the big house in Harris', but further east at places like Barking and Mulcares. 'Mulcares' was interesting. It derived from a family of that name from England or Ireland, who employed my grandmother's father, William Osborne, who was a Millwright, as Estate Manager. By that time the Mulcares family consisted of two spinsters, fallen on hard times, and unable to pay their estate manager's wages. So when they died (or retired to Ireland) deeply indebted to him he inherited the estate in lieu. My grandmother always insisted that the Mulcares were Irish, but now some members of the family claim them to have been English. (I go with my grandmother's memory here because the shop which the sisters ran on the estate was called 'Trescellian House'[4] and though this is more commonly associated with Cornish (three-leaf clover), in the context of the island – Irish place-names; the shamrock adorning Government House in Plymouth, the capital – the story points to an Irish connection. (Trescellian House was, for many years until Hurricane Hugo 'trashed' it in 1989, the main business premises of M.S. Osborne, situated on Parliament Street, in Plymouth.)

Even I came, ludicrously, to be engaged in the workings of metayage. While at the Grammar School (my brothers had by now left the island) I used, occasionally, to accompany my cousin Harold – one of the three current Osborne brothers – to the east with feed for pigs that he kept there. Another brother (Cousin Gen.)[5] owned a hotel in Plymouth and the waste from the cooking was what Cousin Harold drove across the island to feed his pigs in the afternoons. Cousin Harold's main business was the cotton ginnery which he managed; so as well as taking feed to the pigs, he would pop in to Mulcares in the cotton-picking season and buy the cotton produced on family land by the sharecroppers. I would sometimes accompany him. One day, however, he couldn't make it, and I was entrusted to go with the driver (and the pig-feed in the boot of the car) to carry out the dual role of overseeing the feeding of the pigs and the buying of cotton.

Now, there were codes to buying the cotton. First, it had to be weighed.

The cotton was collected in crocus sacks, and a certain amount was deducted for the weight of the sack; I think two pounds. If it was a wet day, however, not only would the sack be heavier, but so would the contents of the sack be; so you had to use your judgement how much to deduct for sack and the weather, as the labourers lifted their produce on to the Stilyards, which is what the special scale for weighing cotton was called: it was hung from a crossbeam in the roof.

I remember the acute embarrassment as I, a schoolboy, stood there in that little hut, arbitrarily deducting pounds from this or that sack of cotton. I was terrified that I would be challenged by these grown men and women; and no one did. I am as uneasy about that encounter now as I was then.[6]

But that was not enough income; the running expenses of the household were heavy – my mother sent to a private school in Antigua, the family having, visibly, to maintain a certain social position in a small island; my brothers and sisters, in time, sent to fee-paying schools, etc. – all with limited input from the Markham family. When my mother returned from the Girls High School in Antigua, a piano was acquired (a Grundig) so that she could complete this 'finishing school' skill.[7] How was all this paid for? Something that secured real income was the fact that the family owned property. There were two houses in the town, in Plymouth, both on Parliament Street, the more splendid one of which was rented out. The other, which the family occupied, had the downstairs let (to Mr. Mills, who sold 'cola' and other soft drinks and ice, and all sorts of sweets and cakes). In the village, in Harris' there were, in my time, three small houses that were let to 'workers', one of whom was the barber who was dumb, whose name was Pilate. We had no idea what rent my grandmother charged for these small houses. So, whatever the reality of the situation, I grew up in an environment of plenty and privilege.

The availability of family transport, I'm now persuaded, was an important factor in its prosperity. Cotton was moved from estate to family-owned ginnery (first at Harris' then Plymouth) in a family bus – which also transported people and produce between country and town. My grandparents owned a car in those days, M 32 (the 32nd vehicle registered in Montserrat to date) which my father, partly because he could drive, used to liaise between estate, ginnery and independent producer. Commercial traffic among the islands benefited the family further when one of 'Cousin James' sons, (Gen) acquired the first of his boats, a schooner.[8]

My brothers, obviously, have sharper memories about privations suffered during the war: saltfish and other imported goods were scarce, or couldn't be had; people often went without meat and clothes were made often of improvised 'cloth' – the sacks in which flour came, etc. which helped to distinguish between 'rich' and 'poor'. But then there was the black-market in cheese, corned beef and even things like cement and paint, acquired from the local Militia. Apparently, people planted millet to mix with flour, and breadfruit 'flour' was made locally. Ham began to be cured locally, butter churned. (I remember the ice-cream churner in our house; I knew they made butter in the house, but I can't remember how.) One interesting detail of the effect of the 'austerity' was that the slaughter of female cattle was prohibited, in order to preserve the stock. (It was also rumoured, when I was growing up, that we developed a taste for brown rice and brown sugar, as we had had to send our white rice and white sugar to England as part of our war effort.)

There was another source of income, and to me it was the most interesting one of the lot: that was the animal pound. It was situated on the other side of the back yard, a round structure of stakes, long grown into trees, and a combination of rough stone wall and crosspieces of wood and board, complete with a front gate that was duly shut at night (one of Sarah's duties) secured with a chain and lock. It didn't need to be completely secure because the animals inside were tied.

How it worked was this: if a pig or goat or occasional donkey strayed on someone's land, that person could catch it and bring it to the pound. Impound it. There, it would be secured and fed and watered twice a day and, if in six weeks the owner didn't come to reclaim it, paying the appropriate fine, the animal would be auctioned to recover the expenses of board and lodging. The auctions sometimes attracted quite a few people – apart from the local butcher, Jim White – because notice of these occasions had to be posted.

My grandmother was Auction-Master, and sometimes employed bidders on behalf of the house. As she got older she gave up the pretence of providing cover for her own bidding, and occasionally an uncle or an aunt (Uncle George, Tan Tan) or Nellie, or me (aged nine, say) was sanctioned to bid for the pig or goat in question.[9]

Apart from these 'fortuitous' animals we kept goats, pigs, chickens which layed regularly, and also provided us with the Sunday roast, often when the vicar came to lunch; there were also a couple of guinea-fowl who would lay eggs layer upon layer: they didn't know how to keep quiet after laying, to preserve the nests. We had, also, some rabbits in a couple of hutches; and cattle which people in the village looked after for us. Latterly, a man in another village (Mr. Daly, at Farms) took charge of one of the cows. At one period I remember having to do the trip there and back (with my friend Roy Lee, who was on a similar errand to collect the milk) before school. This errand was always reserved for a member of the family, the feeling being that someone else might drink or otherwise dispose of some of the milk and replenish the rest with water. As the premium was on 'rich' milk – which was visibly-off-white – the clever rascals were said to top up the milk with muddy water, to simulate the original richness. We never actually saw anyone do this, but the rumour was enough to determine people like my grandmother to trust no one but family with her milk. (My brothers had performed this function before me, when the cows had been kept nearby, at 'Paradise' and 'Farrel's' estates.

★ ★ ★

Why did we leave this set-up? Well, explanations vary. We were comfortable in Montserrat and yet, we looked forward to leaving: however 'protected' by status you never managed to avoid feeling that you were far away from everything, from everywhere; from where things happened; you were at the furthest point from where things in the world came, or from where family went to have a different type of experience: there was a sense – there had always been a sense – of biding time.

First, the prospect was of going to Canada to join my father. That never happened for a variety of (disputed) reasons. One was my mother's fear of splitting the family further, as my grandmother would not, of course, contemplate leaving her home and going to another country, like an immigrant. My mother, too, was safe in the security of her extended family, a centrepiece in a household that included servants (apparently, she had felt isolated in the few years spent in Aruba: the prospect of Canada must have been more frightening, where her only support would be a *husband*. And there were personality differences between mother and father). My father (predatory and self-centred as all the Markhams were[10]) saw some benefit in our remaining in Montserrat as the cost of maintaining his family would continue to be met by my grandmother and her family. So my mother's off-quoted condition for leaving the island, that it would not be before her mother's death, seemed a convenient solution for everyone. I believe my mother set down that condition in 1946. My grandmother died in 1953. Shortly afterwards my brothers were dispatched, one via a scholarship to St. Jose University in Puerto Rico, then to Canada; the other to England. Both brothers ended up in England and, in 1956, my mother, my sister and I joined them.

We left, I think, because the family ground to a standstill after my grandmother died; she was a shrewd businesswoman; my mother was the opposite. (Once, my grandmother opened a small shop in the village and put my mother in charge; and my mother gradually gave away all the goods to poor – or cunning – customers who claimed not to be able to pay.) There was no one, no man in the house to stop the slide of family fortunes: fields fell into disuse, rents were uncollected (because my mother didn't have the authority to threaten that my grandmother had had); the animal pound abandoned and my mother, not fully understanding that money spent had to be earned, promptly bought a car, largely to keep up with the richer cousins. She did try, of course, to cope; but didn't have the temperament for it. On one occasion, provoked by a carpenter who tried, with some truculence, to wriggle out of paying the rent, she lost her temper and slapped him in the face. Typically, she did this in the presence of witnesses, and she was taken to court, and fined.

There was another reason for our going. People in our (privileged) position were beginning to be treated with suspicion in the changed political atmosphere, pioneered by the early trades-unionists: we were part of the employer, not the worker class. I remember being at the count of votes in Harris' (at the infant school) of a political contest involving my cousin Reggie and his trade union opponent; and the family lost. This must have been for a seat on the Legislative Council in 1952, and William Bramble, the winner, went on to a distinguished political career, representing Montserrat in the Parliament of the Federation of the West Indies (1958-62), and, for some years, ably, to serve Montserrat as Chief Minister. But the weekend after that 1952 count, as we were being driven home from Plymouth on the Saturday night, we ran into difficulty. When we rounded the dangerous corner above that very infant school, we found huge stones placed in the middle of the road: though the road was used in the daytime, there were only about three or four cars that used it after dark, two belonged to the Methodist and Anglican ministers, another to cousin Reggie (who lived further east at Tar River) and one was our, newly acquired, Chevrolet.[11]

Altogether, the social environment seemed less benign than before. Maybe England wasn't as bad as some reports claimed it to be.

★ ★ ★

People often ask – and I'm usually at a loss to explain – how I spent my time during those early, growing-up years. And it's true that the image of being essentially alone with an aged grandmother in an isolated big house on a hill in the country, strikes some people as a 'gothic' sort of experience. And even though I can't remember much of it (suspicious?), it didn't (and doesn't) strike me as having been a deprived (except, perhaps, emotionally) childhood. Friends and – over the years, partners – who talk to me about this point out that you can't put emotional deprivation in brackets as if it didn't flow into the rest of the life's sentence; but then, as they say, you can't have everything. So how did I fill the space?

My second memory is more concrete than the first. It is my being on the verandah playing with toys and water. It must have been the middle of the morning: I'm sitting on the edge of the drawing-room floor which was probably raised about six inches above the level of the verandah; and my bits and pieces are laid out on the verandah. Both doors, of the drawing room and my mother's room are open, their (wooden) shutters folded back. I play alone because there are no other children about except the children across the way, at Garden Hill; and though they come to the yard often with their mothers, to draw water and sometimes to borrow things from the kitchen – like the 'mortar-pestle' – they've never been upstairs in our house, and we don't much play together. I remember this session on the verandah because it was the same day that my grandmother decided to send me to school. Though I was only four, she said I was getting into too much trouble playing with water, so school was the best place for me.

The infant school was just across the way on the far side of Garden Hill, the playing field, maybe about five minutes' walk; you could see it clearly from the verandah.[12] I can't remember who took me to the school, maybe Nellie. But when I got there the headmistress, Teacher Kitty[13], a friend of the family who lived near the school in one of the family homes, unrolled a large coloured sheet of paper from the top of the blackboard and asked me to read the names on it. After I had successfully identified

> CAT
> MAT
> RAT, etc.

she said that I had done very well and was ready for school.

As I was smaller than everyone else I had to be helped up on to the seat so that I could be on the same level as everyone else: I was now at school. I can't recall a single other image of my time at that school. (I said this was the second thing I remembered from early childhood. The first was so shadowy that I sometimes wonder if I dreamt it. Or imagined it. It was of my grandfather and, since he died in 1940 when I was less than one year old, I have to be cautious. But I remember him crossing the drawing-room towards my grandmother's (his) room. I don't, of course, remember what he looked like, but I have this very definite image of his going past (and I think it was evening rather than morning) and disappearing: I certainly remember his coffin being moved out of the drawing-room.)

Back to school: the primary school (School No. 2) was in Harris', in the grounds of the Anglican church – an Anglican school. Teacher Mayers was Head; and here the memory is more fertile: What to select?

Doing PT in the road stands out. We would be lined up in two rows, facing the school, facing Teacher Morgan with his back to the school. (Though this was the road, there was no traffic; it wasn't the main road going east, it was a sort of, unpaved, short cut.) Teacher Morgan would put us through our exercises: HANDS OUT. HANDS UP. HANDS IN. HANDS DOWN. And he would do the relevant exercises with great exactness, which we had to match. We would repeat the process several times, throwing our arms out and up and folding them into our chests, until we were told to STAND EASY. Then it would be RIGHT TURN. AS YOU WERE. LEFT TURN. MARK TIME. FORWARD MARCH. HALT. (I found out much later that Teacher Morgan had been in the Auxiliary Defence Forces; so that at school we were getting both PT *and* Civil Defence training all in one.) I can't remember how often we did our drill, maybe about twice a week.

Another memory from that school was not doing very well in a spelling test. (Before that, though, something that troubled me was the prospect of falling off the edge of the school land and into the far valley below. The school was a long, low building, one side facing the church and graveyard and the other – where the loos were – had a little play area. The front was onto the road where we did our PT and the back at the edge of the ghaut, the land falling sharply away. Whenever we had to walk round the side facing the ghaut I always felt that I would lose my footing on the narrow, crumbly path, and roll all the way down into the ghaut, missing the few small trees that would save me from the ravine. Of course, it couldn't have been anything like as dangerous as I remember because (as far as I know) no one ever fell down into the ghaut. But I was talking of the spelling test.)

I was in one of the lower classes and was being shown up by a boy – Daniel, who lived opposite the school – who knew not only the simple things like words which had a 'k' that was not sounded, like 'knife' and 'know' – there was a big banner strung across the ceiling of the school with the words in big letters KNOWLEDGE IS POWER, so we knew all about silent 'Ks' – but Daniel also astonished me by being able to distinguish between words like UNION and ONION; I knew then there was no hope for me. Our playground games (about whether 'Miss Na', who lived at Garden Hill, our nearest neighbour on that side, would be spelt 'Miss Kna' if she lived in a bigger house with land around, and servants), suddenly seemed too 'young' for Daniel. I was very pleased, indeed (at that age, you're not guilty about snobbery) to remind myself that Daniel lived in a very small house, without grounds, and that I lived in a big house on the hill, and therefore my not knowing the difference between UNION and ONION didn't really humiliate me, out of school, that is. (He kept it up, did Daniel, at another lesson where we were allowed to look at newspapers and magazines from abroad, discarding one paper on the grounds that it was a *gazette*.)

I probably remember this, not because I was more than usually class-obsessed, but because at around the same time I was announced to the entire school as being a 'nincompoop'. The sentence: ARCHIE MARKHAM IS A NINCOMPOOP was there, large and damning, on the blackboard; and no one would rub it out. I remember the evening before, as a special treat, a few of us were allowed into the school to prepare a 'banner' for 'celebrating', I think, Empire Day, the following day. About three groups of children were sticking pictures of people from various parts of the Empire on to a large cardboard background. Roy Lee, my friend from the other hill, with whom I used to go to Farms to collect the milk, was part of our team. One of his sisters (part of another team) kept coming over to ask Roy how to spell this or that word, one of which was 'nincompoop'. I was aware that she was writing on the blackboard but thought, vaguely, that this might have something to do with the next day's celebrations.

Nearly every image I remember from that school could be described as positive and negative in more or less equal degree, though, of course, at the time it was the element of humiliation that registered more strongly. Interestingly, most of them had to do with Teacher Morgan, whose lessons are the only ones I really remember.

We were having a history test outside, under the big mango tree. It was either a history test or a reading test; but we were reading from a history book. I liked History and had read the passage before. So when my turn came – we were all lined up in a semicircle under the shade of the tree – I started off confidently, only to lose my place; and had to stop halfway in order to relocate it. Then, in some panic I completed the passage. I knew I would lose marks because Teacher Morgan would assume that I had stopped because I had got stuck on a word I didn't know or couldn't pronounce. In the end he gave me 66 for the test, which I thought was too generous. He must have given me 66 because he was a little bit afraid of my grandmother; or he thought that was the best I could do (I would have been happy with 66 for spelling: even now, as a professor of Creative Writing, my spelling is more than suspect); and I was a little bit embarrassed that Teacher Morgan thought this was the best I could do in history, in reading.

But talking about Teacher Morgan: he's alive, as we said, still on the island, fully-functioning and ninety years old; he's had, perhaps, as much influence on me as has anyone in the family. In idle moments

I try to imagine how he compares with all those literary schoolmasters who have directed, sometimes for the better, the fortunes of people whose names we know, from the character depicted in *Tom Brown's Schooldays* to Frank Collymore in Barbados (influencing the exemplary George Lamming and a clutch of subsequently distinguished writers) to, yes, Roger Scruton's Mr. Chapman in High Wycombe.[14]

Teacher Morgan was tall and thin and independent, an independence which contributed to his never being made headmaster in any of Montserrat's schools (though he did have a spell, in the '80s, as head of a school up the islands).

He wasn't averse to a drink, which earned a certain protective disapproval of some in the village, including my own family; and he didn't believe in God, which provoked appalled indignation in my grandmother. I remember the sessions, in the back yard of our house, when they sparred over this. He would be standing some little way beyond the bottom of the steps. My grandmother would, as always, be sitting on a couple of cushions on the floor of her room at the top of the steps, the door opening on to the yard. Mr. Frederick (a man from the village who came up most days and was given dinner) would be sitting on the steps, halfway up. Nellie would be in the breadroom downstairs, maybe ironing (if this was late-afternoon) or maybe cooking the food for the pigs, having already cooked dinner for the family. Teacher Morgan would have lost the argument with my grandmother and would cheerfully take his leave saying that he would see her, whenever, next week, next Tuesday, say.

'D.V.' (Deo volente) 'God willing,' my grandmother would remind him.

'I shall see you next week, Mrs. Lee.'

'God willing. If you live.'

'I shall live, Mrs. Lee.'

My grandmother would call him ignorant, which was not a light thing to say to the teacher of your grandchild; and would ask him to take care that God wasn't listening to him.

And he would, laughingly, invite her to be logical (Logical, I liked that: no one else in the village invited you to be logical) – he would invite her to be logical, for how could something that didn't exist be listening to important things happening in this yard? He had a way of blaspheming which no one could be sure was blasphemy. When he was excited, he would shout out: 'O Lad O Lad O Lad'. And you weren't sure if he was making fun of those people who usually said: 'O Lord O Lord O Lord' which, in a way, was mockery. We, children, had no doubt that he was seriously into mockery.[15] So there was always a frisson of excitement surrounding Teacher Morgan, which made us, children, suspect that he knew things that other adults didn't know, or didn't care to admit. Whenever he came to visit he seemed always to put the contrary view to the one advanced in the house. He once upset my grandmother by saying that my grandfather had had a high-pitched voice and was short; *that* he had to take back – even though those who remembered grandfather hinted that he was 'not so tall' and had a 'lightish' voice.

But there were more telling disagreements. I remember the conversation on the verandah one evening, where my mother was entertaining a cousin, Enid, down from Nevis. Enid was a teacher and, over drinks, she and Teacher Morgan talked about the difficulty of passing a teacher's exam called 'Method', something that Teacher Morgan had himself fallen down on. My mother and I listened in respectful silence. Then the conversation turned to discipline and, even though I can't remember the details of that, there seemed to be no more disagreement. But then Teacher Morgan admitted that in some cases the teacher, who didn't know everything, could be wrong; and should therefore admit his error to the pupil. Both my mother and Enid disagreed with that. My mother felt that the teacher should 'know his facts', should not be wrong; and Enid, taking a less fundamentalist view, said that, having discovered his error, the teacher should not admit it to the class, as that would affect discipline: the teacher should retrieve the situation by saying that his erroneous statement was just another way of expressing the matter.

Teacher Morgan, of course, gave up defending himself in such powerful company but, in me, he had a silent ally. Even when he beat me that day in school, I was on his side.

The beating came about in this way. We were in Standard Three, I think, or Standard Four in the elementary school in Harris'. Our lesson, with Teacher Morgan in charge, was held outside in the churchyard, among the gravestones, as the schoolroom was usually hot and noisy. (Teacher Morgan noticed that I had carved my initials on the hem of my trousers.

These were trousers that had already given me cause to think. They had come from Canada, courtesy of my father. The light-coloured material from which they were made was called 'crash'; and I remember saying to my friend and neighbour, John Meade, who may by then have been in the top form, that it would be a good idea to make 'crash' the material for a school uniform (The Grammar School in town, where my brothers went, had a uniform). When John pointed out to me that not everybody had a father in Canada to send them 'crash' trousers, I remember being ashamed of being so selfish – a Markham trait?

So it was on the hem of these (short) trousers that I had inked my initials, and Teacher Morgan demanded to know why.

Of course there was no answer, and I had the apprehension of punishment to come. What surprised me was Teacher Morgan's asking if I had inked my initials on the trousers because I feared they might be stolen.

The possibility of the trousers being stolen had never entered my mind; but the idea that there might have been a *reason* to justify putting some marker on the trousers (whereas I had just done it aimlessly), made me again ashamed of myself, and almost welcome the beating for soiling my trousers in this way.

His sharpness seemed never to desert him. Once, when paying a flying visit to the island in the '70s, I dropped by to see him, he seemed distracted and I was pressed for time. So, holding out my hand and looking him full in the face, I told him again who I was. His put-down was sobering: 'I can hear you,' he said. 'I'm not stupid'.

Notes:

1. Uncle George also visited the Dominican Republic and Jamaica. There was no hint of what sort of life he lead in any of these places. Had he ever married? How much Spanish did he speak after 17 years in Cuba? Nobody knew.
2. A sister, Aunt Nancy, also went to live in America. All three died there, without revisiting the island.
3. Cousin Reggie ended up as the highest-ranking Montserratian officer – Sergeant Major – of that war. He led the Veterans' Parade on Armistice Day.
4. Trescellian = three leaf, in Gaelic, Trefoil.
5. 'Gen' was short for 'General' because of his businesslike air of command; and success in commerce.
6. And yet... Every statement, it seems, is in need of modification. That road to Tar River Estate was recently upgraded, laid with tarmac, at the government's expense. R.E.D. Osborne was the only resident at the far end of it who owned a car; and he dubbed the upgrading 'a red-letter day'. It was his brother, Harold, over lunch one day, who referred to the absence of wheeled traffic along the road, and promptly dismissed the tarmac surfacing as a waste of public money. (R.E.D. wasn't present.) It was at these family tables that I was to learn not always to equate what was good for the family with what was good for everybody.
7. No one seems to remember the process whereby the piano was acquired from Germany.
8. The schooners were locally-owned. 'Wally Wade', from the north of the island, owned *The Morning Prince* and *The Evening Princess*; JCL Wall (white-skinned Montserratian, though born in St. Kitts) owned the M.V. *Romaris* (the concertinaed names of his three daughters,

Rosemary, Mavis and Iris) and , later, the M.V. *Caribee*. In 1947 M.S. Osborne and Wall bought the M.V. *Moneka*. These last were ex-World War II torpedo boats, bought from Alstons, in Trinidad. (See Howard A. Fergus, *Gallery Montserrat: Some People in Our History* (Canoe Press, UWI, 1996, Jamaica.)

9. Of a story, 'The Pig Was Mine'. E. A. Markham (*Something Unusual*, Ambit Books, London, 1986, rep. in *Taking the Drawing-room Through Customs* (Peepal Tree, Leeds, 2002)

10. This is, of course, an overstatement. There were other Markhams, the children of my father's brother, Uncle Joe, who grew up in Harris' while their parents were in Curaçao. They – like another cousin, Josephine, discovered much later, in Paris – were exemplary. The 'Markhams' who complicated our life actually answered to the surname, 'White'.

11. The real target was said to be Wilfred Griffin, a member of the white estate-owning family, who was the manager of an estate further east.

12. The beautiful playing field had once been a Botanical Gardens; and some rubber plants managed to survive the conversion, growing in a cluster at edge next to the school.

13. This is contested. Apparently, the Headmistress of that school at the time was called 'Teacher Jane'. But the person who tested me was, as I remember, Teacher Kitty.

14. *England: an Elegy*, Roger Scruton, pp. 27-35 (Pimlico, London, 2000)

15. If, as some think, Teacher Morgan was hedging his bets, the position may have been nearer to that expressed by the character in Rochester's 'And After Singing Psalm the Twelfth':

> And after singing psalm the Twelfth
> He laid his book upon the shelf
> And looked much simply like himself
> With eyes turned up as white as ghost
> He cried, 'Ah Lard, ah Lard of hosts!
> I am a rascal, that thou knowest.

Teacher Morgan died in 2005, aged 96(?)

CHAPTER THREE
MONTSERRAT: THE IRISH CONNECTION

Where is Montserrat? I quote from the history book.

> Montserrat, a pear-shaped island, lies between 16° 40´ and 16° 50´, north latitude and between 62° 9´ and 62° 15´ west, longitude in the Leeward group of the Lesser Antilles. It is about 11 miles (18 km) long and 7 miles (11 km) wide with an area of 39 ½ square miles (102 sq. km). Antigua, 27 miles (43 km) to the northeast and Guadeloupe, about the same distance to the southeast, are its closest neighbours.[1]

The rumour is that Montserrat was more or less created to solve the Irish problem and that Montserrat would be seen to have been useful should the Irish problem be eventually solved. What particular Irish problem might be the subject for another debate. But it is the case that the Irish colonized the place in the 17th Century, and have left their mark. The story goes something like this.

There are Irish settlers on the neighbouring island of St. Kitts. There are also French settlers on St. Kitts. (Note, when islands are small you are deemed to live on them not *in* them, an aspect of our marginalization not often discussed.) St. Kitts – this is 1632 – is formally divided between England and France. St. Kitts is a small island. Events in far-off Europe make it difficult for three foreign nationalities to cohabit in a small place. The Irish are thought by their neighbours to be suspect. Soon, Irish Catholic 'dissidents' (or suspects) find their way to Montserrat about sixty miles away. This is not a voyage of discovery. I turn again to the historian, Howard A. Fergus, Montserrat's trusted and distinguished chronicler.

> The Spaniards did not settle Montserrat. The honour was reserved for Thomas Warner, who arrived there with a British contingent from the Mother colony of St. Kitts – a Leeward Islands' version of the English Pilgrim Fathers. The colonists were English and Irish Catholics, who were made uncomfortable in Protestant St. Kitts. In Montserrat, they found a new shrine for their faith and a haven from Protestant persecution. News of a Roman Catholic asylum in this corner of the Antilles soon

spread across the Atlantic to the British North American colony of Virginia; in 1633, Catholic refugees, pushed out of Virginia by Episcopalian persecution, also came hither in search of unmolested altars. Montserrat was thus unique in being established as an Irish-Catholic Caribbean colony. When, in 1649, following his victory at Drogheda (in Ireland), Cromwell sent some of his political prisoners to Montserrat, he increased the population and preserved its Irish character.[2]

So Montserrat is a haven, selected by the English, with the dual purpose of easing the problem in St. Kitts and having *some* presence in Montserrat in case the French from neighbouring Guadeloupe decide to claim it – for Montserrat is uninhabited. The 'powers' were always doing that sort of thing to outlying islands. So we have the dissidents/suspects from St. Kitts, in 1632, and their co-religionists down from Virginia the following year, etc. Even though Ireland was soon to lose out in Montserrat to England, Irish place-names endure to this day. From the South of the island you go clockwise from O'Garro's to St. Patrick's to Galway's to Kinsale, inland to Molyneaux, East to Harris'. And if the island was sometimes dubbed, 'The Montpellier of the West', it was more generally known as 'The Emerald Isle'. The first slaves arrived in 1651. Their descendants, today, tend to have Irish names – Irish, Farrell, O'Brien, Riley, O'Garrow, Galloway, Ryan and Roach among them. We had for dinner, with the Sunday roast, Irish potatoes.[3]

Montserrat, as I say, was uninhabited, just as it was said to be uninhabited in 1493 when Christo the Italian desperado Colon (1451-1506) on his second voyage to these parts, passed by and, without landing, named it Santa Maria de Monserrate after the monastery of that name 30 miles northwest of Barcelona in Spain. We know from the work of archeologists that the Caribs had been there. (They, too, had named the island.) Their absence on both occasions of European visitation, 140 years apart, is one of the myths beginning to inform a Montserratian literature.[4]

The Irish presence went further than naming. The Montserratian national dish, a stew called 'goatwater' is thought to derive from both Africa and Ireland. Certainly, credible claims are made for its origin in a Connemara housewife's recipe. The ingredients:

2 quarters goat or sheep	4 cloves garlic, minced
Herbs and chible (local	tablespoon whole cloves,
name for scallions and thyme)	crushed
¾ cup cooking oil	1 tablespoon mace
2 tablespoons catsup	3 oz. fresh marjoram
1 hot green pepper	Salt and pepper

Of course, this wasn't the only creation myth for Montserrat. As a child I sat on the backsteps of my grandmother's house in Harris' and heard someone in the yard put forward the very interesting theory that as Columbus landed, the first thing he saw on the island was a rat, whereon he proclaimed, "A rat, A rat"; hence Montserrat. What slightly works *for* this theory is that Columbus, an Italian, speaking also Spanish to communicate with his crew, was very likely, when startled, to utter the words "Ratto" (It.) or "Ratta" (Sp.).

And let's say he wasn't sure what size of rodent he saw *in English*: 'A mouse? A Rat? = Montserrat?' The difficulty, of course, is that the Admiral didn't actually land on Montserrat, believing the information of his Carib 'girl guides' that the place was uninhabited. Much later, another near-Creation story assumed some force. Montserrat was (of course) thought to be a bastion of civilized (English) practice against the man-eating French of nearby Guadeloupe. My grandmother used to tell the story of a relative, a seafaring man returning as a passenger on a boat to Montserrat. The brutal sea-captain diverted the boat in the direction of Guadeloupe where it was rumoured that young children were baked in the oven and served up for dinner. Fortunately, the relative, a man of spirit and superior ethics, engineered a mutiny and (either arresting, disabling or killing the brutal sea-captain) turned the vessel round to the civilizing waters of Montserrat. (When I first had the privilege of visiting Guadeloupe in the 1970s I was embarrassed that as a child of five or six or seven, I had firmly believed that story.)

And yes, Columbus' name for the island (his not knowing that it had long been called Alliouagana by the Caribs) was prompted by the fact of its mountainous terrain, which put him in mind of the equally-rugged location of the abbey near Barcelona.

Montserrat is in some ways an unlucky island having had its share of hurricanes, floods and volcanoes throughout its recorded history. We published a list after the 1989 hurricane:[5]

1667	Hurricane
1672	Earthquake on Christmas Day, destroying St Anthony's Church.
1737	Hurricane
1740	Hurricane
1744	Hurricane
1766	Hurricane accompanied by flood especially around Fort Ghaut
1772	Hurricane
1792	Hurricane
1843	Earthquake (February 8) Worst in recorded history.

Six deaths.

1866:	Hurricane
1867	Hurricane
1896	Flood caused loss of life and cut off the Windward from the rest of the island. (Powson Flood)
1897	Flood which washed away tramrails belonging to Montserrat Company.
1899	Hurricane
1924	Hurricane
1928	Hurricane
1935	Significant earthquake and volcanic activity
1974	Earthquake
1981	Flood on September 3rd. regarded as the worst in living memory
1989	Hurricane Hugo

The latest disaster, a volcanic eruption in 1995 put most of the tiny island out of bounds, exiling the majority of its 11,000 population. When it seemed likely that ones 'home' would never again be habitable, people began to be concerned not only about what was lost, but what it was to lose 'the place where your family is buried'. This seemed psychologically different from the human and environmental disasters that other peoples had suffered. Around the world there are examples of human abuse on a scale and with a ferocity that no one in Montserrat has experienced – groups massacring other groups, governments massacring their own (and other) people. That is much worse than suffering, collectively, the experience of hurricane and volcano where a certain psychic strength might be gained from the experience. In most cases of social breakdown the question to address is that of bad governance. One day the victims – those who survive – might hope for good government. But if your entire geography is put beyond use, the best you can hope for is to be a good migrant. In addition, size matters. Here, you run up against the limitations of scale. With an island of 32 sq. miles you cannot absorb shocks of nature; there is nowhere to hide.

After Hurricane Hugo in 1989 we raised money for relief. But when, after the 1995 volcano, people approached me in England to 'do something', I was at a loss to know how best to react. I recall working in Germany, in an art gallery in Köln, in the 1970s, and one of my duties was to turn aspiring artists away, having glanced, out of politeness, at their portfolios. What struck me as interesting, at the time, was how many of these artists – often from abroad; quite a few of them Japanese – were producing sketches of Köln and other German cities as they had looked before they were destroyed by bombing in the Second World War. By the time I got to Köln the galleries were full of pre-war images of the city; the Directors wanted no more. So, hurricane and volcano in Montserrat bring the Köln image to mind. Something pre-disaster is required. It was not acceptable to take it as read that the capital, Plymouth, buried under ash, should come back to life in some distant future as a place for agriculture, its history of settlement forgotten. I have written some poems, some stories, a play, sensitive though that this must not grow to neurotic proportions; for even on an artistic level grand narratives are, as they say, out of fashion. And would any of this secure food and lodging for displaced Montserratians?

So the volcano needed something more than the fund-raising response to the earlier hurricane, where the approach to persons connected with Montserrat (George Martin of the recording studios, say) or organizations, like the Commonwealth Foundation, produced mixed results. So when, in a refugee camp in Antigua, someone close to me, to the family, now in her seventies, appealed to me to 'do something', I was in a bit of a dilemma.

I had 'done' something after the hurricane in 1989, Hurricane Hugo. Within a couple of months of the disaster, Howard Fergus and I brought out *Hugo Versus Montserrat*, a collection of 'disaster-photos', interviews, poems and bits of 'history'. This took some organization for I was at the time living in the North of Ireland – working as Writer-in-Residence at the University of Ulster – and Howard (later Sir Howard) was in Montserrat carrying out his duties as Resident Tutor at the university centre and Speaker in the Parliament. I flew out a week after the event, spent about a week interviewing people, taking photographs and generally sensing the mood, the morning after, so to speak. Despite the subsequent frenzy of activity – faxes and phone calls between Coleraine and Montserrat, and with the publishers in London – we thought quite hard about the image of Montserrat we wished the publication to present.

It was a book informed by disaster: all the interviews (whether with politicians, the Chief Medical Officer, American expatriates or random Montserratians talking about their experience) related to the hurricane. The same with the narrative and poems, though, to balance the visual images of wreckage, some photographs of pre-hurricane Montserrat were included. But the aim was not to associate storm-damage with destitution and victimhood. The Mighty Arrow's arrow-shaped swimming-pool strewn with tasteful wreckage and Major Browne's impressive library open to the elements of his roofless villa couldn't be confused with the improvised existence that desperate (Third World) people so often presented to the world on these occasions. So the book did have a coffee-table appearance, glossy cover on good paper and high-quality image reproduction. The pre-hurricane photos were important not just for dramatic before and after effect but to establish a visual reference point to before September 17th. 1989, the date in question.

On the back cover of the *Hugo* book was the image of a red T-shirt with letters proclaiming victory over the hurricane.

I SURVIVED

H U
G O

MONTSERRAT. WI,

Hugo printed in huge letters covered much of the front of the shirt, the lettering on the back announcing:

I WENT TEN ROUNDS
WITH HUGO
& WON.

(The storm had lasted ten hours.) These desperate but upbeat images felt right for the time. We were trying to convey the scale of the wreckage and the fact that the people had lost their homes and possessions, yes, but they were not to be treated with pity. You were being invited to give not out of a sense of paternalistic charity, but to purchase instead an attractive and informative publication, for which you could donate more than the cover price of £5.95. (Howard was to sell close to 6,000 copies of the book in Montserrat, a community whose 11,000 pre-hurricane population had been greatly reduced by migration. In Ireland, where I then lived, I was able to exploit the 'Irish connection', inducing, among others, Michael D. Higgins, poet and filmmaker, and Minister of Culture in the Irish parliament, to participate. (At one memorable 'Montserrat' event in Coleraine, Michael D. showed his own film to do with Montserrat and sugar.)

And yet and yet... *Hugo* couldn't get away from being 'disaster' literature. Furthermore, everyone on the island seemed to have been galvanized into writing poems and stories provoked by the hurricane. You couldn't help being uneasy at contemplating this one source from which the nation's artistic imagination seemed to flow.

Six years after Hurricane Hugo, the more lethal volcano struck. I found myself, as I said, visiting a refugee camp in Antigua, 1997. The woman in question now asked me to 'do something' about it, 'to tell *them*' what was happening. She knew what I had done after *Hugo*: I had interviewed her outside her wrecked two-room house in Harris'. But the mood then was different. I had flown out on a plane with twenty or so electrician volunteers from South Western Electricity Board. I remember sitting next to Geoff and Mervyn from Somerset, Geoff checking with me the name of the stricken island they were going out to assist. They made up for this lack of detail by being passionate about cricket and, having witnessed Viv Richards and Joel Garner in action for Somerset over the years, had very clear images in their mind of Antigua and Barbados: was Montserrat like Antigua and Barbados? So, then, I was concerned that the *particularity* of Montserrat be affirmed. When we saw aid packages at the airport in Antigua destined for Montserrat, with the name of the island misspelled, I drew attention to the fact that the island still retained its lexical integrity even though it was storm-damaged. And the experience on the island was one of vitality (the 'green shoots of recovery' were beginning to show). There was almost a sort of frenzy, even, 'men nailing down roofs as if to inflict punishment, saws and hammers; the revving of motors, impatiently queuing up for gas, emergency generators...' This was then. Even the well-dressed – overdressed, pressed – people waiting in queues at the bank or Cable & Wireless taking their turn to ring out couldn't be viewed now as another small demonstration of 'character'. Another such queue after another such disaster would be a parody. Misspelled packages to an island which was in the process of being abandoned was now more than an affront to those people – to what 'geography' would those packages be redirected? I had come out, in a way, to help secure the island's archives, too late to save Basil Morgan's cricket records in Harris', or Louella Daly's choral tapes at Dagenham, or Major Browne's private library in Plymouth. Now, standing before someone from the refugee camp, all of that seemed ill-preparation for this new catastrophe. Nellie – it was Nellie – was then, well into her 70s. She was calm, and youthful-seeming, and in no way self-pitying; her family were OK, both the daughter in England and the granddaughter in Barbados, and she still believed in God. She trusted me. Before leaving to get my flight to London, I promised her that I would talk to *them*.

It took some time. One of the personal consequences of my investment in the book about Hugo was having had to re-mortgage my flat in London. I didn't mind that; that showed, if nothing else, that those of us, from Montserrat who lived elsewhere, weren't immune from the consequences of events 'at home'. But remortgaging your flat was a one-off gesture. And I had, by then, had enough of fund-raising. So, maybe the thing to do was to take Nellie at her word, and try to locate *them*. That's when I wrote a letter, and addressed it to the British Foreign Secretary.

★ ★ ★

But what informed that letter? Over the years writers, academics, businesspeople had debated the question of Montserrat's size and viability as a community. It was obvious that it wasn't large enough in resources to offer a decent living to more than a fraction of its population. This it shared with many other Caribbean islands. And many people in the developing world were similarly disadvantaged by not having the resources at home to sustain themselves. The difference with the Caribbean – and illustrated to absurd degree in Montserrat – was its small size; lack of living space. Schoolboys talked of remedying this 'accident of history' by joining the islands in one landmass, like Europe, like America, *physically*. My mad cousin, Markie, talked of filling in the sea between the islands. So that we could *walk* to Antigua. The older boys who knew about history said what we needed was a Napoleon to unite the islands. What no one seemed to have a view on – the question was never raised to my knowledge – was what sorts of discussions were taking place between our representatives and... whoever they talked to about doing something about the size of the island. (Of course our representatives were English, or British, the present Governor and his predecessors – the Stapletons, the Whillowbys, the Osbournes – we were the colonized, so maybe that's why we didn't think to put words into their mouths.)

So, given the fact that people had to go abroad to earn a living or to be trained for a profession, what could they look forward to when they returned? The thought of a family-member coming back as a qualified doctor or lawyer, or an ordained priest or teacher with a degree, was exciting and a source of pride. And those boys (and maybe, girls) who talked of exploring other areas of scholarship or professional interest were told not to dream. The problem of size soon led to a dilemma no one seemed to have anticipated: an island of eleven or twelve thousand people could support a limited number of qualified doctors and lawyers and priests. Soon, new graduates, if they were to return, would have to replace others in place. This was a situation that bred suspicion, envy, paranoia.

The decision of some of the more highly-qualified Montserratians to stay abroad was strategically useful, but didn't help to enrich the social and intellectual life of the home community. The colonial lesson of distrusting your near-neighbours was well-learnt in Montserrat, as elsewhere throughout the Caribbean. So there was never any *movement* (except when more or less compelled to – as with the short-lived Federation of the West Indies, in 1958) to unite.

Now, after the 1995 volcano, when asked to tell *them* about our position, I saw myself, alternately, as the schoolboy whose dream was to fill in the sea between the islands, and as the representative, going back, if not to the 1650s when the Irish brought in the slaves, if not even to the 1830s and emancipation, at least soon after – my grandmother's time, say – to argue the case against our isolation, our size. It was in this mood that I wrote a letter.

Sheffield Hallam University
9 February 1998

The Foreign Secretary
Foreign and Commonwealth Office
FCO Whitehall, SWA 2AP

FOR THE ATTENTION OF THE RIGHT HONOURABLE ROBIN COOK

'So Where Is Montserrat Now?'

Please consider these random thoughts during your visit to Montserrat on Wednesday.

In response to my original paper, 'Where is Montserrat?' colleagues have been pointing out where Montserratians have ended up in the wake of the volcanic eruption; but also where the two-thirds of Montserratians (c. 20,000) who have always lived off-island find themselves in the world: they are encamped it seems, on four continents.

What has united Montserratians on and off the island has been the integrity of the island as a geographical unit, the stability of which legitimises dream, memory and longing to return. If this stability is threatened, the effect for Montserratians is to be cast adrift.

No wonder people are studying the map, looking at underdeveloped areas of the Caribbean/Americas which might accommodate an entity the size of Montserrat. Montserratians are thinking about their identity, their collective future, their survival as a people in more constructive ways, it seems, than many of the island's representatives, under the pressure of the moment, seem able to do.

The British government might find this idea of an alternative 'Montserrat' intellectually challenging.

1. We do not wish to rewrite or to deny the history of the island. But, to state the obvious, a territory of 39 sq. km. historically satisfying the minimum requirements of plantation settlement can't sensibly

be thought to fit the minimum requirements of statehood, of nationhood – in terms of being able to stimulate the social, economic and psychic environment necessary to a full life.

That has imposed on us two challenges, one short term, the other longer. In the short term, migration was the answer, initially to Panama and elsewhere in the Americas; and then to Britain. (Members of my family have helped to dig the Panama Canal, have been caught up in a war between Haiti and the Dominican Republic (1937) and have fought in both 'European' World Wars this century.)

Less heroically, people have gone abroad to seek employment. (The poets and novelists are now calculating the damage to family life that has resulted from this legitimatizing of the 'sea-split marriage'.)

2. The second, longer-term challenge – consistent with our size, geography and history – is to seek closer political association with our near neighbours. This objective must not be jeopardised by short-term arrangements (a 'Montserrat' in Africa, therefore, is not the answer). Unhappily, a colonized mentality makes us suspicious of our neighbours; makes us, perhaps, distrust ourselves that we might be able to influence a larger political grouping; but if we are reduced to scattered voices, the force of our being able to negotiate entry to a larger Caribbean unit would be considerably diminished. 'Montserrat' is distinctive enough to play a part in a future Caribbean confederation.

Montserrat might be seen as the Carib-Arawak island of Alliouagana that Columbus renamed on his second voyage in 1493, subsequently settled by people from Ireland fleeing persecution in the 1630s (hence Irish place names throughout); subsequently, despite the interest of the French, a British colony.

But Montserrat is also the relationship between the island and Montserratians abroad. The debate between the two has opened up a space which emotionally and intellectually enlarges the experience of the one and reduces the suspicion of foreignness in the other. Those at home are made larger by the experience, those abroad more grounded.

If the island effectively disappears (and there is no corresponding geographical area to which we could transfer our Mont-serratianness) we will be frozen in a historical moment; a source of renewal would be denied us; we would become, in more than a physical sense, refugees.

This leads to the next point: Britain's responsibility for the island:

3. What kind of responsibility?
(i) *Crisis Management.* In the wake of disaster (hurricane, volcano) Britain, like other countries who have the logistic ability to assist quickly, will respond in the expected way. I have no doubt that Britain has done this when required.
(ii) Moral Responsibility. If Montserrat were an ex-colony – Jamaica, say, or Antigua – sentiment might well prompt Britain to do more than other countries providing relief in the wake of disaster. But Montserrat's claims both coincide with and are different from this.
(iii) *Legal Responsibility.* Montserrat is a colony. Montserratians abroad and at home are defined partly by a constitutional process (different from most other West Indians) which leaves us with a pre-independence mind-set. Surely, not to have broken through that barrier – *and to have lost your country and be dispersed* – is a form of intellectual and perhaps emotional maiming. There must, surely, with British assistance, be a search within the Caribbean basin, for an area at least the size of abandoned Montserrat. (Farms in the Americas are sometimes as large as 100,000 acres). This could be leased for, say, 99 years, where Montserratians can congregate physically and mentally prepare for the next stage.

4. This is not a letter of complaint; it is intended to give an inside view. It is intended to release Montserrat from the footnote which is 'British Dependent Territories', a problem which might be tidied up by giving the populations full British citizenship and the right to settle in Britain. This might be a generous gesture to other peoples who haven't lost their territory. To Montserratians this would be to turn them into refugees, *and to deny them their bargaining power in the next phase of Caribbean constitutional arrangements.*

5. It is important that the personal, the organic connection between the individual and the nation be not marginalized; Montserrat is our *place* where we can – with the confidence of not being judged by others who see us as guests – offer hospitality to strangers; where we could be eccentric and odd without exposing the group or the race to which we are deemed to be a part, to the vulgar assumptions of others – or to excite the interest of the police; where you can, within the law, express your more extravagant selves without self- (or other) censorship. In this place you are not consigned to being an ethnic minority. (This place – we can dream – is open to the possibility of hosting international sporting events – like a Test Match.)

6: *Montserrat's Cultural Profile*. Among the Montserratians who have distinguished themselves are the artists: The Mighty Arrow is an internationally-renowned calypsonian. Dr. Howard Fergus, historian and poet, has long brought distinction to the island. Edgar White is one of the region's most significant playwrights. The choral group, The Shamrock Players, also, have built an international reputation. And I have tried to play my part.

My recent publication, *A Papua New Guinea Sojourn: More Pleasures of Exile* is a travel book but tries to engage with the central problems of Caribbeanness, place and identity, questions eloquently raised by George Lamming in his 1960 book, *The Pleasures of Exile*.

The last section is my biography. The letter is Cced to Clare Short MP, Minister for International Development and to Baroness Symons, House of Lords.

★★★

Some time later, I was to receive two replies. One from Bernie Grant, MP, saying that my communication had been passed to him and he would look into it; and a rather formal letter from someone in the Montserrat Unit at the Department of International Development. It was dated 3 March 1998.

Dear Professor Markham,

The Secretary of State for International Development, Clare Short, has asked me to thank you for copying to her your paper "So Where is Montserrat Now?" which you sent to the Foreign and Commonwealth Secretary before his visit to Montserrat.

Your concept of an alternative Montserrat is an interesting one; but, as the people of Montserrat have been quite clear in their wish to see the island populated as long as it is safe to do so, we are providing appropriate development to meet the immediate needs of those remaining on the island and, in discussion with the Government of Montserrat, we are assessing the priorities for a long term development programme.

Yours Sincerely, (signed)

Pat Scutt
V239
Montserrat Unit.

Notes

1. *Montserrat, Emerald Isle of the Caribbean*, Howard A Fergus, (Macmillan, 1989, Second Edn.)
2. Ibid.
3. After American independence, food was imported into the British Caribbean from Ireland. Hence, throughout the Caribbean, imported potatoes were known as 'Irish' potatoes.
4. Cf. poem, 'Kevin's Message to Montserrat' *in Hugo Versus Montserrat,* E.A. Markham & Howard Fergus, Eds. (LLB, 1989)
5. *Hugo Versus Montserrat,* E.A. Markham and Howard A Fergus, Eds. (LLB, 1989)

CHAPTER FOUR
INSIDE GOVERNMENT HOUSE

That was the name of our house, that was the name given to it by the people of Harris'[1], and as befitting Government House my grandmother was dubbed 'Queen Victoria', sitting up there on her 'throne', even though the throne was a box on the floor of her room, looking down on the back yard. My grandmother was not modest of her status; her house was a big house, as I said, twelve rooms, the house on the hill that had survived two hurricanes, having sheltered a good part of the village in the '24 and '28 disasters. The myth is – and there was truth in this, attested by others who were there, yet it had assumed the status of myth – that my grandfather got up on the dining-room table downstairs, in the middle of the night, and preached a sermon. This was Grandfather Lee who was a lay preacher. So there he was at the height of the storm, preaching, and he preached all night, till morning, when the storm abated. Naturally, it was more or less taken for granted that the marathon preaching effort had somehow contributed to the calming of the storm.

The house didn't, in fact, escape unscathed. In '24, it had suffered a crack in the dining-room wall which, for some reason, was never repaired. We all suspected that it was a sign of quiet satisfaction to my grandmother not only that the house had twice survived but that the crack in this solid, stone wall was evidence of the ferocity of the hurricanes that had been visited on Montserrat.

There is no space in an island of 32 square miles to escape from natural disaster, far less to avoid it. Later, I was fascinated to learn how people with hinterland came to deal with *their* environmental disorders: when hurricanes hit the East coast of North America, the official instruction is to retreat, to move inland, to give forty miles, or two-hundred miles to the storm to blow itself out. Thirty miles from Montserrat and you're in Antigua in one direction and Guadeloupe in the other. So when natural disaster struck Montserrat, safety resided in being secure indoors. If the Englishman's home is, in a generalized sense, his castle, the Montserratian's home, as protection against the elements, was secure only for the few. By all accounts, during the '24 and '28 hurricanes, most of the village crowded into three of four 'secure' homes, one of which was my grandparents'. (Sometime in the 1970s, when I revisited, a couple of old men in the village recalled to me the party they had as children, cooking breadfruit in the kitchen of my grandmother's house – that night in '24 or '28 – while the grownups were gathered in watchful prayer, in other rooms of the house.)

I grew up in this house till I was about eleven (1950-51) with my grandmother who died at the age of 86, in 1953. People now say it must have been a lonely house, as I've acknowledged, and of course it was, but you didn't think of things in these terms then.[2] On the contrary, we liked the fact that it was roomy, because the crowded houses were the houses of poor people in the village, who had to 'live on top of one another'; and you wouldn't have wanted to change places with them.

The house over which my grandmother presided from her bedroom facing the backyard consisted, upstairs, of a drawing-room, with piano and bookcase and glass-panels in the windows, as the centrepiece, with a door leading onto the verandah. To recap: next to it was my mother's room, empty during the week. The other front room was the boys' room, separated from my grandmother's room by a passage with a rail on one side, with a trap-door leading to the dining-room below. At the back of the house, separated from my grandmother's room by a corridor, was the large spare room, on the other side of which was the bathroom and water closet. (There was also an outside toilet, tucked away on the other side of the flower garden; and we used that more often than we used the WC.) Downstairs, you had, leading from the dining-room at the centre, the bread-room (ruled over by Nellie) and, beyond that, the kitchen with the cassava-plate for baking cassava-bread, and the small wood-oven – used for the 'small bake', mainly midweek. (Behind the kitchen, outside, protected by a corrugated-iron shed, was the 'big' oven, used on Saturdays by us and, occasionally, by specially-favoured neighbours.)

Leading back from the dining-room was the 'servants' room, on one side of which (under the bathroom and spare-room) was the downstairs spare room (always suspiciously dark), and on the other side, entry to which was under the verandah, the coal room. In normal circumstances – that is, not weekends, not holidays – when I occupied the house with my grandmother, she being lame in the leg and confined to her room, I effectively had the run of the other eleven. (It might be worth emphasizing – and not just through a child's imagination – that all the rooms in the house were large, apart from the coal room and the servants' room.)

Though it wasn't *quite* like this. Sarah, the younger of the two servants, slept in, not, of course, in the servants' room downstairs, but either on the floor of my grandmother's room or on the trap-door to the dining-room (secured at night). I also slept in my grandmother's room, in my own bed, under mosquito netting. When, occasionally, there was a scare in the village – a robbery – John Griffin, a young man from nearby Garden Hill, would come over and sleep in the upstairs spare room. (John would have been in his early twenties, the son of a white planter who owned one of the local estates, and someone whose family came from Garden Hill: he was big (security) and a useful odd-job man.)

The row of small houses on Garden Hill constituted our neighbours on one side, maybe about a quarter of a mile away. 'Aunt Na's' was the first house, then Mrs. Buffong (We all referred to Mrs. Buffong's house, even though there was a Mr. Buffong, Fenton, who used to work the cassava mill for my grandmother, grinding the cassava root for bread: the cassava-mill would be set up on the front lawn for that purpose. Mr Buffong was also the stand-in local cricket umpire. His eyesight was poor, so it was said that 'he gave you out because of the shout.') The half a dozen or so other houses at Garden Hill led on to the playing field and the infant school. Some of the people who lived there used to come to our house for water, filling up buckets and cans from the tap above the trough in the front yard, where Nellie did the washing. So there were people coming and going throughout the day: we didn't feel isolated. (My brothers reminded me, too, that there were lots of visitors during the holidays.)

The back of the house bordered on Mrs. Meade's land. (Mr. Meade had been away, in Curaçao, and had died shortly after he had returned, so 'Mrs. Meade' made better sense than 'Mrs. Buffong'); and John, the son of the house, was my closest friend during those years (and a close friend still, though long settled in Canada). We used to fly kites together standing on a massive, flat rock above our house, and climb the huge sour-grape 'tree' that bordered our land; and make things like baskets out of dried vine roots, and wallets out of 'found' pieces of leather. When, later, it was time for grammar school, John and I used to walk (and then to ride our bicycles) the six miles to Plymouth on a Sunday afternoon. During the 'walking' days John, who was two years older, used sometimes to carry my heavier case, while I took his.

The house was not as empty as it seems. There was Nellie. She didn't sleep in but came early in the morning and left late afternoon or early evening. Nellie, more than anyone except perhaps my grandmother, is the person I most associate with the house.

She was employed to do the cooking and washing and ironing, but seemed to do everything else as well. She made the bread, she bathed us when we were young, she organized Sarah – as she had done the child-maid before Sarah. The front lawn is forever brightened in my mind by the white, family sheets, made whiter with *blue*, spread out to dry, by Nellie. After she cooked the family dinner she would cook, or supervise Sarah's cooking of food for the pigs.

Yes, even though this wasn't a farm, it was the country, and there were animals in close proximity, the animal pound situated on the other side of the back yard, being an important factor.

The house also had a feeling of not settling down to its prescribed function, and this, as much as anything else, gave you a sense, growing up there, that there was more happening than perhaps was the case. Too many things were in the wrong place for you to get bored. The upstairs spare room, for instance, sometimes contained cotton, brought in from one of the 'estates', on its way to the ginnery in town. I remember the hours spent bouncing on the mounds of fresh damp cotton (the seeds still in), to my heart's content. Downstairs, the servants' room housed the cassava mill (cassava mill and cassava box) not servants. (The cassava box was the size and shape of an adult coffin and was made, in the village, by the same man, Mr. Daley, who made coffins. This did cause me some confusion as a child.)

Talking still about things not chiming with their function: even the boys' room upstairs was rarely occupied by me because I had nightmares when I slept in a room by myself. During the school holidays my brothers slept in it, but it was, for most of my time there, empty, though I assumed a sort of ownership of it during the day. Emptiness was something, I can see now, I was always struggling to fill. While my grandmother had her bath at night (attended by Sarah, or, occasionally, by a female relative visiting the house) I tried to stay awake in the drawing-room outside, stumbling over some book from the bookcase. It was important to stay awake because I was, in a way, responsible for occupying all those sections of the house that my grandmother and Sarah weren't occupying: i.e. all but one room at the back of the house. Downstairs was a worry: first, there was that large, spare room behind the bread-room and kitchen. It was always slightly dark and unwelcoming, and was used mainly to store lumber; but I got permission to put my pet goat there some nights. Not only did this separate it from the common goats and pigs, for which the animal pound was good enough, it gave me a sense that something else of mine was filling a (somewhat scary) space in the house.

But, in the daytime, the house was a hive of activity: there was cooking and ironing in the bread-room downstairs and, at weekends, much baking of bread (and cakes). This happened every Saturday, though if the vicar was due to preach at our local church, and hence coming to lunch, a greater effort was made. Or if there was a religious festival coming up, harvest, say, things would be done on a much bigger scale, with the killing of a goat or the roasting of a suckling pig to entertain the inevitable Sunday visitors. When no one was expected on the Sunday we made do with, perhaps, a roasted chicken for lunch – though the bread and cakes were a constant.

The house attracted people. There would be Mr. Frederick. There was 'Jim Brim', a man who had been abroad and returned, there was 'Sea Baby', an old lady who lived on the edge of the village, the last two presenting themselves most mornings for their 'tea'. 'Tea' was probably of the herbal variety, but supplemented with plentiful fresh fruit from the garden – sour-sop, paw paw – and cassava bread.

Other visitors to the 'yard', of a somewhat more elevated (social) position, included Brother Howes, the Pentecostal minister and Mr (Barlow) Daley, who was a Sanitary Officer, as well as a Methodist lay preacher. In passing Brother Howes would sometimes say a prayer, and Mr Daley would read a verse or two from the Bible. Also, I seem to remember a man from the Jehovah Witnesses, who came, occasionally, with 'Good News'. The local head of police visited, to bring my grandmother the latest police news, often, it seemed, to impress on her, how dishonest some people around were. Equally entertaining were the visitors who came upstairs to play the piano, the headmaster of the Anglican school, Edwin White (Teacher Mayers) and one or two others.

People crossing the back yard from Garden Hill to Harris' village would stop for a chat, and there was always the odd 'labourer' come to work on bits of the land (two tasks? three tasks?) around the house, one of whom acted as 'groom' for our horse, Ruby. They, too, would be given dinner in the back yard, and regale my grandmother, looking down from her throne, with the village gossip. So, after all that, it was nice sometimes to feel shut in for the night. We had to make sure that all the outside doors were shut, locked (the seven doors downstairs, plus the animal pound) and three upstairs (technically four, with that to the boys' room). What was more important was to make sure that the little window, from which you could step out on to the front steps (or step in from the front steps) was secure. Then it was quite nice to shut out the world.

What changed things at weekends was that my mother and brothers and sister came home. They arrived from Plymouth on Friday afternoon and then everything was busy. They would bring all the ingredients that my grandmother needed for baking, etc., and presents for me. Despite the weekend baking, the life of the house swung from the back end to the front, with people sitting out on the verandah at night, and lights blazing in rooms that were dark all week. We used the dining-room on Saturday and Sunday, had guests to dinner, had intelligent conversation in the drawing-room on Saturday night and Sunday afternoon, sometimes had someone playing the piano. And this was repeated (though in a more relaxed way) during the holidays.

One change, for me, at weekends, was in the ritual of eating. During the week I had most of my meals with my grandmother in her room (where she usually fussed over whether I was eating enough). Though sometimes I had lunch in the drawing-room or on the verandah; or downstairs in the dining-room, where Nellie would have to report on how much I'd left on my plate. At weekends, however, within the family together (and during the holidays) strict dining-room etiquette was enforced: knife & fork, no elbows on the table, grace. Then you had to ask politely to be excused when you had finished eating and you wanted to leave the table while the adults were still talking amongst themselves. Oh yes, on those occasions, when cake was served for desert, you used cake-forks.

Loneliness apart, was it dull growing up here? Comparing it with people's lives in another society, the solitariness that I inhabited *was* a bit unnatural – even though I listened to the radio from time to time when the battery was charged. But it didn't seem so. There were no men in our house, but that wasn't so very unusual in the Caribbean[3], fathers of friends having gone off to Curaçao or Aruba, or further afield. (My own father, who had had two spells in Aruba, taking the rest of the family second time round, leaving me with my grandmother, was now in Canada, a priest. The expectation was that we would go to join him after my grandmother's death – as my grandmother, proud head of the household, the one with status, would never be induced to leave home for abroad; and my mother would never abandon *her* mother to go and live in a place that she didn't know.)

When I was about six or seven, I suppose, I was aware of this arrangement, mentally packed for Toronto. Ten years later, my mother walked into the drawing-room one afternoon and announced, without consultation (for that was the way in the West Indies between parents and children) that we were going to England.

The 'family', as I say, was always seen as my grandmother's family, of which my mother was the link. It was the branch of the family that had achieved things at home and abroad, and my grandmother would remind me, constantly, of this: even here in Montserrat, our cousins in town who owned stores and the cotton ginnery, and a hotel, and imported cars, and were in politics, were all on my grandmother's side. My father, whose trade was carpentry and who was a lay-preacher in the Methodist church, had married into the family and, all agreed, in that he had done well for himself.

My grandmother, distrusting – with good reason – my father, was always a little wary of me, as I was said to look like him. There were a couple of pictures of him in the house, one, as a soldier standing between two other black soldiers in army uniform, posing with a rifle. The other was a close-up in clerical gear, complete with dog-collar. We were supposed to draw huge satisfaction from the fact that he had fought in the war – on the winning side (he was part of the Canadian, not the British contingent, though I didn't register that at the time), and he subsequently emerged with a theological degree from Canada's prestigious McGill university. (When he went on to acquire two further degrees at a time when my brothers' higher education was in jeopardy, we weren't so impressed.) So it was hard to square the negative mutterings within the family (though not from my mother) of the soon to be Very Reverend in Toronto, with the high regard he seemed to enjoy throughout the island. (When, in the late '70s, I met him at his church on Shaw Street, Toronto, to interview him for a book I was thinking of writing about my grandmother, he put the estrangement from the family down to my mother.) He was a man of limited credibility, difficult to admire. What struck me at the time was how unconvincingly he managed to put his case of wronged innocence and, seeing that he had had decades to get it right, his desperation for his side of the story to be credited was unexpectedly sad.

★ ★ ★

I remember a scene with my grandmother, which puzzled me then, and taught me later not to pretend to have understood her. I wrote it up some years ago when I thought the book about her might materialize.

It was in the old house, of course, middle of the week, nothing unusual. The week before, in the evening, I had taken a chance to send Sarah to the village to buy a sugar cake, and, by chance, my grandmother had called her during the ten minutes it would have taken her to get to Mr. Lee's shop and back. I had entered into the deception in pretending to locate Sarah. But when she got back from the village she promptly owned up to the fact that I had sent her on an errand. My grandmother punished me, as expected, by seizing the sugar-cake from Sarah and throwing it away – and promising a beating by my mother at the weekend. That would teach me for not eating what was put in front of me at home, and sending out to the village for food. So, I was a bit watchful of my grandmother. However, on this night, Sarah was assisting her with her bath and for once, waiting outside in the drawing-room, I didn't fall asleep over my book: *Robinson Crusoe* was an advance on *The Pilgrim's Progress* in this respect. Or, for that matter, *John Halifax, Gentleman* by

Mrs. Craik (I couldn't get into this; even the names of the characters, Ursula and Jael, didn't appeal.) It was the middle of the week, and now that her 'crisis' had passed, we were perhaps back to the old routine.

The wick wasn't burning well in the lamp, darkening the shade on one side, but I could see to read. I had been trying, alternatively, to feel the pain of Crusoe hitting his leg on the sand as he was washed ashore, and to figure out why he had two surnames, Robinson and Crusoe at the expense of a Christian name. I had three Christian names: I was ahead of him there. During all this Sarah came out to say that my grandmother – her bath over – wanted to see me. A quick check. No panic. She had called me a heathen just this morning, but that was because someone told her I hadn't cried at our neighbour's, Miss Bessie's, funeral. But that was just my grandmother's way of speaking. She had often called Teacher Morgan a heathen because he didn't believe in God, but she didn't really dislike him. I checked for the more obvious signs of heathenness: yes, I'd washed my hands and feet. Hadn't cleaned my teeth yet, but I wasn't ready for bed; I hadn't forgotten, I was ready for Mammie.

But as I entered the room I found her, not under the mosquito net but sitting on her commode – used as a seat – in a nightdress and dressing-gown. She had an expression as if she were up to something. (I tried not to keep nails in my pockets, which made holes, which she didn't like; she couldn't get me on that.) I liked the smell of bayrum in the room, so much better than the Canadian Healing Oil which she sometimes used and which got everywhere. I thought about a joke we had been doing to death since last weekend, about my grandmother's new servant. She had got a letter from the Governor, the Hon. Charlesworth-Ross, in connection with registering some land at Mulcares, and he had signed it: 'Your Humble Servant'. We liked the idea of the plump, well-dressed fellow, all superior and fat-cheeked and light-skinned, descending from his official car to fetch my grandmother's ewer of water, or to feed the pigs in the animal pound last thing at night. My grandmother herself, protesting, had been tickled by the idea. That was a bayrummy sort of joke that her present aspect seemed to invite, not a Canadian Healing Oil explanation for wrongdoing.

'Yes, Mammie.'

'The teeth still hurt?' she asked me. I was tempted to correct her: you got the same treatment for one tooth as for three, so there was no benefit in having more than one go bad at a time; but I let it pass in case she thought I was checking up on her grammar. Anyway, that was all in the past, that was this morning when I thought there might be a chance of my missing school.

'You too small always to have teeth hurting. Get the glass.'

'The glass?'

'The glass, the glass.' The glass was on top of the dressing-table. At the same time she was reaching towards the press (which is what we called the wardrobe) – she didn't need to move from the commode to do this – for the hidden bottle. The press also contained the family silver – two huge, misshapen spoons – and books to do with magic I was not allowed to read; so I was already thinking of its new name – wardrobe – to see if that would help to open it up to me.

And then she handed me the bottle.

(My grandmother had been nearly poisoned by that bottle. It had been sent out from Plymouth, as usual, and she had taken a sip and had promptly spat it out; and that action had saved her life. It turned out that instead of her usual bottle of brandy they had sent out a bottle of DDT in a brandy bottle – bottles were always reused, and the original labels weren't always taken off – and after she had poured herself a glass, topped up with water, and tasted the bitterness, she realized the mistake, and spat it out.)

'Here, here. Open it, open it. You teeth wearing out and you don't even grow up yet. The Lord works in mysterious ways. Judge not His ways.'

I braced myself for the sermon, but she had finished.

'Pour, pour.'

So I poured brandy from the glass, and looked round for the water that she diluted it with when, occasionally, she had to take the 'medicine' for her asthma.

'Now, you must gargle.'

The brandy was for me. This was a trap; I had to be careful. There was already talk in the village about someone we knew, a boy 'not even in the Seventh Standard, yet', who was addicted to toothaches. It was well-known that when you had a toothache in the middle of the night, or at a time inconvenient to go to the dentist in town, the only thing to relieve the pain was to gargle with brandy. This boy in the village was so far gone, he had to be taken off the expensive brandy and put on to white rum – the thing that the men in the rumshops drank, which was said to shrivel your liver: that's how far the boy had gone. He was famous for writhing and moaning in front of his mother, but ending up drinking the medicine, anyway; and having to miss school or Sunday School because of the state of his breath. So I had to be careful because it was hinted that if neither brandy nor white rum worked with us, we would have to go back to taking the traditional castor, cod-liver or Canadian Healing oils, for toothache.

I sipped the brandy and made a face, a face intended to convey that the brandy was unpleasant, not that the toothache was unbearable. So it wasn't an extravagantly ugly face, just a moderately ugly face, and that seemed to satisfy my grandmother, a shrewd judge in these matters. She chuckled a little. And as I gargled I felt the full force of the medicine which, as medicine, didn't have to be diluted with water.

'I'm going down, you know,' she said, as if I were an adult. So I had to pretend not to understand. 'Going right down.' The only thing to do was to take another sip of the brandy and pretend to be in pain.

'Then you children will be without me... Baby and the rest of you.' ('Baby' was my mother; it embarrassed me to have my mother referred to in this way.) But then, my grandmother grew philosophical.

'The Lord will provide,' she said.

To which I felt obliged to counter: 'The teeth getting better.'

'Things turn upside down.' She wasn't listening to me, but her mood was lightening. 'Bright ones turn out bad. Your great uncle turn out bad. And your father.'

I didn't say anything.

'You know?'

'Yes, Mammie.'

'Who tell you?'

'Don't know.' I lied.

'Your father was one of the bright ones.'

'Sorry, Mammie.'

'And you just as stubborn. When I hear that you refuse to cry at Bessie funeral...'

'I forget. Forgot,' I said. But of course I hadn't forgotten. I had made a bet with a boy at school not to cry at funerals. My cousin Markie (the one I call Horace, to make him fictional) even threatened to laugh out loud when the coffin was being lowered into the grave but I didn't want to go that far. I wasn't sure if Teacher Morgan was right about there being no God.

'A funeral is a funeral,' my grandmother was saying. 'You have a hard heart. To forget.' Then she sighed and changed the subject. 'Why that child taking so long with the hot-water bottle?' (That child was Sarah.) 'And tell her to bring a glass.'

I was relieved to be doing something, so I went for the glass myself. I had to open up the trap-door to the dining-room. Sarah must have used one of the outside steps to get round to the kitchen or bread-room. From the dining-room, I called to tell her that my grandmother was waiting for the hot-water bottle, and she answered by sucking her teeth, saying something about the fire in the coalpot going out.

Back upstairs, we settled down to our new drinks. My grandmother's consisted of very little brandy drowned in water and mine was, as before, undiluted. I now gave up the pretence of gargling.

She was daring me, teasing me, pouring more brandy into the glass each time I finished. Now, I was emboldened to smack my lips in the way that some of the men did in the rum shops in the village. I calculated that my grandmother had already made up her mind not to have my mother beat me. And if I had a hangover in the morning, she would have to explain it away. So I didn't wait for her to urge me to drink.

'Your grandfather never touched a drop,' she said, simply. 'But God take him, nevertheless.' And now she was direct, dropping the roundabout approach: she wanted to die in peace. Many of the best didn't die in peace. There had been a doctor in the family. And a lawyer. And many parsons, one of them ordained, even. But these things didn't hide godlessness. She was frightened for me. I was even beginning to look like my father. There was talk in the house that I should be a doctor or a lawyer or a priest.

She was frightened of such talk, for such a position, when you were stubborn, could lead to harm. Her brother, Ned, in New York, managed to remain a Christian even though he was a doctor. But he wasn't stubborn or wilful. Like me.

In the end I assured my grandmother, as she demanded – and as a ten-year old, I didn't see what I had to lose – that I would not become a doctor or a lawyer or a priest.

'You swear?'

I swore and raised my glass.

Finally, Sarah came in with the hot-water bottle and took away the glasses to wash them, and I went off to brush my teeth and get myself ready for bed.

The next 'interview' on the subject in my grandmother's room must have been a couple of years later; I was already at the Grammar School. The priest had been with her. This time when I was called into the room there was no promise of brandy; my grandmother was lying under the mosquito net and the room smelt of Canadian Healing oil.

I should be given a chance, she said, not looking at me, her voice registering a new distance between us; for no one was so far gone that he didn't deserve a chance.

'Yes, Mammie... A chance?'

I learnt that a heathen among heathens might still find the Lord merciful. If they were all heathens and didn't know any better, the Lord might not punish them.

I was thinking of all the things I had done to make me a heathen. But she couldn't help me, she said, for the parson had counselled against it. She was wrong to think she could put a little money aside to send me to a heathen country where God might not notice me in the crowd. My family couldn't banish me to a heathen country, that would be ungodly; did I know a heathen country?

'Russia,' I said, without thinking.

'You stupid or crazy?'

Then my grandmother seemed to drift off to sleep.

We never finished the conversation.

★ ★ ★

What did I do with myself? I helped in the house. On baking days I would help to make the mixture for the cake. You started with the big earthenware dish and a wooden spoon, and Nellie would check that it was properly washed; then a dozen eggs would be set out. The usual mix was a dozen eggs, a pound of sugar, a pound of plain flour, a pound of self-raising flour, butter and baking powder, and the spices – vanilla, almond and raw spice – starting with the eggs. Then the butter and sugar, then flour as required, mixing the plain and self-raising: someone would add the requirements as you stirred the mix. The form was to beat the egg-butter-sugar a dozen times with your right hand, then shift a dozen times with your left hand, and repeat the process until you were too tired and one of the adults (or my sister, if she was around) would take over.

(Often, I'd be relegated to 'pounding' the spice in the mortar. My grandmother's cast-iron mortar and pestle was a resource for others in the village, too. To reduce the dried spice to powder, you'd first break it up, put the pieces in the mortar and, with the pestle, start pounding. It's what, today, we'd call low-tech.)

I used to help, too, to grind the cassava. Mr. Buffong, from Garden Hill, usually ground the cassava on the mill, set up on the front lawn. The cassava root would be peeled and washed in the trough, and Mr. Buffong would start by loading the wooden tray at the front of the mill. Then, with his right foot he would press down on the pole secured to the ground at one end and attached to the axle of the wheel at the other, to start the wheel; and then begin feeding the cassava into the throat of the Mill. I would get behind him and help to pedal the pole that drove the wheel. Or sometimes I'd just stand and watch the white, ground cassava pile up in its box (its coffin) underneath the mill. It was fascinating to know that it was poisonous until all the juice had been squeezed out of it in the press overnight; and I often wondered how easy it might be to kill someone, by feeding them this. (After the grinding the cassava mill would be washed and a couple of men would carry it round the back of the house and store it in the servants' room, till next time.)

Then, there was the reading to my grandmother, something that my brothers had done before me. At night, sometimes, after her bath, I was called in to perform this task; it was a test, too, of more than my reading ability; for stumbling over the Bible was not thought to be funny. Occasionally, something from an old newspaper might be asked for, but more usually it was the Bible. Both were difficult because the newspaper had words like 'divorce' and 'rape' that you were supposed not to know – and those you *had* to trip over or mispronounce – and the Bible gave you nightmares.

When I was a little bit older I could help with the slaughtering of the animals. First of all, the chickens: I was allowed to wring the neck of a chicken that we were going to have for dinner, and help Sarah or Nellie to pluck it. From there I graduated to killing the pig or the goat. I soon became expert at removing the hair from the pig: you had a huge pot of boiling water ready and you poured some cold ash from the coalpot over the dead pig (its throat cut) lying on green banana leaves spread on the ground, then you poured the boiling water, waited for a few seconds and, with a large spoon, you started to scrape – each movement of the spoon revealing clean skin.

I also became quite good at skinning the goat, hanging the dead goat upside down on a bar in the kitchen and, more with a balled rag than with the knife, removing the skin (as far as the neck) without a nick. So when I sometimes boast that I grew up on a farm, that's the sort of thing I mean.

★ ★ ★

So there were we, that summer, 1956, preparing for England, my grandmother three years dead, the house in Harris' already in a state of semi-abandonment. I had employed my best 'sign-writer's' hand to address the suitcases, and my mother's trunk. Everything had to hint at our status. The writing mustn't be too flowery but it must be distinctive. My mother had a terrible time deciding what would go into the trunk. Best clothes, of course, but heirlooms, the two big silver spoons that used to lodge in my grandmother's cupboard, crockery and cutlery; her best Bible. The crockery was a problem because we entertained right to the end, and had, of course, to use the best crockery; so the trunk had constantly to be packed and unpacked.

Someone was employed to 'dust' the house after we had gone, perhaps to demonstrate that we weren't abandoning it. At the same time, no one *said* how long we would be in England for. Certainly, we weren't like some people who felt that we'd spend a few years only, make some money and return, because, in a way, we were about to lose our security, our sources of income. The land would be left behind; people who worked for us and owed us favours, and provided favours in return, would be left behind. And what would replace our status in the village, in the island?

But my mother was positive that my brothers were in the right place, in England, and that we'd all get a better education there than in America where West Indians weren't equal with Americans, or in Canada, which no longer appealed.

My mother's style was different from my grandmother's. If my grandmother reclined on the floor of her room or sat on her throne-box, my mother more or less always posed for the camera, even though no camera was in sight, usually. I have a photograph of the family, the earliest I can find, where we are all posing for the camera at the bottom of the steps at the front of the house in Harris'. I can't remember the occasion but, going by the picture, I must have been about six or seven with me and my sister standing either side of my mother, who is sitting. My sister is twice my size, though only five years older. Standing on a step behind us are my brothers, strangely thin, in crisp, white suits. Everyone is serious; everyone looks miserable or terrified, except my mother, who is closest to being relaxed. Even her polka-dot dress brings the only bit of colour to the dress-code, apart from the odd shoes and tie. In the background, you can see the door to my mother's room, as well as the one to the drawing-room and, on the left, the shingles on the side of the 'boys' room.[4]

This picture confirms my memory of my mother as being stylish. At school, in Plymouth, girls in my class used to mimic her walking down the street, head held high, ample purse under her left arm, and a free-swinging right arm. She, quite simply, owned the street. When, shortly before we left home, my mother had an altercation with that carpenter I mentioned, who had rented the downstairs section of one of our houses on Parliament Street, she put a stop to the argument by slapping him in the face. (Obviously, I realize now that we couldn't go to America for, in the film version my mother should play the lady of the house repelling the suitor, whereas in Eisenhower's America – and Kennedy's and Johnson's, etc. America – she would have had to play the maid.) In the Montserrat version the carpenter took her to court and the magistrate (a friend, "Teacher Tom") fined her EC$25, which my mother, proudly, paid.

Her passion for style and saving 'face' outweighed most things. This is true of everyone in Montserrat but my mother had the means, or the family had the means, to carry it off. When I failed an exam at the Grammar School and a couple of my friends who passed came to lunch, my mother embarrassed the entire company by declaring herself 'ashamed' at my failure. Again, although at the time, we couldn't afford it, she acquired a car, a Chevrolet, M86, which was no end of trouble, because the road leading up to the house in Harris' was too rough for the car (and the driver forced it), and because the driver was often uncontactable or drunk; or doing favours in the car for his friends. It seemed, forever, to be breaking down, its engine flooded. But we had our car, others had to use the bus, or walk, or rely on lifts. So even though we didn't know where my mother would lead us, we thought it might be somewhere interesting.

That many of the wrong decisions seem to have been made is easier to see now. Packing for England, we left our books behind, gave them away, but brought cassava bread for people we didn't know that well, people living in places like Manor House.

Notes

1. A distant relative, Mike Morson, then living in Trinidad, writing to my grandmother, addressed the letter to Government House. Apparently, some people in the Treasury in Montserrat were not best pleased.
2. I was reminded, recently, that the daughter of a neighbour, now a member of the family, kept my grandmother company at nights, in the years when I was at the grammar school.
3. See, *My Mother who Fathered Me*, Edith Clarke, 1953; also, the poem, 'Two', by Andrew Salkey, in *Away* (Allison & Busby, 1980)
4. This picture, intended for the cover of this book, was lost during my move from Sheffield to Paris in 2005. The photo on the cover, taken at much the same time, is less formally 'dressed'.

CHAPTER FIVE
DEATH IN THE HOUSE

I remember walking along the main street in Harris'. This was in 1953 so I must have been thirteen though, in recollection, it seems as if I was younger. (Though I sort of remembered the sermon Mr. Ryan had preached the previous Sunday, after the news that Stalin in Russia had died; and if what he said about Stalin was true we were all, in a way, lucky that Stalin had died.) Anyway, I was walking along the main road in Harris'. A usual sort of day, late afternoon, not too warm; I'm still in my 'school' clothes – short pants, clean shirt, socks and probably the pair of shoes I inherited from Uncle Joe – not Stalin, but my father's brother visiting from Curaçao. I hated the shoes, they didn't fit the shape of my feet and, anyway, I would have preferred my own, new shoes. My mother had shamed the visiting uncle into giving me the shoes, so of course I had to wear them. We had all been on the verandah of our house late one afternoon having soft drinks when Uncle Joe – who I was meeting for the first time, I think – said that I was growing up to be a man, and my mother mentioned my needing new shoes; at which point Uncle Joe said that he and I probably had the same sized feet, and offered to let me try on the shoes he was wearing. They didn't exactly fit, but everyone present said that they did; and my mother said that as they were a fit, he had better give the shoes to me. Then Uncle Joe jokingly asked for permission to wear the shoes home, a request that my mother granted; and then I was asked for permission for him to wear them home, which I granted. And a couple of days later the shoes were duly delivered to us, courtesy of Uncle Joe. So, of course, I had to wear them.

I was self-conscious, then, walking through the village in another man's shoes, paying not too much attention to what was going on around me; but as I went past the little rum shop and Mr. Lee's bread shop, just opposite Bethesda Methodist church and Tan Tan's and Uncle Mike's house, I heard some men outside Mr. Lee's shop talking of the recent death in the village and saying, casually, in a light-hearted way, that they expected Miss Dovey to be the next one to go. Miss Dovey was my grandmother.

And, yes, she was 'going'; but this was the second joke I had heard recently about death, dying, and it seemed well-meant and inoffensive. More surprisingly, I thought it was almost a privilege to hear my grandmother being spoken of as if she were something more than a special woman of 86 who was dying. That added a spring to my step. That made me forget Uncle Joe's ill-fitting shoes. I was close to my grandmother; I felt ridiculously privileged. I wasn't allowed by her carers to see her the last week before she died; and that's why, perhaps, I have so obsessively, through the years, set out to revisit those times.

I have written about trying to keep awake in the drawing-room in the evening while my grandmother had her bath in her room; of my working through (dipping into?) the books in the bookcase, *Robinson Crusoe*, *The Pilgrim's Progress*, etc.; of the time that my grandmother encouraged me to sip brandy – not just to gargle with it – for the toothache I faked. She had recruited me as a bidder in one of the animal pound auctions – I must have been about nine or ten – in order to secure the pig in question. She told me stories about her family, the doctor in Boston, the lawyer in New York (they both turned out to have been in New York), and the young sister who, at aged fourteen or sixteen – some say, aged eleven – played the organ on a Sunday in the Methodist church at Bethel.

Of course it wasn't all sweetness and light: during the school holidays she made me practise the piano for an hour every day before I was allowed to go out to play. And she was relentless where loyalty to family honour was concerned. Whenever I came out with an idea of which she disapproved (my asking, for instance, if members of our family had *really* been slaves in the past) she would calmly pose a simple question: 'Are you stupid or crazy?' Naturally, I was always minded to say I was crazy. But craziness was not allowed, as that would be a slight on the family, so, delay as I might, I would, in the end, have to admit to being stupid. That was when she was only exasperated; when she was really angry things could be more tricky – like that night when she threw away my sugar-cake that Sarah had bought for me in the village. To this day I love her without reservation.

We had abandoned the house, the houses, in 1956; and the pretence, from England, of maintaining some sort of establishment in the West Indies ran up against practical problems, so that efforts were soon concentrated on maintaining one of the two houses in Plymouth. But even this 'flagship', Spring Dale, opposite the Evergreen Tree, had gone down-market, from being the residence of the Principal of the Grammar School to being turned into a restaurant (upstairs) and a travel agents (below). Then, within a couple of decades Hurricane Hugo and then the volcano put an end to that, too.

The shock for me, though, was visiting the island in 1970, first time back – first time in an aeroplane – fourteen years after we had left, to find the old house in Harris' was already on its way to being a ruin. Clearly, there were problems with the roof, and bits of the upper portions of the house were beginning to sag; the thing was gradually been pulled out of alignment; it was like – the images, I remember – a ship at sea, listing, like a weird living thing in pain, but silent; it was disturbing, it was *shaming*. Naturally, my mother couldn't be told about this. Neighbours, who didn't always live nearby, claimed it to be dangerous. After my departure, I'm told, they started to dismantle it, helping themselves not just to doors and windows, etc. – and some of the drawing-room windows which still had their glass – but to wood which, some say, could be identified in village houses up to the time of the (1995) volcano. That was some small consolation that the house lived on in this way.

By the time I had visited again, in the late-1970s, the structure was down, a combination of woodlice – the upper part of the building was in wood – and people from the village scavenging. The original structure – our house! – lay bare with its innards open; exposed. My stunned response was recorded at the time.

> Then, a startling thing which sent prickles through my body. We were inside the foundations, we had to hack our way through, break branches (I suffered the sharp but recurring fear of encountering a snake, as you couldn't always see where you were putting your foot; and the occasional ground-lizard scurrying away made you melt). So we were standing in what would have been like the kitchen, though the wall that separated it from the bread-room to the right, had gone: maybe it was wooden, though I didn't think it was, separating it from the big room at the back of the house. Of course it wasn't wooden, that had been the original back wall of the house, the big room at the back having been added in my time. It was never used except for storing lumber and things like that; and my old pet goat which would be brought in there at nights, my grandmother's favour to me, to prevent it being put in the pound, which was a public sort of place that was meant for animals which would be rescued by their owners for a fee, or auctioned after six weeks. Our own pigs were kept in the pound, but pigs were pigs. On top of this spare room at the back of the house was the upstairs bathroom loo, the water-closet. Showering there was a test of nerve, for behind the overhead pipes, you were always likely to find a wood-slave, the most disgusting sort of lizard, trying to keep itself cool. These creatures had a habit of falling off the pipes, but doing so very slowly, parts of them hanging in the air for minutes. It was often too messy to drive them out, too unnerving to kill them, so you took your chances [with the shower] underneath, flesh creeping at the thought of what might fall on you.

Well, this 'upper room' was not open to the sky as expected, but overhung by a giant tree and leaves giving it the appearance of being protected; and sitting in the solid, concrete bathtub – not a crack on it – secure still in its concrete frame, clamped to the outside wall, concrete looking so new – sitting there, tomblike, was a growth. The luxurious [sic] clump seemed too well-positioned, too settled, too arrogant in its placing for it to be an accident…[1]

As you do when things you took for granted are no longer available to you, I began to treasure this house, to revisit in detail its functions, its *function*, to try and determine not just what its twelve rooms were for, but what the whole thing added up to. (It was said that some Jamaicans who came to England at about the time that we did, burnt their houses at home before setting out, in order to ensure that however hard things might turn out in England, they would have to stick it out because there was nothing to go back home to. This was so much not the mind-set of our family – and yet, there seemed less and less to go back to – that we had to start wondering whether what we hung on to as being valuable and valued, pre-England, was as 'unsolid' as those houses left behind.)

There would be no more baking of bread in the bread-room downstairs. Nellie, who did the washing and ironing as well as the cooking, would not be replaced at her ironing-table, her flatirons heating in the coal-pot near the doorway to the back yard. You couldn't think of the back yard without the animal pound which bordered it on the other side; you couldn't think of the back yard without neighbours passing from Garden Hill, taking the back road to the village, and stopping to have a chat with my grandmother, who would be sitting on the floor of her room on a cushion or on her box, above the bread-room, looking out over the back steps into the yard. If it was afternoon, if it was dinner time, there was Mr. Frederick, of course. If I wrote myself into the picture, which I usually did, I would claim that I was the one to point out that there were thirteen steps leading from my grandmother's room to the yard, and my grandmother was so appalled at the bad-luck implications of this that she had another little step added at the bottom.

Two things about this puzzled me then – when I must have been about eight or nine – and continue to puzzle me now: why hadn't anyone before me counted the steps in all the years the house had been built? And, second, if the thirteen steps hadn't noticeably brought ill-luck to the house in the past, then why was *thirteen* so bad? To the end I refused to step on the fourteenth pretend step, in defiance of the reputation of 'thirteen'. (Obviously, the fact that I am not now, with all my 'advantages', the Archbishop of Canterbury, or the Mullah of Bradford, or Bill Gates, or Madame de Pompadour's biographer clearly proves that walking up and down those *thirteen* steps in childhood *had* spoilt my chances of success in life.)

It's so difficult to decide what to recall as being valuable, because someone else looking on this little scene – the back yard with the animal pound on one side, the house facing, the bread-room and kitchen door opening onto the yard, the outside oven under its own shed (corrugated-iron) next to the kitchen, my grandmother sitting above on the floor or on her box, Mr. Frederick on the steps, people passing, lingering to have a chat – would not necessarily make this the lived-in corner of the house. If, say, my mother, brothers and sister were to revisit, they would surely think of the house as having an entirely different *balance.* For the 'boys" room was over the dining room and when my brothers came home from Grammar School at the weekend they occupied the room – and, of course, during the holidays. From the large door of that room you looked down on a space between front and back yards, and the small window at the side opened out half-up up the front steps; so the 'boys' would have had a less 'working' image of the house than my grandmother and I had. (I can't remember my sister's presence very strongly, for she was at school in town – Teacher Tudy Donaghue's private school – during those years, and stayed with a great aunt. When she came home to Harris' she slept in my mother's room.)

Added to that – with respect to where the centre of focus was in the house – the dining room was brought into use at weekends – the vicar or some relative from town visiting on a Sunday. What brothers and sister might have revisited, might be the house I only partially related to. My mother's room, too, was empty much of the week, occupied at weekends and holidays. The outside door to her room opened onto the verandah, looked out onto the front yard ('lawn') with sweeping views, past Garden Hill, towards 'Paradise' in the distance, to the volcanic mountains. In the other direction (east) the view went past the unseen Harris' village to the sea at Trants or Spanish Point two or three miles away.

Access to the verandah was by a more elegant sweep of steps than at the back. I must have counted them but I forget how many: there may have been one or two fewer than at the back because they were grander. So what was my *mother's* view of losing home? – a place where she was both daughter and mistress, drawing a different quality of visitor to the drawing-room, setting the tone but still always financially dependent on my grandmother? What were the *social* restraints? We didn't know. (I haven't mentioned the natural life of the place, the fruit trees, some personalized, named for the children, the profusion of mangoes that made you finicky which ones you chose to eat, plums, pawpaws, soursops and guavas, not enough sugar-apple, though; but gooseberries from which my grandmother made wine, a 'coffee tree', a grapevine that someone had planted at the front of the house and nursed, the few bunches of white grapes balancing the profusion of brown ones produced by the huge 'climbing tree' on the other side, at the border of our own and Mrs. Meade's land. It was important to note, too, that the mountains seen from the verandah tended to be shrouded in mist, much the same, it was said, as in England.) Some time ago I published a collection of stories entitled, *Taking the Drawing-room Through Customs.* The stories were written over four decades; many of them attempting to recover something of that lost world. That's why I'm going to revisit one family scene now to provide something of an antidote to what might be a tendency towards nostalgia.

This was sometime in the 1980s and I was visiting some cousins (on my father's side) who lived at Bethel, further east than Harris': they were family of course, but tending on the whole to be somewhat dependent – a tendency that manifested itself even in England. So, the visit to my father's sister and her son, a man in his forties who had spent many years in England and Germany and (he claims) France, and had long been acknowledged to be mad. He was now back home, living with his mother, who herself was rumoured to be 'odd'; and reports of their managing together seemed more than disturbing. I hadn't seen either in close to ten years. The last time I'd seen him – I'm going to call him Horace, out of delicacy – the last time I'd seen Horace he was in a poor way, resisting, they said, the family's attempt to keep him out of sight, in a 'home' in Antigua. There had been a hint of theatricism about his appearance; his trousers were ill-fitting, the zip undone, his dentures broken – half the plate missing. He looked much the same now and I tried not to focus on it as his mother, embarrassed, did her best to welcome me to the house.

'Do you believe in God?' she surprised me by asking. I had been caught prying a bit, trying to take in the dimensions of the house, shrunken now that the villas in reinforced concrete, inspired by the expatriates from North America, had come and set a new architectural norm. But at the same time the house was pleasant in its proportions, the work of a miniaturist in wood: bees, flies, the odd lizard sheltering inside from the heat. There were portraits of male relatives (one was of my father in clerical gear) on the wall. So I avoided answering the question and instead praised the house, its authenticity. In the end, she sighed.

'God is merciful.' And a memory suddenly seemed to stiffen her features. She looked past me, it seemed, into her own thoughts, and repeated:

'In spite of everything. Yes, God is merciful.'

Horace tried to join us in the dining-room where we were heading, for a snack; and that was when the trouble started. Horace was forbidden the dining-room. He didn't want to eat, he said. Nevertheless, the dining-room was for eating; and he was forbidden the dining-room. Horace wanted to show me some of his writing, because he was a writer, too, and a preacher. And teacher. The mother forbade talk of preaching and teaching in her house because Horace was nothing but a lay-about bringing disgrace on the family, his head full of tricks. She ordered him to take his letters and whatnot out of her dining-room.

'But Mamma, you can't do that.'

'I can damn well do what I like. This is my house.' Further, she wanted him out of the dining-room. 'I don't want him here,' she said to me. I couldn't help observing that Horace wasn't really in the dining-room, but in the doorway: there was no door between sitting and dining-rooms; and I could see that this Mother & Son *play* went a long way back. The mother was saying – while putting cake, drink, etc. on the table – that she didn't want him in her life.

'Go out and get a job.'

'Mamma, I have a job.'

'Lord, Lord, what have I done...'

'Mamma!' Horace turned to me and said something *sotto-voce*, in Latin, and then heaved with suppressed laughter. But the mother was having difficulty containing herself.

'What sin have I committed...?' she demanded. 'I ask, what sort of sin, Oh Lord: I must be the murderer of murderers to be punished thus. Archie, will you tell him that I want him out of this house, OUT OF THIS HOUSE!'

'Mamma.'

(What was one supposed to do?)

'Mamma, why are you behaving like this? It's undignified. And anyway, it's Margot's house, it's not Mamma's house, any more. It's Margot's house.' (Margot, the daughter, the sister, was on another island; Margot was not her real name.)

The mother now spoke quietly. 'I want him out of this house. I want him out of this house.'

'Mamma, you're repeating yourself.'

It was my turn to say something. 'Leave her, Horace... I mean... y'know...' and felt foolish; so I turned helplessly to the mother. 'It's good to see you, Aunt...'

'...Repeating yourself, Mamma.'

'Archie, would you like a little cake? A smile on her face, the stress suddenly falling away. Then she indicated drinks. 'Rum or sorrel? I don't know if you take alcohol. I want him out of this house,' this last said rather distantly now, as she poured the sorrel.

'Mamma.'

'He's only doing it to upset me,' she said.

'Don't let it upset you.'

She finally sat down. I complimented her on the cake and asked if it was home-made; mother and son had a fight over whether the cake was home-made.

'Archie, you mustn't be taken in by Mamma. Mamma...'

Mamma was back on her feet, explosively. 'Don't take my name in vain. Go and get a job. You're 47 years old, go and get a job.'

'Mamma, I have a job. Archie, will you tell Mamma...'

'My arse.' That was Mamma.

'Will you explain to Mamma...?'

'Job, my arse. Archie, excuse my...'

'My translations. My translations are used in German schools. In Hamburg. Nicole, my daughter...'

'Daughter, my arse. What woman would look at you? God, you must have some reason...' (She was looking upwards, beseechingly) 'Some reason, dear God. To punish me so. Archie, I want him out of this house. Take him back to England with you so I can die in peace. In England if you're crazy they don't care, they don't even notice; he was all right in England. That's all I ask, dear God. Take him back to Hamburg with his translations.'

'Mamma, that's a different country; that's a different country.'

'Lord, Lord.'

'You're not being rational. Mamma isn't being rational.'

'I pray to God to be relieved of this burden. The greatest of all burdens. When I hear of their wars...'

'Mamma, you should believe in peace.'

'...their wars, their killings and sinful doings all over the world. When I hear that someone else has to be killed for no reason, I think maybe God is bringing deliverance because there's certain things you can't live with any more. I pray for deliverance. I pray. He's dragging me down. He's dragging his sister down.'

'Margot and I work together. Margot and I are doing... *quelque chose* on the radio. Get it, Archie, get it?' Then he backed it up with a quote that I didn't get.

'I think you should rest.' I said, lamely, to the mother, ignoring Horace; for she seemed about to confront him again.

'Mamma, I love you.'

'I pray... He's sick, he won't be helped; he won't see a doctor.'

'Mamma, I'm a doctor.'

'OK OK.' Then, consoling the mother. 'Don't... Don't upset yourself.' For she was about to explode again. Clearly, it was my visit that was aggravating all this; they couldn't keep up this sort of routine when they were on their own: better to cut this short.

'Try not to upset yourself,' I heard myself saying, declining more cake, and finishing my drink.

'How can I take medicine when I'm not sick?' Horace now demanded in triumph. And they held the silence. The mother was defeated; she'd stopped fighting, and when she spoke the edge had gone out of her voice.

'He's a doctor; he's a linguist with a daughter in Germany.'

'Two daughters, Mamma.'

'…He has a degree in this, and a degree in that. He's a Very Reverend with his gown. And now he's a Syrian.'

'Mamma.'

'He's a Syrian, you know, Archie. A Syrian in a Christian family. Demanding basmati rice.'

'Mamma, you must listen to yourself.'

'…A Syrian. What with his sister trying to hold up her head in the world.'

'Mamma, lots of people eat basmati rice; you don't have to be a Syrian.' He turned to me. 'You don't have to be a Syrian. Archie, Mamma doesn't know about these things. And yet she's laying down the law.' And again to the mother. 'Mamma, I'm not a Syrian. Mamma, you should read.'

(Mother and son are now dead.)

Notes:

1. E.A. Markham, 'Life Before the Revolution', *Misapprehensions,* pp. 59-60, Anvil, London, 1995.

PART TWO

OVER HERE

CHAPTER SIX
ARRIVAL, MAIDA VALE, 1956

It was a wet June night in London, and that added to the excitement; suddenly we were no longer tired, though the second train ride from Dover didn't have the novelty of the first, across France. But the famous black taxi perked us up, and although it seemed slightly smaller than we had imagined, it felt like the real experience; though I wondered if it would take all the luggage. My mother's trunk went in the space at the front next to the driver, a slightly old, white man who didn't say very much; and our three suitcases and odd bits of hand-luggage went easily in the boot. (I liked the word 'boot', we used to say 'trunk' in the West Indies.) Inside, the taxi was roomy, more dignified, we were sure, than the yellow New York cab that friends and family who had been to America had romanticized. I particularly liked the little seats that you pulled down opposite the real seat so that the family sat facing one another. I was annoyed that my brother made me sit with my mother and sister on the big leather seat, while the two elder brothers took the grown-up, pull-down seats for themselves.

But soon, the impressiveness of the buildings, all made in stone, as we headed from Paddington to Maida Vale, made me forget my resentment and marvel at the enormity of London. The lights in each street seemed endless: maybe that's what a real city was like. (We had passed through Genoa, in the daytime; it was dusty and disappointing. We witnessed a scene on the wharf with people on a big boat throwing coins into the water and encouraging young boys to dive in and retrieve them: my mother pronounced it 'shocking'. Earlier, Tenerife had been full of beggars, and my mother had pronounced that 'shocking': in neither place had we seen the lights.)

When we got to Maida Vale (the street was Sutherland Avenue) the driver, to my surprise, helped to unload the trunk and cases, putting them on the pavement. One of my brothers paid him but my mother, who had lots of English money, insisted on giving the tip. She showered him with shillings, florins and maybe half-crown pieces so he had to stop her: 'That's enough,', he said, slightly puzzled, an attitude that impressed me. (Later, perhaps, one was to see something of a paternalistic attitude in all this. Or rather a too-easy slide into bafflement as when, in Ladbroke Grove, the man who came to fix the geyser in the kitchen seemed surprised at our tone, and pitch of voice, at the way we spoke to one another. He said, approvingly, to my mother. 'You're very gentle people. You're Christian people, aren't you!' By which time my brother, Norman and I were minded to contest the notion of being praised for being 'Christian'; but we were in the minority, my mother indignantly confirming that, of course, we were Christian.)

The plumber was certainly right about members of the family being 'gentle', with the exception of one member – me. A character-flaw, nothing I'm proud of, but a stubbornness and abrasiveness that has stayed with me, despite my best efforts, that has, at times, disconcerted friends and partners – indeed, landed me into a fight at school in Kilburn, to the 'shame' of my mother. I can't blame Britain for this; it had already manifested itself in the West Indies.

The suitcases were easy, but the trunk had to be got up several flights of stairs and my brother went to secure help from people who lived, apparently, in the flat below their own: we were going to be on the second floor, the first floor not counting, as it was called the ground floor. The neighbours who were to help with the trunk were from Antigua, the other flats being occupied by English people. (It turned out the Antiguans were sharing our flat.)

It was more or less accepted that the bringing one another up to date would take time; we weren't in any hurry to talk about our three-week journey by sea which already seemed a long way away. In any case, everyone here had taken that journey, everyone, that is, except my brother, Norman, who had come to England directly from Canada. (He had had a year at a university in Puerto Rico, and then had spent some time in Toronto where my father, the Very Reverend, had his church, on Shaw Street.)

We, the newcomers, were more interested in the mysteries of the English flat, like how the gas-meter worked, what happened if you ran out of shillings during the night in winter, and digesting the puzzling news that the heat was not expected to be kept on all night in winter. Other things of interest were whether the neighbours above and below could hear you as you moved about in the flat; and again, speculation on whether it was better to be living above or below your neighbour, whether status came into the arrangement. The thing that seemed most odd to me was that my brothers – and the Antiguans – didn't know their neighbours, who were English, who were white. They knew who they were, passed them on the stairs and that sort of thing, but were not on visiting terms; though the neighbours were said to be polite, when you passed them on the stairs. The best news was that our flat was walking distance from Lords, the cricket ground, and we would go there to see Australia play England later in the month. Next year, of course, it would be West Indies coming to England. My cousin Terry, from the Markham branch of the family (who made up the welcoming party), held out the prospect of going to Speakers' Corner in Hyde Park, also not very far from here, where, on a Sunday, anyone could get up on a soapbox (What was a soapbox?) and criticize the government – or the Queen.

What threatened to spoil this first get-together were my brother Norman's constant references to my being grown up, my voice having changed, etc. so that, in the end, I wasn't that unhappy to go to bed – though I was strangely not tired. Sleeping arrangements meant sharing a double-bed with one of my brothers. (From eleven rooms at your disposal, to sharing a bed; and yet, being in England was exciting.) The other brother (it turned out to be Joe) would sleep in the lounge. My mother and my sister shared the other bedroom. But then, for a year or two, in the town in Montserrat, I had shared a bed with my mother; because what would have been my room was occupied by my father's two nephews. But it disappointed me that my brothers hadn't made better arrangements for us in England. After all, my mother had sent on the money to buy a house in London – we were never meant to be in rented accommodation – but there had been complications about the property that we were in the process of purchasing.

Next morning my brother, Joe, dressed for work in his London Transport uniform, called my sister and me to the window to see an African walking down the street. We had never seen an African and this broad man in his white robes and little cap seemed like someone dressed up for a masquerade, though his costume wasn't especially colourful. So, if Africans dressed like that during normal times, they really weren't like West Indians. We wanted to know how Jamaicans, whom we had heard so much about but hadn't met any on the boat, dressed.

They dressed like us.

So that meant people couldn't tell us apart.

Well, they spoke differently.

Everyone in the West Indies spoke differently, Blackman, our old Barbados headmaster, famously, spoke differently. But how did Jamaicans speak?

Well, they weren't well-spoken like us. But then the English people wouldn't be able to tell the difference. To the English people we were all Jamaicans. (In Canada, it transpired, West Indians were commonly thought to be from Barbados.)

This information didn't exactly please us; and we couldn't work out what to do about it.

The main interest at breakfast was sliced bread. It seemed unbelievably grand, each white slice was the same thickness throughout and the bread was wonderfully moist. It all seemed so much of an advance on the little rolls we used to get at Mr. Lee's in Harris' during the week when my grandmother's stock from Saturday baking had run out. Even my grandmother's bread, however carefully wrapped, would be beginning to go stale by Monday (though this never hurt the sweetbread). This English bread and butter just seemed the ideal combination, you really hardly needed the bacon and eggs which, my brothers said, people didn't have every day, but mainly on Sunday.

As my brothers had to leave for work (Norman worked at a dentist's, in the packing section) they charted out short walks that we could take on our own without getting lost. At the weekend they would take us on the underground, which was different from the train that we had taken up to London from Dover; and we would see the sights: St. Paul's, etc. Someone produced an underground map so that we could study the system and get used to the names of the stations. As Joe worked on the underground, we had an expert in the family.

Now, this working business was interesting to me. I was sixteen, not a particularly good student, and had been off school for maybe about a year waiting to come to England, a schedule which seemed constantly to slip. My strongest subjects at Montserrat Secondary School had been English and handicraft (having picked up prizes for both) though, to my surprise, I had got a good mark in Physics in the last test. My brothers said they would check to see what sort of school would be suitable for me in England. It was to be nearly three years before I eventually got to school.

Instead I got a job. I inherited an overcoat and got a job. I was happier with the job than with the overcoat, which wasn't stylish, and too long. It was handed down, it was my brother's cast-off. (It actually turned out to be a raincoat.)

In one sense I was being treated like an adult, in another as the baby of the family. I was uncomfortable in both roles. My brothers had been away for two years, during which time in Montserrat I had left school, and even got myself a job serving in one of the family's department stores (a richer branch of the family, the Osbornes) with only a mother to boss me around (my grandmother having died in 1953). Now, suddenly, there were these two grown-up brothers back in the house.

The three-week sea-crossing seemed to have affected my mother's confidence, and changed her relationship with me. Before the trip, at home, she would supervise my dress, decide what shoes I wore to church on Sunday, remind me to say my prayers at night. Suddenly, in England, she expected not only my brothers but me to know what to do. (Should I go to school, should I go to work?)

The difficulty with my mother – she got no help from us because we were all preoccupied in doing our own things – was that overnight (or at least in the three weeks on the boat) the *shape* of her life had changed. From being the acknowledged head of the household (after my grandmother had died) with the sympathetic help of extended family who would make sure that nothing disastrous happened to us, she was now on her own, but stripped of power. It was as if she was now subordinated to her sons, not something that a woman from the West Indies would find easy to endure. She didn't know the country; her young sons had been here for two years and thus had to be deferred to in matters of how to cope with England. She no longer had an income. All the rents from land and houses at home seemed to dry up or had been accounted for (she didn't keep accounts, we didn't know what had happened to the 'businesses'; and suddenly money had to start flowing the other way; money had to be sent back to the West Indies to keep houses (including the one in Harris' that had been abandoned) in repair; money was sent back to weed the family graves at Bethel; gifts were sent to various people who had served the family; open house had to be kept in London for people who might drop by, as if we were still in the West Indies; and of course she didn't have a job. She had been brought up in luxury and had never worked; she had no profession, so attempts to provide her with part-time or piece-rate forms of work weren't successful. So here she was, from being the island's trendsetter, fashion-wise, reduced to spending hours in the kitchen doing a job for us that, all her life, servants had done for her. And though she tried, she was no great cook. Despite all that she never, in my presence, expressed resentment. Puzzlement, but not resentment.

There was a Methodist church at the bottom of the road, Shirland Road: should we go to it? My brother, Joe, went to it; but Joe had had ambitions, at one time, to be a preacher. I was fairly hostile to the idea of religion (Norman seemed to object to what he called 'the tyranny of those who use religion to exploit'). My mother, surprisingly, didn't insist. I did accompany her and my sister, Julie, a couple of times, surprised that perhaps half the sparse congregation consisted of West Indians, none of whom we knew. But when the priest referred to this fact, and lightly praised us for being more godly than the English, I was uneasy. I wasn't sure that I liked being singled out in this way; I also wasn't sure that I had come to England to be praised as a churchgoer. So I stopped going, and occupied my Sundays reading the newspapers and listening to the radio and playing my music. (Norman used to go out early in the morning and bring back four or five newspapers ranging from *The News of the World* to *The Reynolds News*) and that would see us through, certainly, till lunch. Occasionally, in the afternoon there would be a cricket match, involving a London Transport or other such team playing at venues like Osterley (near the airport) and Holland Park, nearer home. Sometimes Sunday afternoons would be given over to visits to people who my brothers or my mother knew. These could be in the vicinity, like Sussex Gardens, or as far afield as Manor House. But in the evening we would get back to the newspapers, and maybe listen to the radio. (Yes, Sunday afternoon was also a good time for comedy, *Hancock's Half Hour* and drama, *Flying Doctor*, on the radio.)

It was Norman who taught me to read the newspaper for bias; we would read differing accounts of the same cricket match, and you could tell that the Sundays were less biased than the *London Evening News*, say, because of the attitude that their correspondent, E.M. Wellings, adopted to the foreign players. (Some time later, he was to describe Clive Lloyd's first Test century, in Guyana, as 'meaningless', because it didn't affect the outcome of the match.)

One interesting thing occurred one Sunday morning in Sutherland Avenue: we encountered our first Indian from India (a man in a turban). The doorbell rang and I followed my brother down to answer it. There was this man on the doorstep with a battered suitcase, with lots of little objects inside: toothbrushes and toothpaste, soap, combs, a tin-opener and nail-clippers and, I think, socks and a tie. We weren't really interested in anything as we didn't buy things on the street, but we had to be polite. He slightly misunderstood this and offered to tell our fortune while we considered the purchase.

Soon, he was telling us that we were far from home and that our family across the sea were safe. Our mother was missing us, but she, too, was safe, and would soon be coming across the sea to join us. What was embarrassing was that my mother, having heard the doorbell, was at that moment looking down on us from the second-floor window. To save the man's feelings we bought the smallest thing he had in the suitcase – a cloth to clean the cooker – and saw him on his way. Smugly, we were pleased that we didn't have to stoop to such tricks to make a living in England. Much later, when we saw the thriving Indian corner-shops (after the progressive collapse of the few West Indian businesses that had preceded them in our area) we began to wonder if we, West Indians, hadn't missed the trick of getting ahead in England. Weren't we altogether too fastidious?

There was a pools-winner in our house, the Antiguan sharing our flat. His name was Frank and he had a stammer. (I remember wondering, crudely, if the money made up for the stammer.) But Frank, who must have been in his mid-20s, was very good-natured.

The story is that when he discovered he had won the pools he came out with the phrase, 'He rose... He rose.' Or, was it 'Heroes... Heroes'? (There was amused speculation, in Frank's absence, on what the phrase might mean.) He had won something like £800 and had splashed out on an expensive radiogram and records as well as an £80 or £90 overcoat for a lady reputed to be in 'show business'. He was reputed, also, to have met Shirley Bassey. Because Frank was such a nice guy no one ever asked him to confirm the 'facts'. All this happened just before we got to England, by which time he was working at London Transport, at the Paddington depot, cleaning train engines. Some members of the family played the pools, hoping for Frank's luck.

Within days of arriving, I got a job in Baker Street, making handbags. There were knowing references at the house to Baker Street and Sherlock Holmes, with Norman recommending Conan Doyle's, 'The Hound of the Baskervilles', which had been broadcast on the radio.

If this is a factory, I thought, then factories aren't so bad.

There were only about five or six other people working there, one of whom was a Jamaican woman called Sadie. Initially, the main interest of the job was in travelling to work like a 'worker'. Taking the tube, the Metropolitan line from Royal Oak four stops to Baker Street seemed infinitely grown-up; the knowingness of waiting at the edge of the platform for the train, standing as close to the white line as you dared, with all these people with their *Daily Mirrors* tucked under their arms and women ready to take out their knitting the moment they were seated on the train: it seemed like being part of people in a book.

I didn't myself buy a newspaper, because one of my brothers was bound to bring one home and we could read that in the evening. I generally took a book to work, any paperback novel I found lying round the flat; it might be Erle Stanley Gardner, it might be Peter Cheyney; but reading a book was important for me; though I wanted to be mistaken for a 'worker', I didn't want it to be assumed that this was my *permanent* job; I wanted to hint that I would be going back to school in September.

I didn't like Sadie, the Jamaican woman. One of the men in the factory made a joke about us. (Two of the men wore long coats, one a brown coat, the other a white coat; and they were the men we took orders from; the one in the white coat had an ugly scar on his neck.) The brown-coated man, whose name was Ron, made a joke about us, Sadie and myself, a joke of a vaguely sexual nature, and Sadie's sour response embarrassed me more than Ron's joke had done. At the time I was sixteen and Sadie, maybe, thirty; and her scornful dismissal of our names being linked was something that caused more than a little resentment. (I was also embarrassed for her, too.) A lack of grace, I came, later, to dub it. We didn't have much to say to each other, anyway, and then one day she reprimanded me for admitting that Montserrat had only one grammar school.

This came about when Ron in the brown coat (the one in the white coat had been shot in the neck, in the war) asked about my background before coming to England, and I confessed that my father was a minister in Canada. This was greeted with disbelief as he thought I meant a minister in the Canadian government, rather than a clergyman. And it seemed to me that having sewn that seed of doubt, anything else I might say on the subject would be greeted with suspicion, so, instead, I talked about attending Montserrat Secondary School, which was a fee-paying grammar school and, in order to emphasize its specialness, let slip the fact that it was the only one on the island.

The tactic backfired, of course, as Ron expressed amused surprise that the island boasted only one grammar school whereas here in England there were thousands of grammar schools, all over the place. The conversation ended before I had time to say that the total population of Montserrat was 11,000 people, so that one grammar school for that size of population wasn't that bad. (Thirty years later, being patronized by the Arts Council's Chairman, Lord Rees-Mogg, when I was being interviewed for the job of Literature Director, brought back the experience of the man in the brown coat in the Baker Street handbag factory.)

Sadie's point was that you never gave the opposition ammunition to use against you, even though what you were saying might be true, or might make a sort of sense. In any case, she said, Jamaica had lots of grammar schools, and she didn't want people in England thinking that every place in the West Indies was like Montserrat, with only one grammar school. I hadn't thought of the 'opposition' quite in that way; but Sadie wasn't up for chit chat; she seemed to add a vague sourness to her lack of friendliness.

I remember being surprised that I could dislike anyone as much as I disliked Sadie.

★ ★ ★

At the Test match, at Lords, which I attended with Norman – this was on the Saturday – I was suddenly made conscious of two things: one, that I was willing Australia to win and, two, how indistinct the action on the pitch was, from where I was sitting in the stands.

Both things slightly puzzled me because (apart from supporting West Indies cricket) I hadn't been conscious of any anti-British feeling to date. At school in Montserrat, it was a source of pride that Britain hadn't been defeated in any war (We weren't conscious of 'early' wars, the Battle of Hastings, say, and, though we were doing Latin and aware of Julius Caesar's invasion of Britain in 55 BC, that would have seemed too far back in time to count.) Moreover, some of Britain's pride had rubbed off on me, personally: my father had participated in the last great victory over 'Germany'. And, from my grandmother's family, a great uncle, 'Cousin Reggie', her nephew, had fought for Britain in 1914-18.

But sitting at Lords on that Saturday in 1956 watching England play Australia, I was relaxed at Australia having a magnificent day – Benaud, low in the order, capitalizing with the bat on a good position established by the openers, McDonald (75) and Burke (65) the day before. That recalled the warm-up match we had seen when Graveney, at No.3, survived a caught behind at nought and went on to make 199. (Was Graveney, as my brother asserted, the best bat in England – his claims weighed up by Len Hutton and E.M. Wellings in the *Evening News* – who couldn't get into the Test team?) I was convinced of Graveney's class and hence relieved that he wasn't picked for England against Australia.

With me, the tendency not to support England at sport grew into something of an obsession, to the point that I wanted even apartheid South Africa to beat England. (Later, though, supporting the boycott – yes, you couldn't go to the grounds to see them play, so you had to watch the matches on television – we didn't drink South African wine, entertaining in those days with, as I remember, Cyprus sherry, and a brand of ginger wine that my mother liked.) Decades later when, partly because of England's relative lack of sporting success at international level, I had almost reconciled myself to England winning *something* at sport, a low comedian intervened. Incensed by Norman Tebbitt's (1980s?) comment that supporting England at sport was, for people like me, some sort of loyalty test to the nation, I must have been one of the few people in England (though not in Scotland, Ireland or Wales) cheering for Germany in the Euro 96 clash of the two nations. Later, perhaps mellowing – or maybe a bit more anglicized after 45 years residence in England – I rather hoped that young Beckham and Co. would acquit themselves well in South Korea & Japan in 2002. With regard to cricket, though, I'm still as intransigent as the most fundamentalist Christian.

The other thing that trip to Lords in 1956 confirmed was my failing eyesight. This was hard to accept. No, acceptance didn't come into it; it was hard to *believe* as I was known to have the best eyesight of any of my friends in Harris', to be able to pick out small boats on the far horizon when others could see just sea and waves. When I repeated this trick in Plymouth with grammar school friends, I always came out the winner. (And no cheating.) Many years after that I was driven to speculate on what hidden 'trauma' might have been the cause of this sudden deterioration in eyesight, prompting me to resort to National Health spectacles within weeks of coming to England. (I stopped growing at about the same time, my height now being the same as it was at 15.) The family were always supportive: when, later in the 1950s, a

French Government Minister appeared on television, Norman reassured me that the Minister was wearing National Health-type glasses similar to my own.

To come back to the business of not supporting England at cricket: some of my heroes were the cricket commentators. Not just the legendary John Arlott and Brian Johnston but, with a few exceptions, the present lot – Henry Blofeld, Jonathan Agnew, Vic Marks – also fit the bill. (Their English tendency to support the underdog (often foreign, against England) could be said to be paternalistic, but the best of them acknowledged the greatness of West Indies, when West Indies were beating England. Good men.

★ ★ ★

The general atmosphere in the country was surprising, someone always on the radio or television arguing the point against the government, politicians were made to look foolish in the newspapers, particularly by the cartoonists. Surprising, also, to find so many people in high places supporting President Nasser's nationalization of the Suez canal, in 1956. When the consequent shortage of petrol made it difficult for people to get to work, there was a carnival sort of atmosphere with motorists offering lifts to strangers on the street.

(There was a more informed sort of political debate that took place in the house, often when old schoolmates of my brothers visited. There were a couple of boys reading Law at the Inns of Court and when they visited there was much talk of great justices of the past; the favourite then seemed to be Lord Shawcross, big in the Labour Party, who had said this or that, or given this or that ruling – but I'm in a muddle now to remember whether the man was a hero or a villain.)

But one must guard against nostalgia for the '50s and '60s. Many, *many* things went against the grain and had an impact; and that encouraged a certain caution, a watchfulness to avoid being held up to ridicule, to seek protection in the crowd. (What crowd?) But still to be a little bit apart. What of Nottingham? everyone asked. The riots in Nottingham ('58) seemed somehow more sinister than those at Notting Hill. Nottingham was far away, and something unknown. Notting Hill was on the doorstep and you went up there a couple of days afterwards and everything seemed normal; indeed, people seemed unusually polite. But it was disturbing to find that deep in the country, up there in the north, that large groups of people had come out on the streets to attack black people, particularly black and white couples. And it wasn't the general idea of the attacks that so unsettled – for the odd incident had been reported from time to time, and you knew in reports from America how ugly this could be – though you always prided yourself that this

94

wasn't America – it was the *nature* of the attacks that left you floundering and, yes, *embarrassed* you. It was the idea of spitting, in Nottingham. The reports that people had gathered together to *spit* at people in the street. Grown-up people, men and women, white people, English people, admitting on the radio that they spat at black and white couples on the street. Maybe because of the attitude of contempt that this conveyed, it seemed more *shaming* than other forms of protest; there was something *generic* about grown people spitting at others which made it seem, in our eyes, closer to the experience of living in South Africa, even, than in America. It was from that time that my mother would remind me to be careful, going out at night. Yet it was small cultural rituals that affected me more directly: clocking in for work, for instance.

At my handbag and (later) ladies' belts factories, one feature as you entered the building was the grannie clock, a bit like my grandmother's clock in our drawing-room in Harris'. (Indeed, I thought that was how those clocks got their name – because grandmothers owned them.) The industrial clock had an attachment at the bottom for your 'clocking-in' card. The cards, one for each worker with the name on, were ranged on the side. Having inserted your card you then pulled the lever on the right hand side of the clock, and the time of your arrival would be printed on it. Of course you could cheat and, if no one was looking, stamp your friend's card by arrangement, if your friend was late. But that was risky in these small (often two-roomed) firms.

I did, of course, join the ripple of protest against the 'indignity' of having to clock in. But privately I quite liked the idea. Somehow it made me, at sixteen, a *worker*. When, shortly afterwards I started reading Dickens again (Joe made me pronounce the author's name properly) I was quite seduced by the romance of the murk and grime of Victorian England. (Even the smog of London of the '50s, which caused so many thousands of deaths every winter, seemed romantic: I was young, I wasn't at risk. The day we stood on the platform of Royal Oak station and heard the train come in, but couldn't see it because of the smog, has barely been matched for me, in its romance, by anything I've encountered in literature – outside Dickens, and maybe Zola.) So all this 'factory' culture seemed to me an adventure, infinitely preferable to being marooned on a small island in the Eastern Caribbean, waiting for something to happen.

Allied to this 'indignity' of clocking in was another *workers'* practice I rather liked: that was being paid weekly rather than monthly. (When I got back to school the boast among my more class-conscious fellow pupils was that they aspired to jobs – like those of their fathers, who were solicitors or in business – where they would be paid or would pay themselves, monthly.) By then we knew that in the 'Industrial North', where none of us had been, men in the mines and factories got their pay-packet on a Friday night and brought it home, unopened, to their wives who then allocated the week's spending, including pocket-money for the husband. (You didn't want to go north, of course, you remembered the 'spitting' in Nottingham.) But, for me, in London, receiving the little brown, sealed packet every Friday afternoon, was to be allied to the tradition of men who, in the industrial north, made things – and you still a teenager.

Only I didn't have to hand over my pay-packet at the end of the week. I had a home where I didn't have to pay rent, I wasn't asked to contribute to the general expenses of the household (only to buy my own clothes – being measured up for suits at Burton's on the Harrow Road – and save for the books I would need when I restarted school). I would have been asked at home how much I earned at the factory, but that was just family interest; and hence, with my £9.00 a week I was able to indulge my passion for cinema (I recall having seen only two films in Montserrat), Second World War films, Brigitte Bardot, the new rock n' roll, Dean Martin and Jerry Lewis… I was more uncomfortable with the Westerns and the big Hollywood films. Even though I didn't particularly identify with the Cheyenne and the Sioux, we didn't like the way in which these brown people were portrayed, speaking less good English than the 'white man' even though – as was pointed out in the house – most of the white men were from countries in Europe that didn't speak English. But what was most upsetting was the portrayal of the Indian women, who were always humiliated and never made to look attractive in their clothes. With the Hollywood hits it was less an objection than a puzzle. Walking down the street, whether Harrow Road or Baker Street, or just going to the shops, or on the train to and from work, you came across women who looked impossibly beautiful. And here in these films you were presented with the likes of Doris Day and Debbie Reynolds and Rita Hayworth (what was so special about red hair?) and Bette Davis (certainly, the most off-putting person you'd seen on screen, but then, she may have been very different in real life, you told yourself) – none of them a patch on women you met every day. What was better, a little later, was discovering the continental cinema in Westbourne Grove and at Hendon where they showed French and Italian films – here were women who matched the script.

So, a fair proportion of my £9.00 went on cinema. (The week before Christmas one year – it may have been 1957 – I managed to go to the cinema every night of the week, and twice on the Saturday. In the afternoon it was a Norman Wisdom, the one where he is a window-cleaner, and has to clean endless windows in this building several storeys high, and his little ladder can't reach the top floors; in the evening, I took myself

96

off again to see the latest Dean Martin and Jerry Lewis. The house was preparing for Christmas; I would have been in the way.

Apart from films, my other two passions at this time were books and records. After work on Friday I would drift down the Charing Cross Road and buy a book or a record. Browsing for the book took such a long time that I often had to come back on the Saturday to complete the purchase. Buying the record was in some ways easier, as it was usually something in the Hit Parade. Not Pat Boone or Lonnie Donegan or Perry Como. Not even Bill Haley, but Little Richard and Elvis and Fats Domino and, yes, the odd Nat King Cole. And the record would be played obsessively much of the weekend – with intervals of reading the Sunday papers and listening to the radio. In retrospect, I'm amazed at the tolerance of the rest of the house.

Choosing the book was, as I say, more complicated. Whenever I listen now to *Desert Island Discs* I think back to those times. From Great Portland Street or Goodge Street (where the second and third ladies' belts factories were located) I would head for Foyles. The second-hand department was on the second floor, up by a rickety lift, and I would make for the stacks of plays, and stand there reading. (There'd be the odd, other person crouching, leaning, reading.) Finally, I would buy a play, or a collection of plays – or defer the decision till next week. There were new plays as well as second-hand ones in the stacks, and it was from the new plays shelf that I would find something to read. I was a slow reader and might get through only an act or two of the play, but would come back on the Saturday to complete it, or the following week. I seldom, of course, bought *that* play but a second-hand one for reading at home. That way it was like having two plays for the price of one. (And it was cheaper than going to the theatre, which no one in the house really did.)

I suppose I think of this now as building up a shadow library. I was, the whole time, planning to return to school and there was a residual anxiety about how I would cope in an English setting, not (unlike my brother, Norman) having coped adequately at home in the West Indies. I was conscious then, and later guilty, that we had left the entire family library in Montserrat. Indeed, prior to our departure, my mother had given away the books in our drawing-room bookcase at Harris', so there must have been a semiconscious desire to build up a library in compensation. Soon, clothes had to give way in the chest-of-drawers to books. By the time we got to Kilburn in 1960 or '61, the first bookcase duly appeared.

The other reason for the emphasis on plays at this time was that (after an abortive first novel) I was busily writing plays. Norman, always supportive, hinted that I might do something like Sheilagh Delaney's

A Taste of Honey. (She was my sort of age.) At the time I was trying to match John Osborne's *Look Back in Anger*, a play I didn't much like, but a lot of reference was being made to it by people who knew about these things. I preferred *A Taste of Honey*, though I didn't think it was very ambitious. As I say, I didn't go to the theatre, except occasionally, my play experience being confined to reading playscripts and listening to plays on the Third Programme. (The broadcast of Ionesco's *Rhinoceros*, with Laurence Olivier, comes to mind.) But pride of theatrical place was taken by visits to the *Empire* Music Hall, on Edgware Road.

A couple of years later, at school in Kilburn, I made myself seem somewhat superior to a couple of wealthy students from the Middle East (Ali and his friend) who admitted to visiting art galleries at the weekend on the off-chance of picking up liberal-minded women. I privately convinced myself that liberal-minded women of a higher order were more likely to be wooed by the success in the theatre of the plays I was writing.

You live but you don't learn.

★★★

The in-between school period in London stretched from 1956 to 1959, when I denied that I was drifting; and family were too preoccupied in putting things back together to do more than support my various enthusiasms. I would be a novelist (I wrote a novel at the time, mercifully lost); I would be a dramatist (I wrote plays); I would be a pop singer (I made a record). Meanwhile, I was making ladies belts and handbags; and I got to know London. I don't mind revisiting a couple of those scenes.

Making Ladies Belts in Great Portland Street

At C.G. Spencer's we could attend the afternoon sex show across the street, but Spencer (the boss) and Nancy, the machinist, were so cool about it that I had to pretend to be cool about it too. But that was the second move from Baker Street, up the belt and handbag making chain, so to speak; the stop before that was Mr. Glanz, in Berners Mews, off Mortimer Street, just down from the Middlesex Hospital. I felt very comfortable walking down Great Titchfield Street to work, from Great Portland Street underground, thinking it would be quite good to live in this part of town. I'd look forward to lunch at the little cafe across the road from the hospital where they made fresh chunky bacon and egg sandwiches and served the most wonderful macaroons for afters. Sometimes, I would have a sit down lunch, savouring the feel of the 'workers caff' where young nurses from the hospital in their blue and white uniforms would flit in and out for their takeaway snacks.

There was a man at Glanz who wore a long brown coat like Ron, and he was, in effect, the man who employed me. I remember wandering round the area after leaving the Baker Street job and seeing a sign on the door saying 'Experienced Machinist Wanted'; so I rang the bell and after a little while the man in the brown coat appeared and I said I was an experienced machinist.

'How old are you, then?' he said, with some suspicion.

'Twenty-nine,' I said, for no particular reason. I was, maybe, seventeen.

He looked at me for a few seconds. 'Fair enough,' he said, and invited me to follow him upstairs. (Glanz turned out to be on the second floor; later, he acquired the third floor of the building as well.)

It was a fairly familiar set-up, a room with a couple of machines that looked like sewing machines but weren't, and a couple of other 'benches' where a woman and a young boy sat on stools doing things with bits of leather. (Throughout these years I had problems with the word 'leather': however I pronounced it I couldn't get people to understand what I was saying; and since I had to use the word several times a day, I actually practised saying 'leather' LEAther until I was leather-perfect; so my real lessons in enunciation came about in belt and handbag factories in the West End of London.)

The man in the brown coat introduced me to Mr. Glanz, who wore a long white coat (the style was to wear these coats open, not buttoned) who nodded his agreement, and I was employed. Mr. Glanz was Austrian and spoke with a foreign accent. Before I was shown what to do, the man in the brown coat asked if I wanted to change my clothes, as I was likely to get them dirty. The question was ridiculous as I didn't have a change of clothing, so I agreed that the next day I would bring a change of clothing, something I never got around to doing. I was introduced to the rest of the workforce, to the young boy (who was now putting eyelets in belts, using a pedal to operate the eyeletting machine: he soon confessed that he was on the point of leaving) and to the woman who was called Honey. No, that wasn't a term of endearment, that was her name and she asked me if I wanted a cup of tea. It was slightly unnerving having to call this middle-aged woman, Honey, particularly as she seemed to have no lips and wore very red lipstick which she smeared on the lower part of her face where her lip would have been.

It was really easy to get a job. I don't remember having been sacked from any of these jobs; there was never any particular disagreement. At some point you just got bored and left, and as long as you told them a week in advance, you got your pay-packet to the end. Also, there was no big interview ceremony – some people came straight from the Labour Exchange (nice phrase, eh? Labour Exchange!) and even though they could be rejected by the management, there was always another job waiting for you around the corner.

So, I was put on the skiving machine. (When, later in the '70s, I saw Barry Reckord's play *Skyvers* advertised, I vaguely hoped it might be about making ladies' belts and handbags.) What the skiving machine did was to shave the edges off the leather (*leather*) or suede so that you could fold the ends of the material over, having first applied some glue, and not end up with a bump or a ridge. So, yes, it was vaguely dusty (which was one of the reasons for the long coats) and also you worked with a lot of glue (no-one thought of sniffing it in those days). The man who showed me how to do the skiving had been in the war, and when I put my hand underneath the machine to un-clog the shavings of suede and leather, he put his hand to his chest and said that I'd come as close to losing my hand as if I'd fought in the war. What I didn't know was that a razor-sharp cutting edge which spun round and round and sliced bits off the leather, hadn't been turned off. For years I couldn't believe my luck because the circumference of the edge was barely larger than my hand, and it was hard to credit how, unseen, one managed to fit a hand in the exact centre of that fast-spinning wheel, and extract it without a scratch. For years, too, I fantasized about what would've happened had I lost my fingers. I told no one at home about this.

Two things at Glanz stood out (apart from Honey's fussiness over tea and her disappointment that Elvis Presley, the new singing sensation from America, wasn't 'more handsome'): one was the girl across the way, the other involved the sisters from Cyprus. The girl across the way – there was a courtyard of some kind so she was some distance away, working in another 'factory' – would sometimes nod at us. She may have been doing this as a dare, because she and her friend would then have a laugh. The thing is that you weren't clear who she was nodding to. The sense of elation when you were the only one facing that direction and she nodded was then dashed when you saw her nodding at the man in the brown coat. What was more promising were the Cyprus sisters.

They came to work for Glanz after I'd been there some months: beautiful, continental, heavy-breasted, friendly young women, and I was given the job of introducing them to the eyeletting machine. There was a particular skill to operating the eyeletting machine, not physically, you just selected the colour of the eyelets, put them in a funnel-like container at the top of the machine, fitted the eyeletting hole of the belt on to a small spike at the bottom of the machine clamped to the counter and then pressed the pedal underneath with your foot – and hey presto! That wasn't the problem, the problem was selecting the *right* colour eyelet for the belt. This wasn't too difficult with leather or suede, or with material (cloth) that had one colour throughout. You matched that to the nearest colour eyelet you had, only in a slightly darker shade. No problem. The problem was when the material had a pattern. Many of those belts were made from the same material as the dresses, which we didn't make, and you had to judge a row of five eyelets, all of the same colour, which would carry off the belt to advantage. The most problematic eyelet was the colour mushroom; even a new box would contain up to half a dozen shades of mushroom. And working quickly you had to make sure that the range of mushroom colour in the five buckle holes didn't look *wrong*. I was thought to be a dab hand at mushroom.

So, 'he's the boss,' the man in the brown coat said to the girls from Cyprus, sending me up slightly. But that was all right. That was OK. It was nice working next to the girls and of course they learned the trick of eyeletting in no time. What impressed me was working next to the elder sister one afternoon and to hear her talk about herself and her body in an unconscious way I hadn't encountered before: her breasts, for instance, would reach to here (and she pointed to her waist) if she took off her bra. She didn't of course, take off her bra, but it amazed me that someone could talk to a relative stranger so openly about such matters. I assumed – I had to assume that this was how all women spoke to men when they weren't being overheard. When I left Glanz for Spencer's I wasn't sorry to go, for the sisters from Cyprus had already gone.

C. G. Spencer's was the real belt experience. By then I knew everything there was to know about making belts in leather, suede and material. Spencer was more ambitious than others; he also made the buckles (not the metal bits, but covered them in the right belt material) as well as buttons, which were used mainly to decorate the pockets, etc. of the coats. Spencer had a partner, an older man, Mr. Steinberg, and they were both refugees from Austria. Spencer had been a boy of fifteen when he had escaped to England, and he talked to me a bit about my being lucky not to have been forced to come to Britain, but to have come as a matter of choice. Spencer and Mr. Steinberg, who lived in Maidenhead, had an encyclopaedic knowledge of Europe, knowing what route you took, driving through this or that country and into another: their detailed knowledge of other countries impressed me then as much as anything since. I saw it as a skill. My brother (Norman) used to talk about people who had acquired interesting but not particularly useful bits of information: there was a man in Guyana, apparently, who knew the cricket scores of all the matches that West Indies had played, including those of the opposition in both innings, not only in Tests but in the warm-up matches that the team played against non-Test opposition, home and abroad. This man from Guyana had a routine, lowly-paid job: if he had put that mental energy into learning a foreign language, my brother said, think of where the man could be now.

So, coming back to Spencer and his partner putting all that mental energy into knowing the road map of Europe, I wouldn't wish that they had spent their time learning French instead (they spoke three or four languages, anyway, including French). They also spoke, both of them – as if duty-bound to pass on a skill – of the gentlemanly ways to seduce a lady, and the etiquette to be observed, later, with the lady in bed. Much of this talk was – to use a later expression – to wind up Nancy, who was the other person working there.

Nancy was friendly, and Irish, and lived just round the corner from me in Ladbroke Grove and we used to come home on the tube together. Her husband, Frank, had had an accident at work to his arm, which left the elbow jutting out, so he was at home all day doing nothing much it seemed, but teaching their budgerigar to talk. Whenever I paid my occasional visits to the flat, Frank was always proud of the new words he had taught the budgie to say – words that only he could interpret. At Spencer's though, Nancy always denied, as Spencer hinted, that Friday night was special for her at home. When then, Spencer wanted to know, was the special night at home? Oh, once or twice a year, maybe. So Nancy came to be known as the 'Twice a Yearer'. And she cheerfully answered to that. Nancy's speech patterns intrigued me, the way she would answer a question with a statement. 'Are those belts ready to go out?' 'They are.' 'Are you taking Frank to see this nude-show at the weekend?' 'I am not!' It seemed to me to be a strangely forceful way of speaking that I wasn't accustomed to. And then there was the business of sex across the street.

I can't remember who noticed it first, but there they were in full view, an old man slumped in a chair directly opposite our window, no curtains, only Great Portland Street separating us. Sitting on the floor or kneeling, ministering to him was one, sometimes two young women. It was odd, with the man showing no signs of life, his arms hanging at his side, Spencer parodying him in the office. Both Spencer and Nancy agreed that the girls deserved overtime for this devotion to duty, for surely what they were doing was infinitely more difficult than the regular job of sewing up dresses in the factory, which is what the official business seemed to be. What impressed me with everyone at Spencer's was how they relegated the scene to something of no importance. Even the old man, the partner, Mr. Steinberg, came to the window once, took a look, made a dismissive gesture and walked back to his cutting table in the big room to continue carving out belt shapes in suede, with his Stanley knife.

I spent only about half the day in the factory – the mornings until about half-past ten or eleven and the afternoons till about half-past two or three. Then Spencer would pack a bag of belts and I would be sent off to deliver them – West End late morning, East End in the afternoon.

The sensation of West and East Ends of London couldn't have been more different. I always felt slightly conscious with my big bag walking around those exclusive-seeming streets off New Bond Street (We serviced a very up-market dress shop in Maddox Street) and drifting past Regent Street into Soho, which seemed to be a centre for film. I was amazed at the brazenness of the advertising for the sex industry (Did Mr. Macmillan and those fellows in government know this was going on?) Sometimes, well-dressed women would smile at you as you crossed their path with your bag of belts, and occasionally someone would say that you were their 'luck', being the sixth or seventh or eighth 'dark-skinned' person she'd met that day.

In the East End, on the other hand, I wasn't embarrassed to walk round Old Street and Aldgate with my bag of belts. What struck me was relief that I didn't have to work in *these* factories, which is where the dresses were made. Rows and rows of women sitting behind their machines, listening to a radio somewhere out of sight, a half-drunk cup of tea on the edge of the machines, made you embarrassed for them. It was on those East End trips, I seem to remember, being startled by events taking place in the world; getting out of the train to be confronted at the newsstand by the first edition of the *Evening News: Ghana Independence* (1957) and later (I continued to work at Spencer's during some holidays at school and university) *Bulganin & Khrushchev in London, US Spy Plane Crash in Russia* (1960*), Hammarskjold Air Crash* (this was as late as 1961).

The continued relationship with Spencer, even after I got to university, might seem a little odd now. But Spencer (a foreigner in England with something of an old-fashioned idea of England) saw his workforce as something of an extended family. (I was often late for work and Spencer would tell me, with sadness rather than in anger, that I was doing no good to the image of West Indians, who had a reputation for being bad at timekeeping. I wasn't sure that this was true, because I knew 'boys' who had to go into Paddington to clean the train engines first thing in the morning, and others who worked in factories on the edge of town – the Brillo factory out in, I think, Hayes, Middlesex – who had to take a five o'clock, or whatever, bus to get them there. Presumably, if they got to work late, consistently, they'd be sacked. When, recently, driving round Lisbon very early in the morning I went past two or three bus stops where groups of mainly Africans waited, I was reminded of those early-rising West Indians of the 1950s. So I resist the suggestion that they were not disciplined in these matters – unlike their children and grandchildren, who are English. I struggled to get to work on time, not to have Spencer confirm this view of West Indians.)

Once he gave us a Christmas treat, by taking present and past workers to the theatre to see Stanley Holloway in *My Fair Lady* and then to the Strand Palace Hotel for a special dinner. On these occasions, we would talk about anything but making ladies belts.

I have written elsewhere of how Spencer and old man Steinberg, ragged me about going up to university to read English, which was thought by them to be something you did in your spare time. So in conversation with them I would have to emphasise the more esoteric areas of English I was pursuing, like Middle English and Anglo-Saxon, and downplay the reading of novels. Both Spencer and his partner had a much greater tolerance for philosophical speculation and as that too was part of my course, they grudgingly agreed that I probably hadn't lost out much by leaving C.G. Spencer for a stab at higher education.

One thing intrigued me about Spencer (and about a couple of people I have met since) and it was his claim to be colour blind. I am not talking here about taking the moral high ground, of claiming not to be prejudiced. It was the bizarre notion that a person's 'colour' didn't immediately register when you saw him or her. When a mixed-race young man came to the door one morning asking for a job and was rejected, Spencer was astonished when Nancy and I commented on his colour. Spencer was vaguely upset that he might have unconsciously rejected the lad partly because of his colour. We had to reassure him that as there was no job going anyway, there was no point in his agonising over it.

Talent Failure at the Finsbury Park Empire

I remember being hustled off the stage by a cheerful Hughie Green, of 'Opportunity Knocks', even before I'd finished the second line of the song. So much for my career as a pop artist. But I was too stubborn to give up. (This must have been 1957 or '58 and one had to find new ways of making it, like Tommy Steele and Jim Dale, whom I'd seen recently at the Edgware Road *Empire* singing 'Be my Girl', which was still in the Hit Parade. My song, I thought, was an improvement on the current Hit Parade, combining elements of Jim Dale and Little Richard. On the stage with Jim Dale at the Edgware Road *Empire*, was the masked wrestler Dr. Death, whom we admired, because he had the ability to change shape and size from week to week. Also appearing at Edgware Road on that occasion was the purple-haired Wee Willie Harris who bounced round the place plucking a few chords of this or that instrument of his backing group, sounding a note here or there, more or less revealing to everyone that he couldn't play any of the instruments. *I* would put on a more convincing show! When, later, I saw Laurence Olivier's film, *The Entertainer,* it brought back those Friday nights at the Edgware Road *Empire*, seeing a desperate comic embarrass us all into laughter.

It's hard to know where this passion to be a pop star came from, in that I was never musical and my environment at home was almost entirely devoid of music. In the West Indies, the hymns of Charles Wesley, which we were forced to sing in church every Sunday, didn't count as music outside that setting, and no one in the family played an instrument (except a great aunt, who was said to have played the church organ – at the age of fourteen); although my father and one of my brothers were said to have 'good' voices. What confirmed our family's lack of collective musical talent was the acquisition, before my time, of a piano (from Germany, it was said; the Grundig). It had been installed in the drawing room of the family residence at Harris', so that my mother, eighteen years old and down from finishing school in Antigua, could be shown off to advantage; but she soon got bored with it, having married that same year; and none of us children really learnt to play it. My abiding memory of the piano was that its presence managed to spoil most of our school holidays. My mother or grandmother had enlisted a 'tutor' who came to the house once in a while to instruct us: The deal was that we would then have to practice for an hour every day during the holidays. This inevitably led to my trying to distract my grandmother with all sorts of activity (offering to climb the breadfruit tree to pick breadfruit for the pigs – or for us; pleading to run errands that Sarah, a maid, might have done) until, without warning she would suddenly announce that I hadn't done my hour's practice on the piano. Day after day I would think up more complicated ways of making my grandmother forget my hour torturing and being tortured by the piano, and never succeeded. Later, when I realised that my grandmother's delaying tactics had less to do with lapses of memory and more to do with a way of controlling me, I began to admire her way of operating and to understand how, lame, in her room at one end of the house, she had managed to control not just all the processes of the household, but the co-ordination of activity between houses that she owned, and activity on the bits of land at Trants and Mulcares where cotton was grown. What was most depressing (shaming, even) about the piano business, was to be shown up by the children of the odd favoured neighbour who had no prospect of their own Grundig, and who were allowed to practice on ours; *and who were seen to have talent.*

But in London in the late 1950s, if you were the right age, it was hard not to want to be a guitar-playing rock 'n roll singer. I never got around to the '2 'i's' Coffee Bar where Tommy Steele did his thing, but we heard him on the radio and by the time we got to see him on film, we weren't intimidated. I bought myself a guitar and secured a guitar teacher in Kilburn whom I repaired to every Saturday morning. He was a kindly man who encouraged me to look down on the face as I plucked the strings, because that's what Tommy Steele did as he, too, couldn't play the guitar. But something else about Tommy Steele encouraged me. My brother, Norman, or perhaps one of the family friends from university, visiting, volunteered the information that as a lyricist, Tommy Steele was interesting because the line in his song 'Water water everywhere and not a drop to drink', had been borrowed from the famous poet, Coleridge, friend of Wordsworth. That, perhaps, banished my residual doubts that pop singing was a lowly or unworthy occupation. I threw myself into writing pop songs and reading poetry voluntarily for the first time (mainly Shakespeare) keeping a keen eye for 'Water water everywhere and not a drop to drink' quotes.

The *Empire* Finsbury Park rebuff not withstanding, I had written a dozen or so songs and was looking for a way of setting them to music. We had a cousin from Trinidad, Wilfred Woodley, visiting, a professional musician playing the clubs in the West End and touring Scandinavia and other parts of the continent: he stayed for a while in our spare flat in Ladbroke Grove and I enlisted him to putting some of my songs to music[1]. But in the end he wasn't enthusiastic; his criticism of the lyrics, imperfectly understood by me at the time, centred around the fact that they didn't scan. (I had been trying so hard not to be Charles Wesley!) I had another cousin ('Horace') who played the piano and talked up his own musical prowess, but it turned out that the only thing he knew was how to embellish Glen Miller's 'In the mood'. No help there. So I had to go to a professional. I consulted my guitar teacher who, though he couldn't do the job himself, recommended an arranger in Wimbledon. This lack of his being able to arrange music confirmed a suspicion I had had about this teacher. It was the same reservation one had about those people on the radio offering to tell you how to win the football pools – claiming to have won tens of thousands of pounds for other people – but who themselves lived at obscure-sounding addresses in places like Hailsham, Kent. I liked the idea of Wimbledon (no, not the tennis, you saw that on television), just the fact that I was colonising new bits of London. I lived in Ladbroke Grove (West) worked in the West End and did the East End in the afternoon with my bag of belts; and later had a girlfriend in Mill Hill and a friend in Hendon who introduced me to Chinese food (North). So Wimbledon in the south was expanding my territory.

After Wimbledon, the logical next step was to record. For this I found a record-promoting company in New Bond Street. (Now I remember how I lost one of my ladies' belts jobs: I had taken two days off, the Monday and the Tuesday, to record my 'best selling' *Yellow Dog Blues* album in New Bond Street. The recordings were done on the Monday, but having recorded your 'album' you couldn't really be expected to go back to work on the Tuesday making ladies' belts. So when I went back to work on the Wednesday – this was at Glanz – I was sacked.)

I remember being up there recording these songs: the title 'Yellow Dog Blues' was the only blues number, the others were all hard rock 'n roll, accompanied by an unfamiliar band, doing my thing behind the microphone. The audience consisted of a couple of middle-aged men in suits, one of whom was smoking a cigar. This was early in the afternoon and at the end of my session the man removed his cigar for long enough to say: 'I like his hand movements.' He didn't think much of the songs. Even though there was a vague hint of another chance to record, I was beginning to get the message. So, for a couple of years I swung between thinking I could do better than the Platters ('Smoke gets in your eyes') and the Everly Brothers ('Problems') but dubious if I could match Slim Dusty's 'Pub with no beer'.

My brother, though supportive of my pop music ambitions, effectively urged me back to school. (It was always on the cards that I would go back to school, having arrived in England at sixteen, but there seemed no urgency: I had already written a novel and several plays hoping that this would make the return to school unnecessary.) My brother observed that even though I might be able to do Doris Day's still popular 1956 hit, 'Che Sera Sera' to perfection, people at home in Montserrat would be more impressed if I were to show a similar skill in translating *Caesar's Gallic Wars*. Even though I respected the opinion of people in England, you didn't want to lose face 'at home'.

When I went back to school, at Kilburn, I gained something of a reputation for being well read because, among other things, I knew that Tommy Steele's 'Water water everywhere and not a drop to drink' came, *of course*, from Coleridge's 'The Rime of the Ancient Mariner'; and I've learnt, ever since, to bluff my way through literature.

CHAPTER SEVEN
PLAN B: BACK TO SCHOOL
Learning to Love Jimmy Porter and Emma Woodhouse[1]

I remember my old teacher, Teacher Morgan, with amused affection. I can't help but contrast him with two powerful people from my later school in Kilburn, in 1959-61. I refer to them, collectively, as the Yetton, the sort of creature, perhaps not fully evolved, that imaginative travellers of an earlier century are said to have met on the snowcapped mountains of far Asia. It's interesting, the Yetton. Both male and female exhibits must have realized that they were the last of the species, previous attempts to mate having clearly gone wrong (He, in human life, was the Headmaster, she was Head of English) and they decided, terrifyingly, to marry: the decision provided lively comment throughout the school. The Principal Yetton had succumbed, it was thought, to the charms of the Widow Yetton, attracted, probably, to her indifferent teeth and her lightly-trimmed beard. Widow Yetton and I fought, throughout the A Level year, over ownership of English Literature. We fought over my tendency to be sometimes first in the class in English; fought over my dislike of Jane Austen's Emma Woodhouse (*Emma* being a set text) and over my desire to sit exams at the earliest possible date rather than at the time the school saw fit. Eventually, she gave me a lukewarm reference for university. But this is not to condemn my years doing GCEs at the Kilburn Polytechnic school; I very largely enjoyed my time there. Though you needed to be alert, agile.

A celebrated Russian might have called the years before Kilburn time spent in the University of Life, but I wasn't sure how productively those years had been spent. I knew how to make ladies' belts and handbags, was an avid listener to the radio, particularly the Third Programme; I had read and written some plays, none of the latter being successfully staged; I was a regular cinema and music-hall goer and had made a pop record that was never released; all in all, hardly a graduate from that University of Life. Despite certain bookish conversations with my brother, Norman, I wasn't sure that I had acquired the sort of literary 'taste' that I was confident in defending. I did, however, work at it.

Early on, on my way to work at the handbag factory in Baker Street, I usually took a book to read. The choice of material wasn't entirely accidental: I hadn't started buying books at the time, and the only reading material in the flat in Maida Vale, apart from my mother's magazines, was religious material (my mother's) or books to do with either Bookkeeping or Accounting (my elder brother's), and it seemed provocative to take into the handbag factory the copy of *Great Expectations* that I was reading (and enjoying) at my brothers' suggestion: they'd both done it at grammar school. So I took in Peter Cheyney.

I hadn't heard of him, of course, but then I'd hardly heard of any contemporary writer who wasn't a dramatist, and a couple of Cheyney books were left on the mantelpiece of the next house we moved into before Ladbroke Grove, along with, I think, an Erle Stanley Gardener or a Raymond Chandler. So I took the Peter Cheyney, and read bits of it during lunch; for most this tended to be home-made sandwiches eaten sitting at their workbench, along with a cup of coffee or tea. (I bought my sandwiches at a little café round the corner.)

Peter Cheyney came with the recommendation that he had written over thirty books, crime novels with private detectives chasing down criminals, as well as collections of short stories. I liked the title of the novel called *Poison Ivy*, but the one I remembered wrestling with was called *Dark Interlude*. This was about spies at work after the war, and it was mainly set in France, though with the odd English scene thrown in. One thing I liked about it was Cheyney's trick of suggesting that something was said in French by writing it in English, and merely saying that the character said it in French. It seemed a neat way to me of getting over not knowing the foreign language. Having said that, I was disappointed that more of the action wasn't set in England, as that would have made it, to me, seem even more contemporary. Or, perhaps, closer to my experience.

I didn't, in the end, think Cheyney was a very good writer, though I wasn't confident enough to say why. There were things that appealed. The way he wrote 'farther' when I would have written 'further'. Maybe I could use that. Unless it would make me sound odd. Anyway, I was pleasantly surprised that his main character, an Irishman in France, who is first presented as a drunk, barely able to carry out his low-level job as car-repair man in a garage, is in fact a top Secret Agent able to speak four languages: when he is in a tight spot he recites poetry! In one of the bookcases in one of the houses in France there is a copy of Shakespeare's plays and a *Life of Napoleon*. (I made a note to include a bookcase in my own fictional furnishings.)

But other things in the book didn't appeal; the way the men spoke to women wasn't… well, acceptable. And I couldn't get into the characters through their names. Nago. Guelvada. The Brazilian lady, Eulalia; they all seemed made-up to me. Though the main character, the Irishman, O'Mara – Shaun Aloysius O'Mara – was, I suppose, OK. Talking of *writing*, though, would Dickens have described the heat outside (in France) as 'hot as hell', and inside as 'cold as death'? 'Farther' for 'further' didn't quite compensate for this. Other things – which I had time to ponder on the tube to work – didn't impress: a baddie in the book has a scar of a knife slash across his face. Well, the *Keep Britain White* brigade don't have scars across their faces. And when Cheyney said that something impossible was like 'a man in a dark room trying to find a Negro dressed in black. I didn't know where the hell to start looking', I decided that one Peter Cheyney novel was enough for me. So, it was back to school.

My first day (this was in 1959) was instructive. Having enrolled, at last, for study we were brought together in a large classroom downstairs, and asked to write an essay. The result would determine who would be put in the GCE 'O' level class and who would need a year's extra tuition before joining that class. There must have been about fifty or so of us, the overflow accommodated in another room. Having written our essay we then went to familiarize ourselves with the demands of other subjects, having been asked to return in the afternoon, to the big room, to hear the results of our essay effort. The person in change of this was the person we now knew as The Yetton. (Female)

In the afternoon session she explained that the names she'd call out would be those who would go straight into the GCE class, and that the names would be in descending order of merit, the highest mark first.

'Markham,' she called, and looked up.

After some hesitation I answered. She looked at me, looked away, looked round the room and called again.

'Markham.'

'Yes,' I said, more confidently, putting up my hand.

'Ah,' she said, acknowledging me. Then she said, that in order to speed things up, we needn't identify ourselves, she'd just read out the selected names.

I couldn't escape the feeling that the lady wasn't pleased that I had come out top. I then took in the fact that there were only about half a dozen 'foreign-looking' people in the room, mainly Middle Eastern and Mediterranean, and one other West Indian, who looked somewhat older than the rest, older than me. Oddly enough I wasn't that comfortable at coming first in the essay; it hinted at being singled out, and you were beginning to learn that this was not the same experience as being singled out for praise at home.

These were the years – the Kilburn years – of what I must call *anglicization*. There were never more than two or three 'coloured' or foreign students in the English Language, English Literature, Geography or History classes, and none (other than me) in Latin or Italian. In English (Language and Literature) Thomas, from Jamaica, was the other non-English-born person. In a subject called ABC (Accounts, Bookkeeping and Commerce) there was someone from Guyana and someone from Kenya (both Asians). Later two young sisters from India, enviably good at Chaucer, joined the class and at A Level there was a young man from, I think, Ghana who was very proud of being a Christian. Economics, though, had quite a strong contingent from abroad – mainly from the Middle East.

The 'English' impact was evident in the 'O' Level year. The school, I suppose, was a comprehensive, in that there were pupils there who had failed the Eleven Plus and others, like me, who had not taken it. Among those who hadn't, apparently, was a strong contingent of 'bright' girls from a prestigious school in Barnett, called Copthall's. And, in a way, they set the standard – particularly in languages – that the rest of us struggled to match. Although I maintained my form in English, one other boy, Roy Matthias, contesting the first place, I struggled in many other areas, particularly in languages, in Italian and Latin eventually gaining the barest of passes.

This 'finishing school' environment was as strong as any in orientating me, socially. I had few real friends outside the school; my mother's friends were people you saw, in a sense, out of duty, and even those of my brothers – seven and eight years my senior, respectively – were not people I was close to in a growing-up sense. Indeed, I wasn't even close to my brothers; and my sister, by then training to be a nurse, lived for long periods away from home. So I used to hang around the school all day, use the library or just laze in the common room. Or play table-tennis in that late-afternoon space when school ended and before Polytechnic night classes began: the tables would be set up in the dining-room for a few hours. School was interesting, too, because of the Polytechnic element, older people coming in and sharing the same resources made us feel we weren't at school but at college. Occasionally, a group of us from the GCE class would go to the cinema during the day – the *Essoldo* at the other end of the High Road, the Maida Vale end, being the favourite, until we discovered the *Everyman* at Hampstead. And then, of course, there were the weekend parties. ('Have you ever seen snow?')

Some of the girls from Copthall's were Jewish and lived, like Avril, in Edgware, or in Golders Green, like Pam. An early favourite, Pam invited me to her parents' flat where I was made welcome. Her father had a vegetable stall in the market (Covent Garden) and her mother, at home, was usually forthcoming with coffee and cakes. (And fruit.) There was another friend, Vanessa, who lived in Hampstead and her mother, who was South African, surprised me by her friendliness and lack of overt racist attitude. A little group of us would visit the house in Netherhall Gardens where the father, when at home, would take turns to make the coffee; and Vanessa would feel free to lend out the paperbacks in the bookcase – books like *The Greeks, The World of Odysseus, Plutarch's Lives*.

I was impressed that Vanessa's father, who was a solicitor, had that type of reading matter, that sort of literary interest. (I was doing 'O' Level in Ancient History at the time, reading it up on my own, as it wasn't offered at the school.) I was impressed, too, that Vanessa could lend out her father's books without reference to him – though she would no doubt have checked with him beforehand. This middle-class English-South African family reminded you that people's credibility didn't come ready-made: these were among the most politically-sophisticated people I'd met to date. Though, occasionally, the mother tried a little too hard. On one occasion as we were about to leave the house in a group to go off to a party, or whatever, the mother saw us out and, in a casual sort of way, reminded us to be careful – and not to 'flirt too much'. By that time I had paired up with Judy, from Mill Hill. She, too, was an ex-Copthall's girl. Her mother, who lived apart from her father, was wonderfully tolerant – and a Conservative!

Of course there were limits to toleration. Pam went out for while with an Asian boy from Kenya, and the relationship seemed quite intense; but we didn't know if the parents knew about it. Later, when she got serious about my friend Bill Chinque – Bill was half-Chinese – Pam's parents were not pleased. Yet, I was to be co-opted in the role of guardian for Pam on a trip abroad. This was a couple of years later. At the time she was having a relationship with an older man who was married; he had an up-market antique business just off Kensington High Street. This, the parents didn't know about; and it was clear that I was being used as some sort of cover for the meetings.

This neutering (of me) was something I colluded in, almost like an observer. I was at university by then, in my first year at Lampeter, in Wales; and a group of us, students, went on holiday to Italy. (At school, the talk had always been of cheap holidays to Rimini and Riccioni; but the woman who came to conduct the 'O' Level Italian viva was from Perugia. She was sparkling, bubbly, and did all the talking when she tested me; and then ended up praising my Italian accent. So, naturally, I promised her that I would visit Perugia; but in the end I settled for Rome.) My 'neutering' role was later confirmed when Pam's parents let her come on the trip to Italy, reassured that I would 'look after' her. This was very much in the Hollywood tradition of portraying 'good' Africans and good 'colored' men, generally as desexed, so that white women would be safe in their presence. I had some problems in colluding with her to deceive her parents over this: she *did* come to Italy with us but cut short the trip to nip back to Paris to meet her man. Ten days later, she rejoined our returning train from Rome (I think at the Gare de Lyons) and we coordinated our stories about Rome. Very Hollywood, I thought, with some satisfaction.

But this was later. I was surprised how much I enjoyed being back at school, and in particular, the two English classes, Language and Literature. In Language I was lucky in the 'essay' slot because, along with the list of essay subjects, was usually the option to write a short story: I always chose to write the story and often had the satisfaction of having it read out by the teacher. One of our English teachers was Geoffrey Stern (later of LSE fame, now, alas, dead). I remember being very proud of a one-word comment in the margin of a story to which Geoffrey had given a high mark; and showed it round, only to have it pointed out that the comment wasn't, as I had supposed, about the sophistication of my literary effort, but of my inability to spell the word, 'subtle'.

I particularly enjoyed the literature class where the main books were *The Old Curiosity Shop* and *Macbeth*. Just about everyone in the class preferred *Macbeth* to Dickens. And this I couldn't understand. But I had an ally in Thomas, the Jamaican. Thomas had a clerical job at British Rail – in the Paddington office – and was in the process of buying a house in Queens Park. We were the only two 'coloured' pupils in the 'O' Level Literature class, and tended to be at opposite ends of the class in terms of grades – opposite, also, in where we sat in class, Thomas at the back. But we shared certain traits: if I was a slow reader, Thomas was funereal, and had some difficulty getting to the end of *The Old Curiosity Shop* in time for the exams.

But in response to Dickens Thomas and I were as one. We loved being plunged into the Victorian world which, in a sense, we were closer to, coming from the West Indies, than were the English students from Golders Green and Dollis Hill. Their fascination with England was going up to the West End at the weekend and drinking an expensive 'continental' coffee at the 100 Club in Soho. Even in literal things Thomas and I knew the world of Dickens. When, for instance, Kit's mother, Mrs. Nubbles, in the middle of ironing, brings the hot, flat iron close to her face to test its heat, Thomas and I had witnessed it in our own homes. (The times I had seen Nellie do that in the bread-room: I could still see the four or five irons being heated on the hot coals in the coalpot, near the door that opened out into the back yard.)

Yet, there were warning signs at our admitting to knowledge which others were keen to dub as backward or unmodern. (One girl got terribly excited when she glimpsed the cover of my *Teach Yourself Logic*, misreading the key word as *Magic*. How to choose between her gushing enthusiasm and the 'cool' of another girl who vowed that she would commit suicide at the age of forty? This quiet, beautiful girl claimed she would have done everything she planned to do by that age; she had a distaste for being old, and a dislike for old people, including her parents.)

On a more mundane level, you didn't want to give the impression that you grew up without electricity (the caution from Sadie at the handbag factory wasn't forgotten), for before the end of our time in Harris' the village got street lighting, and in the house in town we had electricity. I was sensitive about this, too, because I had run into so many West Indians and Asians who tended to make the wrong assumptions about how we – my family – had lived at home, drawing from their own experiences. This was true, too, of Thomas: his version of growing up in the West Indies didn't really correspond to mine, though being in England you learnt to play down the differences. Privately, though, you were determined to present *your* West Indies to the world.

In class, our criticism of the Dickens book centred largely on deploring the sentimentality (which we secretly liked) of the 'good' characters, and the over-writing of the death and burial, in all that snow, of Little Nell. I think now that it's possible that Thomas and I overemphasized our love for Dickens because no one else in the class liked the book much. We even noted that Dickens, like us, but unlike almost everyone else in the class, was born outside the capital – even though Portsmouth was a lot nearer to London than West Indies was.

What amazed me, looked back, was the gap of what one must call 'sensibility' between the O and A Level years: in the latter, one was saying much the same sorts of things about Jane Austen and T.S. Eliot that I would probably say now; whereas when, some time ago, I returned to *The Old Curiosity Shop* I could get through it only by regarding it as a children's book. As a teacher how else would you approach stage-baddies like Quilp? (If Richard III is a stage-baddy in the Premier Division, then, surely, Daniel Quilp, the ugly dwarf who makes faces to scare young boys and women, whose notion of domestic assault is to pinch his wife, etc. – Quilp is barely in the *League*. At school we didn't, it's true, register that there was no real sex in a novel of 500 pages (you expected sex in *films*, that's why films were modern), but we were fascinated and appalled by the character of the old man, Nell's grandfather, who by his gambling disinherits the child and sets out with her across England, begging. Thomas and I felt a cut above the class for we saw in this what we would now call 'emotional bullying'; *they* saw it as being simply 'stupid'.

Recently, I dug out my old copy of *The Old Curiosity Shop*, the Everyman edition with its reassuring, dull-green cover, and its mediaeval-Victorian notion of comfort printed at the front:

> Everyman, I will go with thee, and be thy guide!
> In thy most need to go by thy side

full of annotations and ticks and underlining; and with lots of little, wafer-thin, white, oblong bits of paper with notes and scribbles wedged between the pages, undisturbed for over forty years. My first interest in seeing this was to note how my handwriting has changed (as, indeed, has the signature). Found, also, was a yellowing, folded sheet of paper, much larger than the rest with 'vocabulary' (and some words) scribbled on the outside. Opened up, it revealed something in typed capitals, which I give complete:

IF I DEFINE AN AUTHOR AS A PERSON WHO MAKES HIS LIVING BY PUBLISHING IN BOOK FORM ORIGINAL COMPOSITION SO CALLED IF WE CAN AGREE UPON THAT I WILL PROCEED FURTHER TO SAY I THINK THE PERSONS WHO COMPRISE THAT CATEGORY ARE UPON THE WHOLE A VERY FORTUNATE CLASS THE GREAT MASS OF MANKIND PASS THEIR DAYS IN WORK AND IT IS ONLY AFTER THEIR WORK IN THE FIELD OR THE MILL OR THE OFFICE HAS BEEN DONE THAT THEY FIND TIME TO PLAY SO MANY HOURS FROM EVERY DAY OF THEIR LIVES HAVE TO BE SACRIFICED TO A TYRANT THING CALLED WORK UNWELCOME MONOTONOUS AND UNREMITTING WORK NOT TILL THAT IS SATISFIED IS THERE ROOM FOR RECREATION OR FOR PLEASURE THAT IS THE LOT OF THE COMMON RUN OF HUMANITY THE FORTUNATE PEOPLE IN THE WORLD THE ONLY REALLY FORTUNATE PEOPLE IN THE WORLD IN MY MIND ARE THOSE WHOSE WORK IS ALSO THEIR PLEASURE THAT CLASS IS NOT A LARGE ONE NOT NEARLY SO LARGE AS IT IS OFTEN REPRESENTED TO BE AND AUTHORS ARE PERHAPS ONE OF THE MOST IMPORTANT ELEMENTS IN ITS COMPOSITION THEY ENJOY IN THIS RESPECT AT LEAST A REAL HARMONY OF LIFE IS NOT THE AUTHOR FREE AS FEW MEN ARE FREE IS HE NOT SECURE AS FEW MEN ARE SECURE THE TOOLS OF HIS INDUSTRY ARE SO COMMON AND CHEAP THAT THEY HAVE ALMOST CEASED TO HAVE COMMERCIAL VALUE HE NEEDS NO BULKY PILE OF RAW MATERIAL NO ELABORATE APPARATUS NO SERVICE OF MEN OR OF ANIMALS HE IS DEPENDENT FOR HIS OCCUPATION UPON NO ONE BUT

HIMSELF AND NOTHING IS OUTSIDE HIM THAT MATTERS HE IS THE SOVEREIGN OF AN EMPIRE SELF SUPPORTING SELF CONTAINED NO ONE CAN SEQUESTRATE HIS ESTATES NO ONE CAN DEPRIVE HIM OF HIS STOCK IN TRADE NO ONE CAN FORCE HIM TO EXERCISE HIS FACULTY AGAINST HIS WILL NO ONE CAN PREVENT HIM EXERCISING IT AS HE CHOOSES THE PEN IS THE GREAT LIBERATOR OF MEN AND NATIONS

I have no idea where this came from but it must have resonated with me at the time. On the front of the folded paper is scribbled 'Vocabulary'. Then: 'And she could feel its palpitation'; and the words 'malignant', 'equivocal', 'admonition'.

Some of the white strips of paper were aide-memoires to the big scenes of the novel. 'Quilp's tea party', 'The Wackless' party', etc. but most were reminders to focus on the details of the scene. 'Describe Schoolroom, parlour and kitchen.' (This of the schoolmaster in Chapter XXIII). 'Describe Boys day school'; 'Describe Pxxx Jarley's Caravan' p. 191). These were obviously essay questions where the big scenes were used as the basis of teasing out some of the book's themes. Though, 'Describe slum' (p. 205); 'Describe Sally Brass' and many other notes just said 'Describe'. The teacher – if, indeed, this was teacher-driven – chimed with my own tendency to be fascinated by these strange, remote scenes being brought to life and the unlikely characters who populated them. 'Important, Swiveller!' was another note. Also, 'In a drunken state told Quilp that the [illegible] gentleman was seen in conversation with Kit. Quilp followed.' (This, between pp. 348-9).

Then there are the lists, my weakness. 'Name the Characters in the Punch show: 1 (blank) 3: Punch's wife & child, 4: hobby horse, 5: doctor, 6: foreign gentleman, 7: radical neighbour, 8: executioner, 9: Devil. *9 persons & dog.* The biggest list appears at the end of the book (pp. 540-41) headed 'Journey of Nell and Grandfather', and there are ten items. (1) Slipped through Quilp's watchful eyes in early morning. (2) Got refreshment from poor, old cottager – and his daughter and her children – who said his dead son had been a soldier. The woman washed Nell's blistered feet, and they were the cause of the travellers' getting a ride. (3) They met Short and Codlin in churchyard (Grinder's lot – to the races). (4) Jolly Sandboys. Jerry & dancing dogs. (5) Meet Schoolmaster. Harry West. (6) Mrs. Jarley. (7) Valliant Soldier Gen Groves, Isaac List and Joe Jowl. (8) Men on barge. (9) Man and finance. (10) Meet Schoolmaster Jakes (?) then to village near churchyard.

I can't remember what mark I got for O level Eng. Lit; but I passed.

Talking of Kilburn as a sort of finishing school doesn't seem absurd to me, even though some of the 'finishing school' touches may have been socially questionable. I took it for granted that my closest friendships would be formed there, and that within that group – the bright girls from Copthall's, Avril, Pam and Judy, my part-Chinese friend, Chinque, from Hendon – my own family's middle-class background would be more-or-less reflected. So, evidence of 'otherness', particularly in terms of speech, was de-emphasized. (Pam, good-humouredly, tended to pick me up on it, anyway.) Whereas in the more foreign-tenanted Economics class we talked sometimes about the redistribution of wealth, in the near-English environment of the Literature class, I learnt to redistribute my *stresses*. *Pam*ela became *Pamela*, because the person whose name it was pronounced it so, and the Yetton insisted on it. With that went a more general redistribution of stress, from West Indian to English – *Char*acter became *Character*. *Alu*minium became Alu*mini*um, etc. The stress was now thrown onto the first rather than the second syllable of 'concert' – all this learnt, not just in the classroom and common room, but at the homes of Pam or Judy or Chinque. The notion of securing 'best' tables in restaurants was new to me: how could you be humiliated at the Ritz or at Claridges by being given a table near to the kitchens? (Chinque's elder brother, who was a waiter at the Ritz – and an Oxford graduate – enlightened me.) This gradual conversion into 'Englishness' meant (without particular resistance on my part) taking on new prejudices. It was quite liberating to learn, say, that the Scots were mean, that Italians were hopeless fighters, the Japanese imitative and that (when not in their company) the Jews were dubiously into business (despite Marks & Spencer), or tended to live above the shop in Burnt Oak – despite Marks & Spencer. I remember one day being in the dinner queue at school with Judy and Avril and the usual crowd; and the very friendly dinner lady asked Avril if she was English.

'Yes, I'm English.'

'Oh, I didn't think you were English, I thought you were Jewish.'

'I'm Jewish. But I'm English.'

'I thought you were Jewish.'

'But I'm English all the same.'

'That's right. But you know what I mean.' Then she turned to Judy. '*You're* English.'

We were all on Avril's side, and not just because of her embarrassment; there may have been a class thing at work there as well. And yet there was ambivalence: on the one hand I wanted Avril (and Pam) to be accepted unreservedly as English, because they were my 'English' friends. Also, we wanted there to be different categories or versions of 'English', so that the thing wouldn't seem so monolithic, so unbreachable.

At the same time you knew that if you were white-skinned and foreign

117

– like the Hungarians who had come over in '56 – it would be good to make some distinction between the newer and the older 'English' to prevent them lining up against you, the black-skinned, who would be kept permanently out of the club. Until this was sorted out it was *useful* to have the dinner-lady question Avril's Englishness, and *important* to rally to Avril's defence.

And we played cricket. The school team played at the Welsh Harp on the North Circular. I was (surprisingly) a valued member of the team. We played on a Wednesday afternoon, and usually got beaten. Occasionally we combined with the ex-Poly team, which was stronger, and there, though bad at batting, bowling and fielding, I was usually picked because I was West Indian, and hence assumed to be good – despite the evidence. (It was there that I began to develop the theory of 'benign racism'.) But Judy came to see me play. In my cricketing whites she said I looked like Johnny Matthis.

★ ★ ★

If these were fairly overt ways of becoming attuned to the culture, there were more private concerns that challenged, however nebulously, my sense of being fully fit to compete with my new contemporaries. (To know all the names of the stations on the Central Line – though not on my 'own' line, the Metropolitan, to which I related – was a trick that had impressed my fellow belt and handbag makers, but we had moved on now.) I knew nothing of nature; odd, for someone brought up on an island, and in the country. But apart from fruit trees and the odd shrub I now realized that, unlike my sister, I didn't know how to identify flowers that everyone else seemed to take for granted. I sort of knew the names, but couldn't really match the flower to the name. Trees, flowers, the same with birds. (My boasts of having tended the flower garden at Harris', with its border of crocuses, though true, seemed increasingly hollow.) Keats's nightingale. Wordsworth's daffodils. The argument that we were ill-served, in the Caribbean, by being forced-fed this foreign literature would gain some force if the contention were that we were never provided with enough 'context' fully to appreciate these texts. During one of the summer holidays, while at was at university, I took a job delivering flowers, driving a van backwards and forwards across London. Hydrangeas. Clematis. Ah! This was the whiff of hyacinths in that garden that diverts the attention of the young man from Eliot's Lady; this is the scent from the bowl of lilacs in her room.

The thing about becoming more attuned to things English meant letting go of certain West Indian attitudes that 'at home' we thought were English but here in England were seen as quaint.

You soon got over the embarrassment of saying that you would *send* your books back to the library, or *send* your clothes to the laundry. People in contemporary England – or at least the people you knew – tended to perform these duties for themselves. It is true that the odd person in Hampstead or Edgware had an au pairs from Denmark or France or Germany; nevertheless the children took their own borrowed books back to the public library.

What took a little getting used to is what we would now call the linguistic politeness of Londoners, who would apologize to you when you jostled them in the butchers or at the bus queue. It didn't seem ironic. And explanations that the habit was learnt during the war, through having to take your turn for scarce supplies, or to secure your place in the underground shelter, didn't ring entirely true; for other people had had shortages – as we had with imported stuff in the West Indies – and that made you, if anything, to be sure to be first in the queue. Indeed, you used your connections to avoid the queue.

But did all this saying 'sorry' mean anything, or was it just a pleasant ritual? And why should it be more than that, anyway; it was an expression of the *culture*, like saying prayers in other countries before going to bed and getting up, and at mealtimes. Though you had a feeling that inherent in the act of queuing was a sense of fairness which would make you decline to take more than your fair share, were it offered.

Though you couldn't be sure. One Saturday evening at the Post Office in Ladbroke Grove, I was given a pound too much in my change by the young woman behind the counter. On discovering it when I got home I thought, over the weekend, what I might do with the extra pound but – I expect, partly to impress the youngish woman – returned the pound to her on the Monday morning. She was confused, then puzzled, then surprised, which made me think that this sort of thing didn't happen often.

Then there was the idea of democracy, something I hadn't thought about much. Back at school, even though you were aware of class difference, maybe in the way people spoke, you no longer judged people as worthy or unworthy on a class basis. And yet that wasn't as liberating as you hoped, for you were aware that for most people in England being 'coloured' or black put you in a *class*, separate from – and lower than – the working class: how to relate this to an idea of democracy? So you found yourself throwing out endless hints of the elevated social position of your own family, you even made reference to the fact that you were going to school full-time, not part time, as were some other students from Asia and the Caribbean. But then the undermining of your own position struck you: here were you accepting the legitimacy of all these English students to transcend definition by class, but at the same time you were throwing in on your side, a little value-added extra here and there, as if one's position were *inferior* to theirs and needed topping up.

It wasn't an easy lesson to learn, coming from a society where you instinctively saw beyond the person to the family, and where the decision on long-term friendship had something to do with the family's status. (I remember at home being reprimanded for playing with children in the park at Garden Hill because they were poor and ill-dressed, and I was on my way to a (smart) function. Of course this didn't solve the problem that in *this* democracy there seemed to be separate (and unequal) rights for people who were black.

Certain 'colonial' attitudes continued to embarrass me. At the cinema, at the end of the film in those days, the National Anthem was played, and film-goers were expected to stand for the duration. My first fight with Judy was over the National Anthem. We were in the cinema. At the end of the film, the National Anthem struck up. Like most people in the cinema I stood up, Judy remained seated. I urged her to stand. She refused and suggested that I sit down. After some hesitation I crouched, hoping others would think that I was standing and that Judy would accept that I wasn't. Moral courage was not – and still is not – something that comes *naturally* to me.

Being with Judy, with that group, was instructive. One always felt included and slightly exposed at the same time; one was never shown discourtesy by any parent and yet, outside the confines of these (largely-middle class) homes one always felt somewhat uneasy, more than a little exposed. OK, in public people didn't know you; but you were never going to make yourself *knowable* to the bulk of people on the street; yet you couldn't remain *hidden* and anonymous: you'd be noted, noticed, glanced at (particularly if the woman on your arm was white-skinned): you were made to feel that the London, which you knew better than most of your school-friends, didn't really belong to you. (Or worse: you didn't belong to it.) There was embarrassment here, but there was resentment, too. I ran into a girl, who had worked in one of the dress factories I used to deliver belts to. She had come over from Hungary in '56 with, as I remember, a story of torture at home. When I ran into her, about four years later (in a little bookshop on Charing Cross Road, called *Better Books*), I had no idea who this attractive Englishwoman was, who knew my name. On reflection she still did have a bit of an 'accent', but having left the dress factory behind – or outside its context – she, and her white-skinned partner, would pass unnoticed in the crowd. It was hard not to feel some small resentment towards this very pleasant young woman, who no longer had to bear the badge of 'otherness'. Even her friendliness was a challenge: it was as if she and her partner were making me feel welcome in England.

The homes of friends might be mine, more or less. But Ladbroke Grove, where I lived for some years, couldn't be said to be mine, when a declared fascist lived in the house next door. And would I have accepted that street in Ladbroke Grove as mine, had it been offered to me, if that had meant ceding the rest of London to others? Judy lived in Mill Hill; this was pleasant in a quiet sort of way, but too much like Outer London where people hid behind net curtains and knew who came and went along the street. (Everyone knew the address I was heading to.) Edgware might welcome you into its clan, but the questions asked made you realize that you were being seen as an experiment, something exotic come to town. (In all of those places I put thought-bubbles in the heads of the parents – and sisters and brothers – to be given voice the moment I left the house. But there was a strange inhibition to put people you knew on the stage, in the same sense that you didn't want to put your family on the stage. It wasn't so much that it was bad manners, it was more a feeling that for a writer it was the *easy* option: in those days you felt that the writer should *invent*.)

Bill Chinque's place in Hendon was a good blend of the English and the exotic; a mixed-race family that seemed totally relaxed in its ownership of both cultures. (Bill was to pull me up on my slippage into the phrase 'Red China', in reference to Mao's China. And although Chairman Mao, we now know, was rather worse than we had imagined at the time, Bill was, in a sense, right.) So, to ownership: Pam's place in Golders Green was fine because Golders Green, even though designated as 'Jewish', seemed pretty cosmopolitan to me, with its Indian and Chinese restaurants, and cinema which showed more interesting films than the *Essoldo* on Kilburn High Road. The address to beat, though, was Vanessa's at Netherhall Gardens, in Hampstead. Now, *there* was a place to live.

It was at Pam's place watching television one afternoon that a realization finally hit home that I – that my family – weren't properly part of this society. (One always knew this but held the thought at a distance.) Pam's mother referred to something advertised on the television. Whatever the product was she had bought it and was being vaguely dismissive: it hadn't lived up to the image seen on television. It had never occurred to me until then that TV advertising had anything to do with the lives of people we knew, not in the way in which they organized their lives. (My mother had bought goods from mail-order catalogues, but when she was disappointed in the product, she more or less accepted that the mistake had been hers, at the point of ordering.) The TV adverts I was conscious of at the time were mainly for toothpaste and soap-powder and margarine. There were ads, too, for cigarettes and cars and petrol. The toothpaste ad was the first one I really noticed: in it a young woman with a very white face and good, even teeth was brushing her teeth the wrong way (up and down rather than across) while there was music and a sort of jingle in the background. Now, all my life we had been taught to brush the other way (across), something I had done assiduously night and morning, year in year out; and already I was beginning to have problems with my teeth. And still it didn't occur to me that the woman on the television was maybe brushing the *right* way. I didn't relate to the smoking Ads. No one in the family smoked, nor did Judy, unlike some of the girls at school. (In some of the motor car ads the men smoked pipes.)

The ad that resonated with us at home in Ladbroke Grove was the one where grown people claimed not to be able to tell the difference between Stork and butter. The stupidity of this was hard to explain. The taste of margarine was so different from any brand of butter you came across that the whole thing seemed like a joke. We didn't have problems with margarine – we used that, too – but why pretend it was the same as something from which it was as different in taste as was an apple from a mango? So we just didn't take the notion of TV advertising on board.

Even those adverts for cars or petrol showed people driving out into the country. Well, we hadn't driven out into the country. My exploration of 'country' stretched no further (I'll stick with 'further') than Wimbledon in the south (to see a man about arranging music), Osterley (towards Heathrow airport, for cricket), Stratford, in the East End, on the Central Line (occasionally, for theatre: Joan Littlewood, not Shakespeare) and Mill Hill (Judy) – though I associated this last, also, with reading through most of Molière as, changing buses I waited, endlessly, for the 144 at the corner of Golders Green Road and the North Circular. So ads with cars advertising petrol by driving out into the country, didn't relate to us. True, we knew the odd person living in Birmingham or studying in Edinburgh (or Ireland), but, apart from my sister, we hadn't been much outside London. So the notion of all that *England* outside London belonging to someone else made you feel that your patch in the country was *small*.

Pam's mother belonged because she bought things advertised on the television, and expected them to perform as advertised; the jingles were meant to impress her. Similarly, with Judy's mother. In our house in Ladbroke Grove we simply *talked* when the ads came on, or went downstairs to make a cup of tea.

It will be said – it has been said – that it was the relative absence of black faces on the television that led one to being so disengaged; yet, I wonder. There *were* black people on television quite a bit of the time, particularly on the news, people being humiliated in Africa or America, or black people from America who were singers or musicians; and endlessly on the newsreels in the cinema – and I seem to remember the comment that, apart from the singers, black people were, on the whole, badly-photographed. The image of black people portrayed was, more or less, negative, and although you identified with the *shame* of all this, you didn't really think that the situations portrayed were similar enough to your own, to want to identify England with America or with Southern Africa.

There were, of course more positive images: a charismatic Egyptian president, a dignified Indian prime minister, a relaxed president of an independent Ghana paying a State visit to Britain,[2] hosted by the Queen. There was the young and handsome Cassius Marcellus Clay; but these positive images hadn't filtered through to the advertisers.

But a transaction was being entered into between them and their customers – Judy's mother, Pam's mother and no doubt thousands of others – but not with my family; in an important sense, for the advertisers, we didn't register. Scribbling, scribbling, I couldn't bring shape to the mass (the mess?) of images in my head. I walked around all day with a loose-leaf notebook, adding to the mess. My mother, amused, referred to the notebook as my 'dictionary'. (She laughed and laughed at her own joke.)[3]

My closest friend was Bill Chinque ("Guangua" when, on the phone, he felt like stressing his Chinese identity). His mother was half-Scottish, living apart from her husband in Hendon. Like me, Bill was the youngest in the family, the same sort of age-gap existing between him and his brothers, as between me and mine. His two brothers, who were not always around, seemed very sophisticated; the waiter at the Savoy (I can't remember now whether it was the Savoy or the Ritz) dressed formally, as if *he* were being taken out to dinner. One evening, wearing his 'Oxford' hat he condescended to put us right about D.H. Lawrence, whom he rated; and about the philosophy of 'Peanuts', the Shultz cartoon, which he rated more.

It's difficult now to remember why we had the fight, Chinque and I, but I seem to recall that it had something to do with a ruler. (No, not measuring ourselves.) I was the oldest in the English Language class (Thomas wasn't taking that class) and Bill was the biggest – 6ft. *plus* even then. Bill would demonstrate his toughness, during break-time, by smashing his fist into the notice-board in the common room to the appalled fascination of those around – particularly the girls. We had got into the habit of arm-wrestling on the desktop, and had both worked it out to the point where neither could subdue the other. Then there was this thing about the ruler. In the class. Threats were made to sort it out during break, outside.

The mistake was that the threats were overheard, and during break when we drifted downstairs for a snack and a drink, we were reminded that we had a fight on our hands. Neither of us had the least intention of fighting but it was increasingly clear that we weren't going to be allowed to get out of it.

Pushing, shoving – who knows – but Chinque's glasses fell off, cutting him on the cheek in the process; but mine stayed on. We were about to shake hands when our supporters demanded more; fortunately a teacher came up and put a stop to it. In order to show the teacher that we were above it all, Chinque and I *did* shake hands there and then. (I was enormously impressed by Chinque, as he had offered to shake first.)

But we had to be marched off to the Principal's office (the Principal hadn't yet transmogrified into the male Yetton, but he was well on the way), and he told us how appalled he was by our behaviour, and demanded a written explanation before he decided whether we would be expelled. Before obeying the instructions to go home until further notice, Bill and I spent some time in the common room composing a statement, synchronizing notes, both of us more concerned about the reaction at home, should we be expelled. We each took our share of the blame for the 'incident'; and when the Principal relented next day and agreed that we could stay on at school, Bill invited me to visit his house in Hendon. (Pending that, he offered to teach me to play chess, and opened out the tiny chessboard he always carried on him.)

★ ★ ★

As a student I laboured under two disadvantages: I was a slow reader, as I've said, and I had a poor memory. I often told myself that were I to write an autobiography, given my life as a writer and academic, I would entitle it: *Against the Grain*. My memory was so poor that at school cultural events (in Montserrat) I couldn't be relied on to perform the smallest part, satisfactorily; the 'recitation' was a nightmare, the obligatory Longfellow ('Tell me not in mournful numbers/Life is but an empty dream!') or Thomas Hood, tripping me up. To this day I have difficulty memorizing chunks of Shakespeare, and cannot recite my own poems. Altogether, it was a bit of a handicap in passing exams, learning foreign languages, being effective in academic life. I have huge admiration for my sister who is able to recall, with seeming ease, verses learnt early in life.

But – there's always a *but* – is being a slow reader so very crippling?

I come back to *Martin Chuzzlewit* and *Anna Karenina* and *Ulysses* knowing that I *must* turn the television off for a month or so; and emerge triumphant that *Ulysses*, say, is a much easier and more enjoyable read than last time round when I read under the pressure of time. I'm persuaded now that slow-reading (the opposite of skimming, of gliding over books with the eyes) is part of the sensuality of the exercise; is, in fact, an act of seduction; and I now cheerfully accuse my fast-reading colleagues of experiencing something akin to a one-night stand, or a fast-food lunch, when they read. Shamefully, they seem not to mind.

Notes

1. See Chapter Eight, for 'Jimmy Porter'.
2. Though an African priest, rather comically, proclaimed GHANA an acronym for GOD HAS A NEW AFRICA
3. But tabloid 'wit' wasn't entirely lost on her. When, later, in the 1970s the Romanian tennis star, the flamboyant Ilie Nastasie, was dubbed 'Nasty' by a largely benign press, partly because of his stagy questioning of line calls, my mother, too, chimed in with 'Nasty?' – the question-mark, and the suppressed giggle, suggesting her own (suppressed) fascination with an adult acting so strangely, in public.

CHAPTER EIGHT
A PLAY BEFORE BREAKFAST

I dig out the playscripts, going back to the mid 1950s. True, there was an early novel attempt from that time but for me the play was the thing. The fascination with theatre was all-encompassing, producing unperformed (unperformable?) scripts throughout the whole of my life. In addition to writing scripts I was, from time to time, active in the 'business' of theatre, being president of Dramsoc at university, after university being part of an amateur theatrical company in West London (John Elsom's *Theatre* 69, where we wrote group plays and performed them) and, in 1970, I had a year in the Eastern Caribbean directing with my own Caribbean Theatre Workshop. So plays were being written while I was at school in Kilburn.

Plays constituted my most essential reading matter. Despite the Peter Cheyney effort and novels serialised in the newspapers (*No Love for Johnny*, a contemporary drama about a politician, *Dr. Zhivago*...) it was plays, plays, plays. Though this might be an overstatement. I used the local library – the Ladbroke Grove library – on a Saturday afternoon, and sometime in the evening, until closing time. The intention, as I remember, was to do my 'Chaucer homework'; but, usually, I spent most of the time browsing – a habit that's become something of an obsession: it was at those spacious tables that I guiltily read short stories. (You could sit at the table and read a couple of stories from a collection and not have to take the book out; as you had your set-texts at home to read. Nathanael West was a prized discovery at the time.) My brother and I read *Dr. Zhivago*, and quite liked it, but weren't sure how to place it against the great novels of the past, of which my brother had greater knowledge than me. But it did win Pasternak the Nobel Prize, and we were encouraged that something that seemed so down-to-earth and – in a sense – manageable was thought to be worth the Prize.

I developed the habit of reading plays in the morning before breakfast. Always an early riser (too early to play my records in the house) I found the next best thing would be to read a play (or a bit of a play) while the house was asleep and before my mother was ready to make breakfast.

During those GCE years my play-reading even became a little bit structured, for I would sometimes read three plays (acquired from the Foyles second-hand department), say, by one author, or it might be plays by authors from the same country. Or the same part of the world. So having read Ibsen and Strindberg I found myself reading something by a Swedish author called Par Lagerkvist. (Par Lagerkvist, mysteriously, had won the Nobel Prize for literature, in 1951.) I had discovered classical Greek Drama and had read Sophocles and Aeschylus; so, naturally, I sung the praises of Euripides. I disingenuously pretended that this would help me to pass my O Level Ancient History exam. But it all had an impact: in my first year at university, fellow students were impressed that I had read, among others, a 'fairly obscure' German dramatist called Gerhart Hauptmann. I had read him before breakfast, in Kilburn.[1]

But, of course, this was all in the service of writing my own plays. The one I'm looking at now is called (I'm afraid) *A Meaningful Relationship. Part II*. (A One Act Play). I have no idea what happened to *Part One*, and no memory of it. Reading it through, what strikes me is the clipped, artificial formality of the dialogue, and the fact that nothing happens throughout the play; there is no action, no movement towards crisis, and no sense that the people involved are engaged in any dilemma that matters, though emotional weight is assumed. It is easy now to understand the endless rejection letters that greeted my plays over the years. I was, alas, also to miss out on a chance at engaging in a more professional type of theatre.

That was at Bristol, in 1964 or 65: I was being interviewed for an MA in Theatre at Bristol University, the attraction being the Bristol Old Vic to which the successful candidate would be attached. The interview was conducted by a dauntingly eccentric man called Glyn Wickham, who had a terrific reputation as a theatre scholar, contributing to prestigious volumes, like the *Cambridge History of the Theatre*.

Wickham, a shy man, lived up to his reputation, by leaning back in his chair, in the book-lined room, avoiding your eye, and painfully reaching for non-intimate words, like 'peregrinations'. Anyway, the point here was that among the people waiting for the interview was a silent, duffel-coated, somewhat older man, later to be identified as Edward Bond. He got the place.

Back to my false start: *A Meaningful Relationship, Part II*. I seem to remember there was talk among my group at school about the 'colour-values' that the 'characters' names suggested. There was someone called Vivienne in the play. Was this a 'yellow-purple' or a 'bluey-green' type of image? We had no idea how people in the real theatre talked about these things.

Yet you took the thing seriously. I was on the point of congratulating myself on how well-typed and presented the play was when, tucked into the pages, there was this note from Judy.

> Dear Archie,
>
> I have finished at long last and
> I am on the way to ring avril [sic] to find out
> the address. If she hasn't got it I'll
> send it to you.
> I know it isn't very good
> typing and I'm sorry. I hope you
> succeed in your aims.
> I apologize also for this
> scribble but I am in a
> hurry to get this off in the
> post.
>   Hope to see you soon.
>
> from
>
> Judy

The letter (apart from being strangely formal) isn't dated so it must have been around 1962, when I was at university in Wales, hence the necessity to write. The embarrassment is that Judy would have laboured over so poor a script, perhaps accepting my valuation of its worth. I had had a go at typing up my own plays, and even my friend, Chinque, had assisted. But when I started sending them out to managements I had decided that they needed a more professional look. In one instance I had employed Pam (who, I think, had a part-time job somewhere as a typist) and agreed to pay her £5 for it. I was late paying up and Pam was not pleased. It took me some time to realize that Pam would not have derived the same degree of satisfaction in having been associated with my script as I had done, and therefore the £5 resonated more with her than it did with me. Others have helped, over the years, with this typing-up task, not least my fellow-Montserratian, Mary Griffin, the visual artist (who taught Art in a school in South London). I recall her coming all the way to Shepherds Bush (the late '60s?) and typing up some early stories – maybe bits of a novel – and being very careful with the ellipses to reflect the interrupted conversations. At the time, round about 1962, the BBC Radio Wales took an interest in another play, set in West London, I was surprised that their main recommendation for revision was to make more of the Notting Hill riots of a few years back. I was wary about being labelled as someone who wrote about 'black' or 'race' issues (and to being told what a 'black issue' was). Whatever the reason, maybe a bit of intransigence on my side, the play was never broadcast.

At school, in Kilburn, we had a small literary group that met in the common room once or twice a week, to read a play or discuss a book. I remember during one session when our play was *King Lear*, I did Lear's speech on the Heath in an Indian accent. Pam's response was puzzlement, because Lear wasn't Indian. On another occasion when we were reading *The Tempest*, Pam was dismissive of the comedy, the Antonio-Sebastien exchanges in *Act.2 Sc.I*, on the grounds that they were unfunny. 'I'm sure he (Shakespeare) could do better than that,' she protested. And to reinforce the point, turning to me she said, *Archie* could do better than that. (I didn't let on that I found the punning in that scene quite witty.) But Pam was OK. We didn't just read Shakespeare; we read John Osborne.

But this was an improvement on the usual commonroom culture, which tended more towards bragging and jokes, among the 'boys'. (A sample 'joke': 'So this woman goes to a psychiatrist. You know what a psychiatrist is. So she goes to the psychiatrist; and says. Doctor, I have a problem. So, he says. Come in. He then takes off his clothes and rapes her. That solves my problem, he says. Now, what's yours?') Though there were more neutral jokes. ('My wife and I went on holiday last summer.' 'Jamaica?' 'No, she went of her own accord.') In a weird sense, hearing this in the common room at Kilburn, told by a sallow boy from Dollis Hill, one was made to feel that Jamaica (West Indies) was being affirmed. There wasn't any general sense among us at the time of the West Indies (as opposed to Italy, say, or the Riviera) as a holiday destination.

I didn't like *Look Back in Anger*. Oh, yes, there were some good jokes, the one about there being no dry-cleaners in Cambodia, and about T.S. Eliot and Pam. But I identified with the wrong people in the play, with the Major, Alison's father – despite his reference to Gandhi as a 'dirty little man', and found the self-pitying, loudmouth Jimmy Porter hard to take. Oh, yes, I liked the fact that so much was made of reading the Sunday papers (and I took Jimmy's criticisms of the literary reviews on board – even though I didn't quite believe the bits of them he read out in the play. But I was impressed by his references all those writers, and his love of (classical) music: he was a graduate, after all – even though it was of something called a 'white-tiled' university. Later, when I got hold of the text (I never saw it in the theatre, but was depressed by the film) I was nevertheless pleased that a bookcase and rows of books featured prominently in a one-roomed flat. And yet, I thought the baiting of Alison by Jimmy was outrageous. Jimmy seemed the worst sort of lout – going through his wife's handbag, going through her things when she's not there, a vindictive bore calling other people vindictive – the worst sort of character whom you wouldn't let inside the house from his sweet-stall, never mind into the drawing-room – and to have him possess your *daughter*, and subject her to a servant's life at the ironing-board! (And then, to do the same to her friend – until the daughter returns after a miscarriage, for more of the same.) No question, I was really in sympathy with Alison's father, Colonel Redfern. I would certainly have supplied the missing scene in the play where the Colonel horsewhips the young (and at 25, he wasn't so young) well-read clown for abusing his daughter. At the very least I would have provided Jimmy Porter with a woman who could stand up to him both verbally and emotionally, as every West Indian woman I know, in that circumstance, would have done. Jimmy Porter was the sort of man who beats up women who befriend him on the pretence of challenging the system to which they belong: the only attitude one could have to that type of fellow is contempt. But that's not the way other people saw the play. Harold Hobson in *The Observer*, and more particularly, Ken Tynan in *The Sunday Times,* hailed it as entering new territory, leaving behind the over-familiar landscape of Rattigan and Bernard Shaw. (I had heard a Rattigan play on the radio and rather liked it, and Shaw's ideas were stimulating. I didn't realize then that the plays lacked drama and tension.) And John Osborne only 26! I didn't think 26 was that young. I had plans to overtake Osborne before *I* was twenty-six.

A Taste of Honey, by Shelagh Delaney, was another matter. There may have been things we noted with interest about the film, the northern accents – the play was set in Salford – and the fact that it involved a black man getting a young, white girl pregnant and abandoning her: we didn't like that last bit. But there were other factors. (The fact that Shelagh Delaney had been nineteen when the play was first produced challenged me more than the twenty-six year old author of *Look Back in Anger* did.) The interracial aspect of the play was perturbing because the boy, Jimmy, from his speech, was not your 'labourer' new to the country making a fool of himself with women on the streets of London. This lad's family hailed from Cardiff; he was well-spoken, and doing his National Service. (Shirley Bassey came to mind: *her* family was from Cardiff.) Yet, this lad, abandoning his pregnant girlfriend, was letting the side down. This was how the English people expected 'us' to behave. But as a *play* I much preferred *A Taste of Honey* to the rant of *Look Back in Anger.* The only hateful man in the Delaney play was the spivvy new husband of the main character's mother. And the verbal battles between mother and daughter affected rather than enraged you.

The mother is totally selfish, it's true, and treats her daughter as an afterthought, but she's good-hearted. And there's genuine affection there. The daughter, Jo, is spoilt, but then, who brought her up? I also noted with interest that they're not colour-prejudiced. Jo doesn't become bitter in a racist way when her black lover deserts her while she's expecting his child; the homosexual friend doesn't seem to mind taking on the mother of a black child, and even Jo's mother, Helen, in her little outburst at the end (when she first hears the news of the baby's parentage) is more exaggerated than unpleasant. Delaney, one felt, studying the text, though she wasn't the one to *beat*, she was one to watch. When, a few years later, Norman told me that Delaney was befriending 'members of the London underworld' in Soho – 'Legs Diamond' being mentioned – in order to write a new play, I was *sure* she was one to watch.

This was a new and troubling thing, how to write about race, because you weren't sure whether you were writing about race or about colour. Well, you were writing about *both*, but in a new sense (a sense of uncertainty) of where you, personally, figured in all this.

In the Caribbean, and particularly in Montserrat which was less racially-mixed than other islands (It astonished me to learn that over a third of all Trinidadians were Indian and a half of the Guyanese) our consciousness in this area was focused on *pigment*. Light-skinned people OK, darker-skinner people less OK. So the whole *thrust* of social-advancement and upward mobility had to do with 'compensating' for *degrees* of blackness. And there were well-tried ways of doing that. My great Uncle Reggie was very black, but he was rich, owned land, stores and was into import-export in a big way; was a war-hero, and a member of the Lodge. Other people managed it in other ways. Getting into education. When a black 'boy' went abroad to be educated and came back a 'professional' he was no longer a black boy but a doctor or a lawyer, and his wife was likely to be lighter-skinned than himself. There was a rumour that a black man on one of the islands had bought an hotel which had had an all-white client policy. Having bought the hotel he neglected to change the policy, but simply invited himself and his friends to dine there. The implication was that the management were still free to exclude other black people who didn't qualify in terms of status. (Or family.) So one's whole experience of race-policy in the West Indies was that it had to do with pigment, yes, but ultimately, with *class*. It was liberating, in a sense, when you came to England to find that people didn't make fine distinctions about pigment. And, in a sense (except, perhaps in the case of Jewish and maybe Irish people) about *race* – though, with the Irish, it was probably more complicated. Anyway, what they saw, what the English saw, was *colour*. When I was first mistaken for an Indian by an Englishman, I just assumed it to be a joke. But that wasn't the only time it happened.

So I was confused how to approach this business of race, this business of colour. My brother brought home a literary magazine that a Barbadian working at Cable & Wireless (where both my brothers then worked) had edited. The centrepiece – or the feature that was drawn to my attention – was a piece about an abortion by a white woman of a black child. The abortion was messy, and described in great detail. I disliked the piece. Maybe squeamishness (I may have been reading Jane Austen and T.S. Eliot by that time), but I disliked the implication that the fate of a child in an interracial relationship was abortion – and messy abortion at that. I could have understood this in *A Taste of Honey*, because in that context an abortion would have made sense; it wouldn't necessarily have been a racial act. But in this Barbadian short story there was no reason for it other than that the child would be black. I may have been influenced by the report of a young girl in Birmingham, a girl from Montserrat, who had had a 'back street' abortion and had died. We weren't encouraged to talk about it at home; but you were beginning to wonder how all of this might figure in your work.

I'd drawn a portrait, in a little play, of a man from an island like ours. I called him Philpot. He was a man of no social pretensions, middle-aged, a guard on the London underground, and on a Sunday he puts on his best suit, and goes hospital-visiting. In this case it was at the St. Mary's Hospital in Paddington, where my mother had had an operation. I put him in a sharply-laundered brown suit, and the portrait of Philpot was much lauded in the commonroom at Kilburn. The suit had to be brown because we noticed that some West Indians had white suits, which they wore to church on Sundays, and the joke among English members of the congregation, was that the West Indians wore white suits perhaps because they liked cricket. It may not have been a joke, it may have been sympathetically meant. So, naturally, I distanced Philpot from that white suit. O, yes. Philpot didn't go to the hospital to visit someone he *knew*; he specifically sought out those beds who had no visitors. He was showing the sort of imagination that people of his colour and class were supposed not to have.

★ ★ ★

I couldn't settle on the right image for the writer, *of* the writer. T.S Eliot was the most distinguished living writer we were aware of in England, but he was, in a sense, like someone who was dead. One wanted to be a writer who would be turned on by Elvis and Little Richard. Agatha Christie, who turned up on the television, big and blonde and flowery, also didn't fit. Bertrand Russell, though ancient, was better, but he didn't write plays. There was a big, solemn fellow, called C.P. Snow, who came on the television and talked about science and about Russian writing. Most unattractive. So it was back to John Osborne and Shelagh Delaney. Someone mentioned Dylan Thomas, the Welshman who drank himself to death in America. Why would you want to do that? My brother rather liked the self-taught, beatnik Colin Wilson, who slept in a sleeping-bag in the park, while writing his 'existential' book; but I wasn't so sure. A writer, I felt, was someone, who possessed a grand library, which was also his study, containing a shelf or two of his own books. His plays, of course, would be performed to glittering audiences in the West End.

★ ★ ★

Emma Woodhouse was a challenge best left for the classroom. I couldn't warm to this twenty-one year old mistress of the house bossing everyone about; and the Yetton hinted that my lack of appreciation might have something to do with my failure to appreciate Jane Austen's irony. In those days that was tantamount to labelling you 'foreign', and I resented it. Surely, when the author very early on describes Mr. Woodhouse, Emma's father, as having been a 'valetudinarian' all his life, having looked up the word, I didn't just think, hello, there goes a 'dictionary' word, here's the author showing off a bit. We thought things like: maybe the word would have been used in their circle in drawing-rooms at Hartfield in the early 19th. century. Or even, Great Yetton, maybe Jane Austen was establishing some little distance between herself and her character, inviting us, the readers – gently, this being Jane Austen – to judge him. I thought I understood something about Jane Austen's irony. I was more concerned not to make the mistake of a couple of jokers in the class who persisted in writing the author's name as *Austin*. However poor you were at spelling, it seemed to me disrespectful to get the name of the writer wrong – unless the writer were foreign, where you might have something of an excuse. (I'd had the experience of doing O Level Ancient History; the Greek names were not funny. 'You need to write them down,' Avril said.) To come back to the Yetton: no one accused Jane Austen of not knowing her grammar when she wrote, on the first page of the book, that Emma 'was the *youngest* of *two* daughters'. Enough.

Victoria Cross

Pam recalled, some years later, my approaching her in the Polytechnic library upstairs, and asking her to write something for the school magazine.

She confessed to being relieved that my request wasn't for something more intimate. Pam was, perhaps, the most sought-after girl in the school, and after she'd had a fling with a very handsome Asian from Kenya, both foreign and native males seemed to position themselves in competition for her favours. Pam was flirtatious, the boys tended to be literal-minded: there was a lot of baffled hurt-feelings as a result.

My idea for a school magazine (something that neither Kilburn nor any other school I attended had had) was, I think, just to demonstrate that I was good at English. There was no particular discussion leading up to it, as I remember; just my announcement that we now had a magazine, that I was the editor, and was still working on a title for it. There were no models. I had not at that stage knowingly read a literary magazine (apart from the one that my brother had brought home, from his Barbadian friend): if there were literary magazines in the library I wasn't aware of them. The magazines around our house in Ladbroke Grove were the property of my mother, the sort of reading matter you got in the doctor's waiting-room, *Women's Realm, Woman, The Reader's Digest.* I was sometimes sent to pick up my mother's copies at the shop across the road, and occasionally read the stories in them. But they weren't meant for me: there was nothing about rock n' roll, no extracts from novels that you sometimes got in the newspapers.

My mother's magazines contained no discussion of contemporary plays like *Look Back in Anger* or *A Taste of Honey.* (On second thoughts, I didn't quite like the association of 'honey' and black skin, in that play.) I was vaguely out of sympathy with the portraits of women who seemed to have all sorts of guilty secrets or mysterious illnesses that their husbands or families didn't know about, but that you needed prayer or miracles or something strange to resolve or to survive. Those few stories which touched on racial issues didn't appeal either: they were usually set in America and presented an image of 'colored' people which I found embarrassing. Cut off, equally, from the literary scene here and from what later came to be called the 'black community', I had no idea how writers in England were approaching the subject. (Even the phrase 'literary scene' is a later acquisition.)

So, there was no *plan* for the magazine. It would include a short story (which I would write) and perhaps other short stories; an essay, by someone like Matthias, whom I suspected of being better-read than I. I had been reading Bertrand Russell, the popular essays in *The Conquest of Happiness* and *Power,* and I just didn't have the *knowledge* to write that sort of essay, and I couldn't think what else an essay was if it wasn't a display of knowledge; that's why I always wrote the short story in class, given a chance. So, Matthias for the essay. And a 'review' of one of the books we were doing for A Level would get the thing noticed in the school. (We might approach The Yetton for that one.) There'd be some artwork, cartoons, maybe, like those in the *Daily Mirror* and *Reynolds News* to liven up the pages; and Pam would be enrolled to type it all up: she'd be part of the project; no payment needed.

Poetry was the big challenge. Poetry for me, at this time, meant Shakespeare and T.S. Eliot: *King Lear* and *The Tempest* (as well as *Macbeth* from the O Level class) and Eliot's *Poems 1909-39*, set texts, taught by The Yetton. Eliot was altogether too learned and cool and difficult. The Yetton said you had to read Jung and Freud and (particularly) Sir James Frazer's *The Golden Bough* in order to understand Eliot. We claimed to have read Freud or Jung, though we hadn't done more than flick through a few pages of either; and we didn't even know where to find Frazer. So I, for one, was for keeping poetry out of the magazine. When a poem, 'Lies', by the new Russian popular writer, Yevtushenko, appeared in one of the English newspapers and was widely-circulated in school, I found myself not liking it much; it seemed to me altogether too obvious: I wouldn't have printed it in the magazine. (Much later, on holiday, down from university, I was presented by Pam with a new selection of Yevtushenko with the injunction to read, not 'Lies', but 'Zima Junction'. That was OK, but I did wonder if it was the Jewish theme that had impressed Pam.)

Yet, if you were going to be a student of literature and be taken seriously, you'd have to get your mind round Eliot which, in a sense, was what contemporary poetry was for you. The sheer amount of background knowledge needed to understand Shakespeare and Eliot was something that was unacquirable. (We tried to make a little distinction between understanding and *appreciating* these poets; but that wouldn't help us in the exams.) Here was the Yetton telling us in one class that we had to read Tudor history to understand Shakespeare (we were ahead of her there) and in another that we had to know about Austrian psychoanalysts to understand 'The Waste Land'. (This 'doing English' business might yet prove to be as hard as training to be a doctor or a scientist.) We couldn't even get past the 'minor' Eliot poems, like 'Burbank with a Baedeker: Bleistein with a Cigar' and 'The Hippopotamus' without being caught out by hidden traps. The anti-Semitism in the former had to be pointed out; with the latter the 'hippopotamus' wasn't what it seemed. Here, it was hard to have to take on board images from the church service in Montserrat that one had long rejected, the image of a house (the Church) built on rock (as opposed, presumably, to being built on sand); the blood of the lamb business – to be 'washed white as snow' to gain Heaven; and the hippopotamus growing wings to pull him out of the mud, etc. Surely, if all this seemed close to *Women's Realm* and *The Reader's Digest*, what to make of the following?

The 'potamus can never reach
The mango on the mango tree;
But fruits of pomegranate and peach
Refresh the Church from over sea

I needed no encouragement to convince me that we seemed to have set out here, without irony, a sort of colonial-colonized relationship, and that the image of the colonized should be contested. But that, I was told, was not what Eliot was about.

Those other poets, like Yevtushenko who seemed easy to decipher, didn't engage me much as poets. (We had encountered Chaucer at O Level and had Wordsworth's *The Prelude* as another A level text. But with Chaucer the fascination was with *transliteration*, not with the poetry (a struggle rejoined later, with Anglo-Saxon).

Oddly enough Wordsworth's Lake District settings seemed more remote to me than Shakespeare and Dickens, and the commune with 'nature' seemed too close to the small-island life I was so relieved to escape from. So, perhaps for that reason, Wordsworth's was one of those texts I failed to explore. (The Yetton's plug of the young Wordsworth getting drunk one night with his poet friend, toasting the French Revolution, was OK, but not really enough to swing it.)

I can't now remember the rejected titles of the magazine before I settled on *Victoria Cross,* but this was clearly influenced by my reading of Lytton Strachey's *Queen Victoria*, which we were doing for A Level. It wasn't the Yetton but Stanley, a mature student from Israel (maybe he was English but had spent time in Israel and had been in the army there) who now ran his own business here and had come back to do A Levels – it was Stanley who educated us about the sophistication of Strachey's prose, and not just the more obvious thrill of his debunking the Establishment. The ironic title of my magazine – which was a play on *Queen Victoria;* a homage to Lytton Strachey; a memory of my fascination with the London Underground system; a random comment on the military thing; the desire to be clever or witty – was intended to set the tone of the publication.[2]

In the end we managed three issues. When, later, at university, I started reading literary magazines, I realized that I hadn't had the faintest notion of how to 'edit' a magazine.

Notes

1. Gerhart Hauptmann (1862-1946) wasn't particularly obscure. His novels and plays earned him the Nobel Prize for literature, in 1912.
2. This was a note I discovered recently. But it was made much later than the time discussed, maybe in the 1970s, when I first thought of revisiting schooldays:

'Albert Saxe-Coburg-Gotha seemed, in some ways, to be West Indian, prim, proper and wanting to keep up appearances: a combination of self-importance and wanting to marry 'above' oneself betraying the element of self-doubt under the veneer of confidence, feeding the 'neurosis' of wanting, in some way, to be significant. Also, familiar, was the fact that Albert, coming to England to 'make it', was coming to a country made less foreign by the fact that his cousin and future wife was Queen of England. In our case, England was made less foreign because this was the 'Mother Country' and in whose wars ones family had fought and – perhaps better than Albert – we spoke the language.

When arrangements were being made to establish Albert's personal household in England (?), Strachey writes (p. 88). "He had a notion that he ought not to be surrounded by violent Whigs; very likely, but he would not understand that the only alternatives to violent Whigs were violent Tories." While The Yetton used such information to draw attention to the strong-willed nature of the young Victoria, who took no notice of Albert's sensibilities and with the collusion of her Whig Prime Minister, Lord Melbourne, imposed a Whig household on Albert, I was more interested in Strachey's depiction of the British political class (of 1837-40) as 'violent'. Paradoxically, it made my place in England that little bit more secure-seeming than if the people surrounding Lord Melbourne and Sir Robert Peel hadn't been 'violent'. This put them below our family in social grace. By extension I was drawn into speculating whether the people surrounding Macmillan and Gaitskell might also be violent: I began to be less *emotionally* intimidated by England, though, perhaps, more watchful of it. The fascination – the frustration, the need to belong and to resist – at this time, *England*: did everyone born outside the country have it? Victoria and Albert are just about my sort of age. Strachey makes me unafraid of them. That makes me confident of my chances in this society.

CHAPTER NINE
OSWALD MOSLEY AT THE FRONT DOOR[1]

Because my mother, to my knowledge, never commented on the Mosley visit, we tended to speculate. She was sitting at her window, as always, looking out. It was a Saturday afternoon, in 1959, and the crowd had gathered, filling the space on both sides of the public loos. Mosley's helpers – maybe Geoffrey Hamm, his second in command, who lived next door to us, among them – set up a little structure, a podium, in the street outside our front door; and Mosley climbed up on it, bringing his head level with my mother a few feet away, at which point he tipped his hat to her.

I heard the scattered cheers. I was focused on my book; but I looked up and saw the gesture. My mother sat at her window, unflinching, apparently unaffected. At that point I joined my mother, briefly. I had been sitting on the bed inside, running through either some Latin or Italian homework, vocabulary, I seem to remember, taking nothing of it in. This studied casualness was the idea of my brother, Norman. We mustn't shut the window, we mustn't lock ourselves away; we should even use the front door and weave our way in and out of the crowd, going to the shops on Goldbourne Road for small items we didn't really need.

We were lucky in one respect; our cousin, Terry, was visiting from the army, and he was in uniform. So my brother urged him to go out in the street and stand among the crowd, in his uniform, to prove a little point, a gesture that Terry – with exaggerated cool – was willing to make. He stood towards the back, but prominently, apparently in rapt attention, while the fascist spoke. The point that Terry was supposed to be making didn't need to be spelt out. Here was a black man in uniform geared to defending the country, fighting its wars, not one on the dole. Or, as the fascists would have it, living off the immoral earnings of their women. Alternatively (and the second point doesn't cancel out the first) here is a black man, a trained soldier, able to defend himself if trouble started. *And again*: here is a black man, a soldier, known to this house, emerging from this house and presumably returning to this house after the meeting; you may have targeted this house, you may have brought your rabble to this address, but this house, the family in this house, the friends of this house are not a push over. Look, apart from this young man in uniform, are two, three other young men to be glimpsed, able to protect their mother. None of this was, as I say, spelt out. And the meeting – the rally – passed off without physical violence.

Another reassuring feature of the meeting was the fair number of West Indians grouped more or less at the back of the crowd: it was the first time in England that I was conscious of being reassured to see a sizable number of black faces in a crowd.

So, this was our most graphic experience of Mr. Macmillan's You've Never Had It So Good 1959 General Election.

We talked about it so much that it's difficult to know now what sense we made of it. The unpleasant feeling of being targeted – the only black-owned household in the street, with Geoffrey Hamm as neighbour: should we consider moving house? By that time we had improved our environment somewhat; the rag n' bone family downstairs had long gone; the West Indian grocery downstairs had come and gone and, consistent with one of Mr. Macmillan's election promises, we now had a betting establishment downstairs: a few men who seemed to hang about the shop, didn't have far to go to the public loo.

The proprietor of the betting shop was Mr. Brown. Before Macmillan's promise to legalize the trade of betting on horses and dogs, promoters weren't allowed fixed premises, so Mr. Brown (and others like him) did their trade from the pavements; now they had a shop front. To be fair to Mr. Macmillan, he did promise other things in his campaign to get re-elected, one of which was the building of seven new universities.

That Mosley lost and lost badly made us, in retrospect, not unhappy that he had held the rally outside our house, and that we had faced him down.

But what was my mother thinking through all this? We didn't know. One had always had a certain sensitivity, if you like, to putting the family on the stage. It seemed a form of exposure, it seemed a betrayal of privacy, it seemed – as we say – bad form. Much later, towards the end of her life, I had tentatively started probing my mother to reveal more of her secret life; but she was usually reticent, protective of people, including her husband from whom she was long divorced; she preferred to recall good times had in growing up in a house, the only child of elderly, devoted parents; of the privileged treatment encountered at Antigua Girls High School all those years ago; at being a beautiful, much envied bride at eighteen. But nothing much of the disappointments of England – though she loved to demonize politicians in the news that we rather liked, people like Tony Benn and Arthur Scargill.

Yet you felt that this reticence was a way of protecting us in some way; for my mother was known to be forthright with her opinions, not just in the West Indies but in England. I've recounted how embarrassed we sometimes got, in the early days, travelling on the underground together, when she would glance at the headline of a passenger's newspaper and pronounce it 'Shocking'. Sitting together one night, looking at an old French film on television, we observed someone cycling at great danger through occupied villages to return with the prize of a baguette, and my mother promptly pronounced it 'nasty' because the bread wasn't wrapped. It was of the same order of slackness as eating in the street. And yet when Mosley came to the house she said nothing.

Mosley's speech had been predictable, though delivered with restraint and politeness. We were misled, he told my mother, in having been brought to this country on the promise that the streets of London were paved with gold; and now that we were here we knew that this was not the case. We should feel aggrieved that we had been encouraged to leave our own countries where the sun shone, and where it was warm, and brought here to this country where it was cold, and where we were unhappy. Surely, it was time to admit the mistake that had been made, and to return to our own countries where the sun was still shining, and where we would be happy again. This might not always be easy, for we were in poor, low-paid jobs (except the few who were dishonest and criminal); and we would not be expected to have the financial means to return; that's why he proposed that the government help us to do so.

And more of the same.

We, the brothers, had ideas about Mosley's visit. We were on the front line. We resented the fact that people elsewhere in the country, black people in Brixton, say, were appropriating this position to themselves. Weren't we living in the proximity of Notting Hill during the riots, wasn't Kelso Cochrane, the carpenter from Antigua (who lived opposite us in Bevington Road) stabbed at the corner of our street; didn't Mosley come to our house; didn't Geoffrey Hamm live next door? I began to distrust rhetoric and writing that appeared stagy rather than considered concerning these matters; but perhaps more worryingly, I began to question whether a black person living in this society, could ever escape being on the 'front line'.

This is not a fanciful notion; for Geoffrey Hamm pursued me to university. I was then at Lampeter reading English and Philosophy. (Before going up, I varied my choice of subjects to study, at this or that proposed university, including, I think, Economics, which was one of my A Level passes; but it was more or less obvious that I would do the humanities. And I must say Philosophy captured my imagination more in those days than did the study of English which, in the first year, consisted mainly of Middle English and Anglo-Saxon.)

Geoffrey Hamm seemed out of place in the lecture hall where we took notes on Plato's *Republic* and Aristotle's Laws of Thought and the British Empiricists and Kant's (impossible) *Metaphysic of Ethics.* Here was this faded, ill-kempt man, with a folded newspaper seeming to make an economic case for Nationalism. In retrospect I was relieved that I was not called at question time, as my ironies might have been lost on the speaker; indeed, I might have tripped myself up on them; but what was dismaying was that here was the fascist's bagman holding the stage that – who? — John Spears, the Chaucerian, Gilbert Ryle, the Philosopher and a radical South African Bishop had graced before him. What was more perturbing, though, was that within three years Geoffrey Hamm had managed to cross the breadth of England, from Ladbroke Grove to, as it were, track me down at Lampeter. (It seemed like a plot for a thriller worthy of Peter Cheyney.) So, really, you couldn't hide. This was a small country and you couldn't hide. Or, this was an Open Society – so, there was a danger here, too, Karl Popper – and you couldn't hide. Or, once you had made yourself visible, you couldn't hide. And there was a suspicion that out there – OUT THERE – there were people worse than Geoffrey Hamm, ill-disposed to you, and from them you couldn't hide.

So, was I doing the right thing reading English and Philosophy? Would A.J. Ayer's Logical Positivism come in handy on the rough streets of London? Was it important to pass my exams on the Philosophy of Religion?

★ ★ ★

I didn't know then and I don't know now how sophisticated it is to be sophisticated. The Surrealist painter Marcel Duchamp, perhaps best known for his *objets trouvés* (a marble lavatory bowl submitted to an exhibition as a piece entitled '*Fountain*'), is said to have had a special doorway built in his apartment, with two doors, so that it was always both open *and* shut.[2] To the same degree you're not sure how much access – and what sort of access – to accord Geoffrey Hamm. To the Geoffrey Hamms. There is access in terms of proximity, his living next-door to us in Ladbroke Grove. Eventually, we moved house, though Hamm's presence may not have been the sole cause; for, after all, we didn't know who our neighbours would be in Kilburn. Bringing Hamm to Lampeter was a mistake for he was never going to be interrogated; he was being given a platform, in a lecture-room, protected by the tradition of courtesy given to lecturers; protected by the, then, good manners of students; he would have been more 'appropriately' treated on the street corner, with hecklers and interruptions: the debate about how to deal with this was, for me, not far advanced.

The one small consolation of all this is that I doubt whether Geoffrey Hamm would have recognized me in the audience at Lampeter as the person who had lived next to him in Ladbroke Grove. (I was, I think, the only black person present; though there was a Mauritian friend in the room, who was Indian.) Hamm would no doubt have had a *sense* that he recognized me (for don't they all look alike?), but he would probably have dismissed the thought as this was a university and hence an unlikely setting for a scion of the black family above the betting shop next door in Bevington Road. But then that, too, might have given him a moment of panic – the look-alikes lurking in the most unlikely parts of the country. (Perhaps there had been one, too, in the Falkland Islands!)

There's a play here; there's a play everywhere.

★ ★ ★

But was 'finesse' enough? From the start you waged little battles you hoped to win. One such was at the shop, a grocery cum general store, half-way down the Harrow Road on the way to Royal Oak station, where my brother Norman and I went to do the family shopping on a Saturday morning, when we lived in Sutherland Avenue. At the time, there was talk by someone my brother knew, a young man from Barbados with a beard, so they called him Castro, who claimed that the owners of the shop were racist. We were never given any details, any evidence of racism, but Castro had formulated a plan to counter it. He would continue to use the 'racist' grocery but would refuse to speak to the proprietors, an elderly husband and wife team. Instead, he prepared his shopping-list and silently slid it on the counter and waited to be served.

We didn't trust this. We could see the point of continuing to patronise the 'racist' shop, as the next viable shop was all the way down on the Edgware Road, and why make yourself inconvenient because of a racist. But did the idea of silently putting your shopping list on the counter really appeal? What if the racists thought you were dumb? Or foreign and didn't know the language! They might not recognize that you had been in before and had *spoken* to them. When we visited the shop the following Saturday my brother and I had a plan.

Looking for a strategic moment (while my brother did the ordering) I made a joke. The man paused, not understanding. Then he looked briefly at the woman, as if to confirm. She said they didn't have it, assuming I had ordered something strange. Stung, I repeated the joke.

The husband said, more confidently now, that they didn't have it. That shut me up.

But my brother was more resourceful. Husband and wife continued to be polite – if a little tense – serving him. Having completed the shopping, my brother got ready to pay. Then he caught sight of a sign hung prominently on one of the shelves.

PLEASE DO NOT ASK
FOR CREDIT
AND BE DISAPPOINTED

My brother pointed to the sign, and asked, pleasantly, if he could have the sign on credit. It took a while to sink in. After briefly checking with each other, husband and wife decided to see the joke; and laughed. How did we do? we asked ourselves, on leaving. We didn't know.

★ ★ ★

How secure, I ask myself, did my mother feel, on the inside of her front door?

I've learnt, over the years, not to be too certain about knowing my mother's mind. It is agreed, in the house, that she didn't tell jokes, and I can't remember her telling us a joke – other than referring to my 'dictionary'; and when she laughed at ours, it was usually a consensual laugh: she knew she was expected to laugh and she did, usually. And yet, sometimes when her women friends were around, and exchanging what might be gossip in the next room, you would hear her laugh, the sort of unrestrained laughter you had never quite elicited from her. There were times, in those days, when I thought of coming up with the joke of jokes that would make her laugh and laugh and laugh. But it never really happened.

I'm thinking now of the rightness, or not, of an assumption we always made about her. She had never returned to the West Indies; nor expressed – to us – a desire to do so. Everyone else from the region that you met, from whatever walk of life, talked and dreamed of going back, if only to visit. And, of course, increasingly, many went back to visit. It was taken for granted in our house that because, unlike most other migrants from the islands, my mother's fortunes had declined rather than been enhanced, it was a matter of pride to her not to go back a relative loser, rather than someone who had conquered England. (A couple of women who had been servants in the house back then, and had come to England and had done well – or had bettered their position – would visit her in the early days, expensively-dressed and with upbeat

143

stories of their new lives in Birmingham or wherever; and my mother seemed never to understand or resent the slight that may have been intended. Indeed, she expressed herself genuinely delighted by their success. So we thought we knew why, 'deep down', my mother never expressed a desire to return home.)

And then one day my brother made a chance remark of how bad a sailor my mother was, the bad time she had had, heavily pregnant, on the boat from Aruba when the decision had been made to send her back to Montserrat so that I should be born British rather than Dutch. I knew of my mother and the sea; she had taken me, when I must have been about eight, to Antigua, to visit friends. The launch took five hours to complete the thirty miles, and not only was my mother sick on the journey, she was terrified. Many years later, the three-week sea-journey to England had had a similar effect on her – and, indeed, on my sister. My mother had never flown in a plane. I now encourage the suspicion that the prospect of a return (imagined) three-week sea-journey to the West Indies would be as much a disincentive to my mother, as the 'shame' of going back with her status reduced.

So I am cautious in pretending to know what was going on in her mind. (One of the small ironies of all this is that before she died she insisted that her body be returned to Montserrat for burial. It was taken there by plane.)

Yet, my mother was not divorced from 'community' or a suggestion of the extended family. She kept open house for friends or members of the Markham family who had, apparently, nowhere to go; and treated them as welcome guests. Even though she ceased to be financially head of the household, whether at Kilburn with Norman and his wife, Rosa, or later, in the East End of London with my sister and her husband, Bernard, her centrality in the household was affirmed. There was never a suggestion that she might, in her later years, be put in a 'home', in the way that English families (inexplicably) treat their elderly parents. In addition to that, my brothers resolved that my mother would accept no benefits from the state; so she preserved both her pride and her sense of not being indebted to her hosts.

An important sense in which my mother played her part in the 'extended family' was her role in helping to bring up my sister's first child, Gwen, during those years when Julie, as a nurse, worked in various parts of London, and sometimes out of town.

★ ★ ★

A Note About Racism

How do you write about racism?

Let me first dip into a very personal protest note that I've delivered here and there (with examples to fit the occasion) against 'Type-casting in the Arts'.

In 2001 I had the pleasure of listening to a short story of mine dramatised on BBC Radio Four. It was interesting and instructive. Interesting, because the central character, a woman from the Eastern Caribbean, a returnee from England, was played by a superb actress with a Jamaican accent. The accent (suggestive of the experience and texture of a different society), speech rhythms and emphases seemed sometimes to work *against* the 'light' ironies of the piece. (Would a Scouse accent, by the same production team, have done for a comic drama set in South Yorkshire? That's one question. Another might be: would either of the above be lightly cast for a comic drama about cockneys in the old East End of London?)

Was this – this altering of the *tone* of the thing transmitted – a one-off? Or confined to one *genre*? If it were there would be no need for this essay. Or we might be accused of over-reaction. The ethnicizing of Caribbean/West Indian into 'black' has happened, and attempts to define 'black' in the arts (now as a political colour, now as a way of facilitating inclusion; again as a way of asserting separateness) has been a feature of the last few decades. One has to be sensitive to the challenge of operating in a racially-conscious society which is, at the same time, racially incurious. It is a climate that privileges the production of farce and tragedy (or melodrama), and is less nurturing of the range of social interaction and emotional response in the space *between* farce and tragedy, where most people's lives are lived. 'Black' persons, we are told, constitute about 7% of the population of Great Britain; hence 'black' is obviously marginal to the norm, and seen as 'other'. That a practise of typecasting was flagged up by the arts magazine, *Artrage*, in the mid-1980s, under the somewhat sensationalist title, BLACK ARTISTS, WHITE INSTITUTIONS, showed the need, then, to invite debate on the issue. Evidence of typecasting 'black' seemed to be prevalent in all the arts.

In 1988 Picador published *The New British Poetry*, six years after Penguin's *Contemporary British Poetry* with, in its introduction, a somewhat smug confession of 'Englishness'. *The New British Poetry* had four editors, each responsible for introducing 'an important strand in contemporary British poetry', the strands being 'Black British Poetry', 'Quote Feminist Unquote Poetry', 'A Treacherous Assault on British Poetry' and 'Some Younger Poets'. The suggestion of openness in this formulation seemed unrealised as 'black' and 'Feminist' seemed confined to their respective ghettoes. The editor of 'Feminist' (Gillian Allnutt) aimed to 'give away' as many women as she could to other editors. But 'other editors' failed to reciprocate: if it could be argued that no men successfully passed the 'feminist' test, was it obvious that no 'black' poet could be said to be 'feminist', to be making 'a treacherous assault', or to be 'Younger'? ('Young.)

In the visual arts, a 'landmark' exhibition at the ICA, in the Mall, was happily representing Black visual arts in Britain as a *Thin Black Line*, the paintings mounted in the corridor and staircase of their building, not managing to subvert the (no doubt) intended irony of the labelling. Revealing, also, was Gallery director Sandy Nairne's book, *State of the Art: Ideas & Images in the 1980s*, following the Channel Four transmission of the corresponding arts programme, in 1987. The project was divided into six categories of art. 'History, the Modern and Postmodern', 'Value, Commodity and Criticism', 'Imagination, Creativity and Work', 'Sexuality, Image and Identity' and 'Culture and Power'. The seven black artists represented were all placed in the category featuring 'Identity'.

To look, finally, at a recent poetry anthology, Andrew Motion's *Here to Eternity: An Anthology of Poetry,* published by Faber in 2002. The decision here to make the Asian and Caribbean-heritage writers in Britain 'other' continues as before. (Indeed, I might have chosen anthologies from three or four major houses of the period, that were no better.) In the Motion twelve black British poets are represented by thirteen poems. (If we are into head-counts, as in the old days, that is an advance of sorts.) What is revealing is they are still largely represented as outsiders, as guests, as people with no emotional of psychic claim to the place where they have long lived, and for whose freedom some of their families had fought.

Three examples might suffice to make the point. James Berry, born in Jamaica. Fleur Adcock, born in New Zealand and Peter Porter, born in Australia. Reading the entries of Adcock and Porter (both long resident in England) you get the impression that they have assumed a sort of ownership of the place in which they now live. Then we come to James Berry, longer resident here than either Adcock or Porter. His poem – we haven't come around to talking quality, that's the irony of all this – his poem is an *angst*-ridden twisting and turning for a place to settle. This man, who has written some fine poems, who has been resident in this country since 1948, is represented by something calling for his 'water hole'. *Plus ça change.*

Back to the 1960s, and our main narrative. Jomo Kenyatta, President of Kenya, came, unexpectedly, to our aid, then. He was visiting England and being interviewed on British television, in the middle of which he made a mild protest. (He had been treated discourteously in the street, but not in the studio.[4]) 'You make me black,' he said, to the somewhat baffled interviewer, who protested, lightly, that the president *was*, indeed, black; and not through British intervention. Kenyatta, an African, living in Africa had no reason to assume that the human norm was white.

And, yes, in a sense, Kenyatta *was* a black man; but of all his other competing identities (male, successful nationalist leader, post-graduate, President, growing impatience with the political opposition at home, etc.) it wasn't obvious that his being black subsumed all his other identities. A self-defining African living in Africa would not have subscribed to the notion that he, that she needed an enabling adjective or adverb to secure the noun of humanness. *Ah, but the context!*

This was England. Most people in England are not black. Well, in that case, while in England we might tick the black box in compiling the Kenyan president's identities. No one much objects to labels if they don't entrap you in a too-narrow a space *for ever and always*, and deny or de-emphasize your other selves: a wife, a mother, a daughter, an executive, a neighbour, etc. – all the same woman – does not find the need to agonize over which of those identities she must stick with to the exclusion of others.

Of course there is the social context. If you are part of a minority grouping (however arrived at) you often find that one of your roles in the society is to make the majority (however arrived at) feel good about itself. (Traditionally, the powerful tend to appropriate the assets of the weak; more recently, the unscrupulous in power have proved successful in off-loading their anxieties, like Aid.) So where does that leave us?

Still avoiding the question: how do you write about racism?
Easy, some said at the time. By evoking South Africa and America. Easy, too, by looking around you in London at the KEEP BRITAIN WHITE stickers on the trains, the graffiti on the walls; the fact that some of the graffiti was misspelled gave more comfort to white liberals than to black people who had to walk past the insults. There was no shortage of 'material' for your 'book'; reports of acquaintances having difficulty at work, could be transcribed; chance remarks overheard about the children of mixed-race couples could be rebutted; spitting in Nottingham dramatised: it was as if your subject were laid out for you. So, was it the environment of racism in England that was preventing me writing the play with a black bank manager, set in London? (Black people were known to get together to play the pools, theoretically, to improve the chances of winning; why couldn't they get together to start a bank? With a black bank manager. Though that would be segregation of sorts. And wouldn't that be risky?

Would white people, in time, patronize the bank? Wouldn't white racists attack it, burn it down, as they were doing to black churches in America?

In my last GCE year, I had read a lot of Bertrand Russell. Not just the 'popular' books, *The Conquest of Happiness* and *Power* but – prompted, I suspect, by the knowledge that one of the boys from Edgware had read it – the massive and daunting *The History of Western Philosophy*. (That raised my stock in the common room, carrying around this big, expensive, volume.) The thing is, reading Russell confirmed a view I long held that the acquisition of knowledge (allied to writing plays) was the way to go.

So you were unconvinced that racism was the only subject for you, the *given*.

But it wouldn't go away. So soon you were saying to yourself: given that it won't go away, how do you justify writing about racism? Coming back to Russell, who castigates America for its criminality, yes, but for its racism, there is a passage in one of his books where he is critical of white racists in England in their treatment of black people, and then goes on to make a throwaway mark about the 'loudness' of West Indians in public, militating against support for them. Well, Russell wasn't referring to my family, who were the opposite of 'loud', he wasn't referring to any of the people we knew; so black people needed to be defended, too, against their defenders, like Russell. (At work, in the belt factory, at Glanz, someone had asked me something that I didn't know the answer to, and in order to emphasize how much ignorant of it I was, I said, 'I have no conception of it.' I was immediately ridiculed for the 'borrowed' phrase. ('Where's that come from?') The Ron character was right, in a sense, in that the language may have been inappropriate in a belt factory; but it was clear he was making the point that this was not the language he expected a black person to use. At home in Ladbroke Grove, the sentence would have passed without comment, indeed, would have been used by my brother as a matter of course, whether we had visitors or not. So were West Indians, generally, to be denied the particularity of this family's experience (and that of most of the families we knew), and presented as 'loud' in the Russell version; or as people who didn't use 'borrowed' educated vocabulary? People seemed altogether more relaxed about West Indians looking forward to the Saturday night out at the Hammersmith Palais (to pick up women) than about those who might stay in and do the Latin homework, and look forward to university. What is equally reductive is thinking that the West Indian can't be *both*.

So, if racism was the big theme everything about the way it was handled made you uncomfortable.

One of the enduring victories of the racists was their success in convincing their victims to take responsibility for racism. In the case of the Atlantic slave trade it would be hard to know who the descendents of the abolitionists were: it was left for black people in America and increasingly in England to protest against racial prejudice and to point up the evils of slavery and the slave trade, and its continuing to colour attitudes governing black and white people.[3] You could, more or less, accept that this was the grand theme for America, because America was composed of warring groups of foreigners, and black people being a sizable group there had the right – and the need – to fight their own corner. But surely, in a more 'settled' European context to go down the 'ethnic' route would be a form of defeat. It would be a mistake because one would always be in a minority, and – truth to tell – because one wasn't sure that one had more in common with some black people than with some people who were not black. Perhaps most importantly, coming back to the point that Jomo Kenyatta had made on television – one would be accepting an adjective ('black') to reinforce the noun (man/woman/child), and hence be seen to be ceding something *essential* about you, to others. Very soon, in England, one was accorded the status of 'ethnic minor', member of a class (or tribe) of an 'ethnic minority'. Within that class one's 'subject' was 'identity'.

This uneasiness in allocating responsibility for racism in whatever form was reinforced later in the academy where I was to run across scholars from the Commonwealth, with a background in History, tending so often to research the Atlantic slave trade and its effects. (Was there nothing else in the history of the world that captivated their scholarly interest?) I met no white person at that stage for whom their ancestors' trading in slaves was the consuming scholarly interest. So it was not a surprise that I was occasionally taken to task for having read English at university, and for liking Jane Austen. (This was after I had escaped the literary crudities of the Yetton.)

But life has to be manageable if it's to be managed. If many people were talking about racism in ways which seemed to me to entrench racism, could one approach the subject, not head-on but, as it were, glancingly. There was a sort of racism which, though not overt, was obvious; and this tended to be perpetrated by people who would be horrified to learn that they were racists. And as one had always seen these 'unconscious racists' as potential allies, they consumed a great deal of my intellectual and (writing) energy. The latest examples of this that comes to mind are my chance meetings with a colleague at the university where we both worked. He had an interest in aspects of 18th and 19th century literature, among other things, and I had an interest in Creative Writing, among other things. 'Other things' we had in common were a fascination with the English 'essay' – from Bacon through Emerson to Orwell – and cricket. Now, whenever we bumped into each other in the corridor, or in the kitchen, my colleague would inevitably, introduce the question of cricket. That wasn't a problem as cricket was and is a keen interest of mine; but for my colleague in the English department our un-timetabled interest was *cricket*. The play about this form of racism has been written – and rewritten, but has never found its way on to the English stage.

Again, recently, I was invited by the BBC to contribute to a series of talks on the radio, writers being offered a series of subjects – mainly about writing and the play of the artistic imagination – to reflect on. Unsurprisingly, my brief (along with two other 'black writers') was "Multiculturalism".

In a recent essay about how American writers depict their society, Toni Morrison observes that 'racism is as healthy today as it was during the Enlightenment.' If this is a statement few sensible people would contest, what is equally depressing is how globalized the religion of racism has become.[5]

Notes

1. Oswald Mosley, Leader of the British Union of Fascists was imprisoned during World War II. Geoffrey Hamm's 'punishment' was to be sent to the Falkland Islands, as a teacher. After the war (in 1948) Mosley formed the equally unsavoury Union Movement. See also 'The Mosley Connection', in *Meet Me in Mozambique*, pp 93-111.
2. Marcel Duchamp (1887-1968) Dada, cubist, etc. artist, born in France, moved eventually to America, became a US citizen. He submitted *'Fountain'* to the New York *Salon des Independants*, in 1917 (signing it. *R Mutt.*). It was rejected.
3. In those days, with evidence of white racism everywhere, you thought that the debate about racism needed to be restructured. And, of course, you still think this. What one was unaware of at the time, was the collusion of African coastal elites in the trade, raiding the interior and marching their prisoners, sometimes hundreds of miles, and keeping them, sometimes for months in deplorable conditions, before handing them over to the European slavers, for an even more gruesome journey. An important part of modern Africa's liberation, would be the way in which its thinkers confront this aspect of Africa's past – and in some instances, its present.
4. Martin Webster of the British National Party greeted the President with the offal from a dead animal.
5. Tony Morrison, Playing in the Dark: Writers and the Literary Imagination (Vintage, NY, 1993, p.63)

PART THREE

AGAINST THE GRAIN

CHAPTER TEN: STOCKTAKING

1

'Taking stock' sounds a bit better than stocktaking. I know that businesses do this from time to time, shut up shop for a week or so during the process of checking what they had in store. I did assist one person in this, the wife of a man who had opened a small shop on the ground floor of our house in Ladbroke Grove; it was a fairly dispiriting process, surveying the small range of goods on offer, though the items catering to West Indian tastes – brown rice, pigtail, salt fish and Carnation milk (tins and tins of it) seemed to keep the trade going, somehow; but the general lack of organization made you fear for the future of the business.

One had mixed feelings about this. You shared your mother's view, more or less, that one shouldn't open a business, selling foodstuffs, bang opposite to the public loos in the street. It had always offended her sensibilities that she had to look down on the loos when she sat in the front room upstairs looking out, which she did most days. The couple downstairs were from Montserrat and were known to some members of the family.

Another thing I was unsure of was having a shop catering largely to West Indian tastes. There didn't seem that many West Indians about, to provide the clientele – though we were told that they came from distant parts of London to shop there. The feeling in the house was that an ambitious shopkeeper would have done better to compete with the English shops on the Goldbourne and Chesterton roads, shops that didn't really know about selecting fresh fruit, so that what they imported was nearly always off, and you ended up throwing most of the stuff away. Our next-door fascist, Geoffrey Hamm, occasionally came into the shop; and we were convinced that he came in not to buy foodstuff he needed but to pry, to look for evidence. Though this had nothing, really, to do with us. Anyway, I must have had this in mind as I did my own stocktaking: Where do you go from here? sort of thing.

Where you went from here was to university. I had had a go at several careers and had failed them all; failed to be a successful playwright and novelist, failed at rivalling Tommy Steele and Jim Dale on the pop scene (and don't even talk about Bob Dylan and Elvis), failed even at turning the making of belts and handbags into a High Street business that bore your name; even though, towards the end at CG Spencer, the man, had offered me a partnership: though, was this serious? The reason for this failure, you told yourself, was not lack of talent but that you were insufficiently well-trained and well-educated, insufficiently knowledgeable of how things worked in this country. Where to look for assistance? You had to look to university.

It was more or less expected that that would happen, anyway, despite my years out. My brother had been to university in Puerto Rico and had moved on to Canada before completing the course and, as he was the brightest member of the family, we were all solicitous for him. My other brother, Joe, was doing a correspondence course that would, presumably, end in a degree.[1] But both their education had been interrupted and they both switched from their original jobs, having passed the Post Office exam, and now worked for cable & Wireless, earning a decent living. My sister was training to be a nurse. But talking of educational expectations, my father, in Canada, had acquired three university degrees, and was a Very Reverend. Before that my great uncle Ned had been a Doctor in New York, and Great Uncle Bird *nearly* a lawyer (as some of our sub-Continental friends might say) in New York. So, yes, though it was considered natural that I, not really having to work or pay rent, would continue the tradition of higher learning in the family.

Friends now find it odd that no real pressure was exerted to get me back to school sooner. I put it down, I suppose, to the extent to which everyone in the family was preoccupied to stabilize the position, both financial and social, after disruption: regrouping in England took some time. (A small but contributing factor in concentrating my mind on education was that the year I went back to school I got my Call Up papers for National Service. Two or three boys whom we knew got theirs at the same time, and were happy enough to go off to fight in Cyprus, something I was personally ambivalent about. My cousin, Terry (one of the Markhams – the one present at the house, at the Mosley meeting) had been a volunteer in the army and had signed up for, I think, nine years; but I felt I had more options than Terry. You were excused National Service if you were in full-time education, and I wanted to prove, seriously, that I was in full time education.)

But even here I had a fight on my hand, to clear the way for university. I was in the Geography class at Kilburn when at the start of one lesson Mr Greening, the teacher, announced that there was a timetable clash with Latin, and as there were very few people proposing to take Latin at O Level and lots of takers for Geography, it was decided to drop Latin from the full-time curriculum.

I sat back waiting for the protests; there were fifteen or sixteen of us in the class, but no one seemed bothered by that. At that stage my aim was to go to university to read English. It was known that in order to achieve that you needed, among your relevant GCEs, a classical and a modern language at either level. Italian was my modern language, Latin the classical. Without Latin I wouldn't get in to university to read English. I assumed that others in the class would have similar ambitions, but in the silence that ensued, I had to speak up.[2]

No one else expressed dismay at the loss of Latin; I was alone. In the end Greening suggested that there was a Latin class taught in the evening, and my best bet was to join that. I couldn't understand why my fellow students had so little ambition for themselves. This served to confirm certain notions of England that had long been growing: the realization was that it was not England that would help me achieve things; it was despite England that one would achieve things. I was beginning to see England as something of a hurdle rather than as an opportunity.

Not that this was a sudden or dramatic revelation; it was part of an oscillating tendency – now to keep your head down, now to take a risk. For, in truth, England was neither wildly exciting nor hugely disappointing; but something of a mixture that left you confused when you took the time to think about it. You felt both lucky and somewhat aggrieved, lucky that you had escaped the terrors of a West Indian childhood of God, church and family status; aggrieved that no one you met took you at your own valuation, even that people tended not to laugh at your jokes. In retrospect these must have been the travails of growing up anywhere; but I wasn't in touch with many people of my age, out of school. Later, George Lamming, the Barbados novelist, was to tell a cautionary tale about – was it ownership? Was it ambition? – that seemed real to me: it was the image of a black man and a white woman contesting the same space in London.

So, the story goes: this young English (white) couple, secure enough in their little postwar house, are having a lie-in on a Sunday morning. Eventually, the lady of the house gets up, puts on her dressing gown and comes downstairs, maybe to make a cup of tea. She goes into the sitting-room and is about to open the curtains when she sees, to her surprise, a black man lying on her couch. She doesn't know the man. She recovers from her surprise and asks.

'What are you doing here?'

And he bestirs himself and answers: 'I live here.'

This scene, I've since thought, would make a powerful opening for a play, where the protagonists would lay out their arguments for ownership and the audience gain some illumination (or at least be made

155

uncomfortable) as a result. But George leaves it at that, a sort of metaphor for the confusions attending host and guest at the time.

It's true that both host and guest might feel aggrieved at the circumstances that caused them to contest their present living space. The guests were to a certain extent misled about their possible reception in the 'Mother' country, and the hosts could claim not to have been consulted about being required to give house-room to people they might not like especially, people who weren't in the normal sense, fleeing persecution. The debate, when it came – often on the streets – was devoid of intellectual honesty or historical background, and allowed *both* host and guest to be able to claim to the sanctity of victimhood.[3]

In the *play* one might have enlarged the frame of reference, pushed it back a few years past the 1948 docking of the *SS Empire Windrush* at Tilbury, with its 498 'Jamaicans'[4] – past that, to the war years, say. Then, the black man on the couch may well have been in an air-force uniform, and with revised dialogue.

Another Line in Stocktaking

'It's always tempting to compare things that might not be alike. That's probably why your similes are rarely accepted by your opponent in debate. Or, for that matter, by your fellow-guest at the dinner-table when the conversation gets heated. Even with partners, disputes often come down to the quibble of semantics (Is it a quibble?) or definition – one person's synonym being blocked or countered by the other's antonym. The same, too, with family members recalling the past.

So to this home, blessed with lovingness, caringness, a protective family embrace shielding one from the outside world. The same home differently looked at becomes harsh and smothering, an unacceptable limit on a person's – a child's – freedom. I'm thinking now of conversations with my niece, Gwen, my sister's eldest child who grew up, mainly with her grandmother, in the family homes I'm writing about. Gwen, a lawyer, is nearly two decades younger than me, and consequently would have a different perspective on things. Here's the point of making comparisons, that I hinted at above.

I was the product of a West Indian childhood. Gwen was an English child of West Indian parents, born and brought up in London. So, as an English child she recalls the frustration of not having enough time to herself, of having to do too much housework, of not being allowed out enough to play, to visit friends, etc. (She remembers being enrolled into the old ritual of making cakes at weekends.)

So let's step back a bit: a West Indian household in London in the 1950s was under a certain amount of invisible pressure. (The *visible* pressure was obvious. The reported joke of a Labour party parliamentary candidate at the time, vying for the 'immigrant vote', was: 'We want their vote, but we don't want to shout about it.') There was a feeling among these 'immigrants' that it wouldn't do to step out of line, to expose yourself, to be identified and be targeted – a warning that black people in America had learnt to take seriously: adults felt they needed to impress this on children. Gwen, being the youngest in the house, would have felt this. A child born in England, presumably carried less psychological baggage than the adults, brought up in another society.

Allied to this, ours was never a touchy-feely family (no hugs, no real bedtime stories, no sharing of secrets). A West Indian child would not have found this unusual; an English-born one might sense its lack. The compensations – stories of a grander existence to the present back in the West Indies, of sun and sea and communal respect; of people in power who were family; of fresh fruit in the garden, etc., might not always resonate with a child who just wanted to do things her friends did. For her 'emotional security' it may have been more important to be asked, 'Did you make any friends at school today, darling?' than to be on the lookout for slights encountered *out there*.

So, are we getting closer to that troubling comparison of a difference of being a West Indian in the West Indies and being of West Indian parentage in England?

It is too crude to say that the West Indian child's fate (in the home) was to be seen and not heard whereas that in England the child demanded more to be heard and less seen. But there is something in this in that a child in the West Indies was more likely to accept the diktat of parents (and of adults, generally) whereas the English-born child expected to participate in decisions that affected her, expected to *negotiate* conditions in the household. (We might parody the excess of 'democracy' in some English homes where both parents and children end up paralysed by the range of choice laid out before the simplest decision could be made. Or worse, where lack of adult direction leads to a form of child-tyranny. But why live at either extreme of commonsense?)

The *play* in revision at the moment is not about a black bank manager in England (a stale, stale idea of little interest to me now), but of the relationship between men and women in this context, in that context where men display the sort of emotional intelligence so that women don't feel silenced or bullied or abused; and the women don't end up isolated, or resentful or in analysis – or in the clutches of religion.

If I were permitted a footnote here I would probably say that we were a 'virtual' family where the *idea* of family was paramount, because at no time did all main members of the family actually live in the same house or island or country. My sister and I (separately) were brought up apart from the main family unit, the father, in my time, was always elsewhere – Andrew Salkey's classic 'sea-split marriage.' 'England' was a brave attempt to regroup. It worked in some sense, but it was never organic. This was not an unusual 'West Indian' experience.

★ ★ ★

A Nurse in the Family

My sister writes:

'I started training as a nurse in London in the early sixties. After spending eight weeks at the School of Nursing we were allocated our first ward. My first ward turned out to be a T.B. ward. In those days nurses got only one day and a half off each week. Sunday is the start of the week so if one is off on Sunday, you may get Monday morning off, then you start work Monday afternoon, at 1.p.m.

After leaving the training school on the Friday, I went to the ward that I was allocated to, to check my off-duty. The Sister on that ward told me I should start Monday afternoon, so I went home for the weekend. Little did I know that an amendment list had come out on Saturday, and for some reason my name was on that list to go to another ward. Of course I was not around: I was at home enjoying the weekend with my family.

I returned to the hospital early on Monday to start duty at 1.p.m. only to be told that I had to go to another ward; a female T.B. ward. I went to the ward and introduced myself to the Sister, who promptly said: 'I don't want you. You should have been on duty here on Sunday morning.'

I was speechless to hear this; I turned and was about to leave when she called me back and instructed me to go on to the ward and support the Staff nurse who, she said, would show me around. Tears came to my eyes for the rest of that day every time I thought of the words the Sister had said to me: 'I don't want you.' What helped me to survive that day was the luck that the Sister was off-duty that afternoon and not due back until the following afternoon. However, after working on that ward for five days, I ended up in the sick bay on day six with nervous diarrhoea. All the tests they did came up normal, so after a few days' rest I was sent back to the ward. The thought of working on a T.B. ward was bad enough, but I was so afraid of that Sister – who I thought of as a dragon – that it gave me sleepless nights.

I spent eight weeks on that ward; the dragon had me with her:

if she was making beds I was with her; if she was taking blood I was with her; coffee-break, lunch-break, I couldn't get away from her; and then after eight weeks a change of ward, and I thought Christmas had come early. However, before I left the dragon had to sign my Report book, and to give comments on my performance. To my surprise she gave me a very good report; she also told me that I would make a very good nurse – and that I should not let her down.

Throughout my training my first ward was by far the most stressful. I worked with other Sisters who were obviously racist, but by then I was much tougher and able to handle them in my own way. After three years I changed hospitals. I moved to a much smaller hospital where I got to know almost everyone by name. Even though this was a so-called 'Cottage Hospital' the principles of what I learnt were the same. The good thing about that place was that there was a Matron in charge, and one that was approachable: if any of the nurses had a problem it was comforting to know that we could knock on her door and be listened to. While I was at that hospital the M.P. for the Borough, Reg Freeson, booked in for surgery. I was working on the ward at the time and was personally involved with the care. After his recovery he invited the entire team to dinner at the House of Commons. That was a memorable occasion for me.

After I left that hospital I spent a year in Gloucester, on a course. Most of the people there, once you got to know them, were friendly; the one thing I didn't much like was having to do split-duty.

I recall a surgical ward that I worked on. There was a patient with an infected wound, so badly infected that it smelt, especially first thing in the morning. So after reporting for duty I would get the dressing-trolley ready, and change her dressing as soon as possible, before breakfast; so that the other patients could enjoy their breakfast. Two of my colleagues on the same ward (they were white) avoided doing the woman's dressing because it was so unpleasant. Of course I didn't do it because I *liked* doing it but because it was more pleasant for all of us to work once it was done. The patient, however, looked forward to my doing her dressing, and I certainly did not expect any reward. But one day as I was about to go off on split duty the patient asked me if I was going into town. I said yes, and she then gave me some money and asked me to buy her two boxes of chocolates, which I did. When I returned in the afternoon I gave them to her. To my astonishment the two nurses who did not want to change her dressing came into the office with the two boxes of chocolates that I had bought. The thought that I was used as a messenger by

159

her (and for those two) made me very angry, indeed; but I couldn't show my disgust.

On another ward in the same hospital there was this lady who had been hospitalised for a long time; she had problems with her legs, and it was necessary to keep her on bed rest. Because of the length of time she spent there she got to know a lot of what goes on in the ward: some of the things she said showed that she was racist. One of the things she said to me was: 'Nurse, I like to see the little black babies. Their eyes are so wicked.' She said that with a big smile on her face.

On the children's ward a little girl aged between six and seven came in and her face was covered in freckles; she didn't want any black nurse to touch her: she felt that her freckles would get worse if a black nurse touched her.

After leaving Gloucester I worked for about two years as an occupational nurse. This was at a Government Training Centre at Bromley by Bow.(?) There, they trained people of all ages to learn new skills. I enjoyed that very much, but they closed the centre so I had to move on. I did agency work for a while, then finally I worked as a District nurse. This was challenging; most of the time you worked alone, unless there was a very ill person who required two nurses to lift and change them. Working alone you're often required to make on-the-spot decisions, which could mean the difference between life and death for the patient.

Visiting people's homes could be a challenge. On my way to a diabetic patient one morning, to give the insulin injection I got in a lift to go to the 4th. floor. The lift stuck between floors, so I was trapped for about twenty minutes before the fire brigade came to the rescue. On another occasion I went to a patient who was very confused: in her case a nurse had to visit her daily to administer the medication. One day when I visited her she let me in and then put the deadlock bolt on the door. When I was about to leave I couldn't get the door open; I had to phone the Council Office, who eventually sent someone round. Once, when another nurse visited her, the patient called the police claiming that this person had come to rob her.

There was another lovely lady whom we visited once or twice weekly. When I arrived she opened the door, she had her hair in curlers, rolled with five-pound notes, five of six in all: I had to think what would have happened if someone else (less honest) had called on her that day.

I had a very terrifying experience with a large Irishman, who must have weighed between 14 and 15 stone. He was unsteady on his feet and fell on the floor the morning before I got to him, but was able to pull himself to the door to open it and let me in. But he couldn't get up; so I tried to help him up; but because of his size I didn't want to take the chance of hurting myself. So I told him to hang on while I phoned for help. But as far as he was concerned I was a nurse, and should have been able to lift him. So he resorted to the most offensive language, pouring out the curses. I just had to stand there and listen to this until help came. I reported the incident; but nothing much came of it; the only good thing was that I didn't have to visit that patient again.

Apart from those 'minor' incidents, which I now call the funny side of nursing – because, looking back, they were not so funny at the time – I can now laugh about them. The good thing about nursing is that you get satisfaction when you see people under your care, recover; and some of them are very grateful for the help you gave them. One of the low points is the shortage of staff which makes you stretch yourself beyond where you can give of your best.

I have no regrets following my nursing career, but having said that, I have two daughters and I have discouraged them from taking up nursing; because I was so miserable when I was training that I didn't want them to go through that. At some point they both wanted to be nurses, and were fascinated with the uniform. When my elder daughter continued to show interest in the profession I said to her: 'Do you know you would have to touch dead people?' That quickly cured her of the romance. She eventually became a solicitor. Nursing is not glamorous. My younger daughter trained as a dental nurse and, after university, went to work in the forensic science laboratory at the Home Office.

Throughout my nursing career, family support was paramount. Also, some of the colleagues with whom I worked in different hospitals have remained my friends to this day.'

★ ★ ★

The prospect of university didn't of course, mean giving up the ambition to write professionally; university would be a means to accomplish that. There was just too much confusion over how to present people on the stage, and one needed the clarity of *knowledge*. I had written something with a bank manager as a character and was told, by a visiting West Indian actor whom we knew, that my sketch was unrealistic because the scene was set in London and the Bank Manager was black and there were no black bank managers in London. It was difficult to point out that that was the point of the sketch, difficult particularly because our friend had grown disillusioned with the dearth of parts for black actors on the English stage, and was on his way to America to try his luck there. I didn't want to have to resort to setting work in the Caribbean in order to show black people in leading or responsible positions; I didn't see why I shouldn't make the Prime Minister of Britain black. I didn't quite know where to go to discuss these things. Maybe university. I also didn't see why all my characters should be black.

Walking along the street I sometimes played the game of looking through the other person's eyes, the person walking towards me. Through my eyes I saw a white person. After a very short time in England when walking along the street I expected to see a white face: if I saw a face that wasn't white then that was noted with special interest. So, the white face, then, was becoming the norm.

But then what of the other person, the person coming towards me. That person would be looking into a black face. That person would see something different, strange to them, exotic.[5] I thought of the thought-bubbles coming out of that person's head. I didn't like what I read there. So I thought it was incumbent on me to revise the dialogue coming out of the heads of persons met on the street.

After a certain number of black faces – how many black faces over what length of time? – that person would cease to see those faces as strange and exotic. Different, perhaps, but no longer strange and exotic. It would matter, the way I conducted myself, to modify the dialogue coming out of the person's head. It would be good to change places with that person from time to see how this was working: which of us had the richer experience of walking along the street? That should be the subject of the next play. Thinking back to Jomo Kenyatta I wouldn't make my characters wear an adjective just because they were not white.

(There'd been a moment of indecision, in the house in Ladbroke Grove some years back, when I decided to write off to America for a correspondence course in writing; and one of the tests they posed (or it may have been the first lesson), was to present a portrait, in writing, of yourself. This caused me unbelievable difficulty because I had no clear idea what I looked like. As a young boy, I never really remember looking in the mirror much, even though, I am now reminded, that there was a large mirror in the boys' room at Harris'; and as I didn't shave, I still wasn't in the habit of looking at myself in the mirror; when someone at school in Kilburn drew a portrait of me with a forehead lower than I would have liked I was disappointed. (We had been reading Shakespeare. A 'low brow' wasn't something you celebrated.

But the point here is the confusion about colour. In my 'self-descriptive' piece to the Americans do I include the information that I was 'coloured'?

There were some St. Kitts friends at the house, one of them renting a room upstairs: they were light-skinned and felt newly vulnerable in London. They argued that the information was not relevant. This was England and not America and therefore ones colour should not be relevant. Worse, the feeling was that America was so segregated, separate and unequal, like South Africa, that admitting to being coloured (or 'colored') would be to tempt them to send you an inferior pack of instructions of how to write a short story. I think, as usual, I compromised, and said I was born in the West Indies, was British and living in London.

One of the things that had informed our friends from St. Kitts (three beautiful young women) was that they carried a fear of rejection, and tested it from time to time. When they went to the J. Lyons corner house at Marble Arch one Sunday afternoon for 'tea', they took the precaution to ask the waiter if they served 'coloured' people. The waiter, graciously, pretended to be surprised at the question.

★ ★ ★

My mother was a worry because she felt the loss of status keenly. She never complained. Except about the cold, but she never hid the fact that she had had five houses 'at home' and had had five maids (though not at the same time) to do her bidding and that when she laid out her shoes on the broad front steps of the house in Harris' the shoes covered the entire step. We knew she felt she had come down in the world and we suspected she felt that we, her children, had let her down, though she never criticized the Very Reverend in Canada. She had her group of women friends, all from the West Indies, who came to visit, but we usually took that as a signal to escape the room, or the house. If I have difficulty in painting her portrait it's because I fear she harboured painful thoughts about our standing in this country, and we weren't in a position, really, to do anything about it. (Some time later I heard a story about a South American dictator, exiled in America. His mother – everyone has a mother – his mother had gone mad, and when she looked down from her exile on the busy streets of whatever American city they were holed up in (Miami?) and saw the big cars and big shops and prosperous well-dressed people everywhere, thinking she was still at home, she praised her son's success at bringing so such development to his country.

Of course my mother was the most mentally-clued in of all of us, and that's why we suspected that our fantasies of getting the better of England didn't fool her. Yet she was generous – judgemental but generous, a strange mix – and, to the end, she feared for us in England.)

Not that much was spelt out in the family, so you picked up the hints. My brothers were quite often surprised that there were things about the house in which we grew up in Harris' that I didn't know;

the pruning of the fruit trees in the garden, for instance. Of course I had a vague sense of someone coming one holiday and cutting into the bark of the odd mango tree, sticking a freshly-cut twig from another mango tree into the cut and taping it up. This 'pruning' which was done apparently summer after summer by friends or cousins who were studying science at the Tropical Science College in Trinidad and demonstrated an interest in science that other people in the family seemed to be sensitive to; leaving me behind. My sister's long-standing interest in Botany – her drawing of leaves and flowers was much admired by visitors, even when we were children – came into this wide category of interest in science which I alone, unable even to identify flowers by name, seemed ignorant of. When my brother, a propos something trivial, called me an ignoramus, in the most kindly way, I was minded to take it to heart. This, remember, was the age of the Sputnik. Americans and South Africans were talking about eugenics. Hitler had happened. (Yes, there would be stray reference in the house to Darwin and Einstein, in a general way; and to Newton; but you knew no more about these figures than people in the street did: you certainly didn't know what the First Law of Thermodynamics was – though, like other people, you could refer to it. Most of the names of scientists I knew I had discovered by reading Bertrand Russell, and through the BBC. Even now, 40 years later, I wouldn't know – to reach for a couple of minerals at random – what cobalt was. Or tantalum.)

So was my interest in art, in the humanities – shamelessly proud as I was of my O Level in Ancient History, as I had prepared for that without tuition, worthy of some praise, yes, – masking the fact that I was taking the soft option: was it too late to change tack and veer towards science which seemed, somehow, to represent more of the world that we would encounter in the future. Or, indeed, that we had abandoned in Montserrat? If the house in Harris' were to be reclaimed wasn't writing about it very much second best to going back and pruning the fruit-trees?

But did I have the talent for it?

I didn't much go to the theatre for the first two or three years in London, which is odd, since I was so obsessed with playmaking, having a very strong visual image of plays heard on the radio. Trying to make up for it later by obsessive theatre-going and stage-directing – as well as doing graduate work in Drama at university – still didn't have the desired effect of making my plays stageable. Though liking the drama as an idea we had a somewhat old-fashioned idea of the *stage*; if the playwright was to be admired, the actors were suspect; we couldn't quite understand why some of them had become superstars; we were baffled why one or two of them had been knighted. No one in our house went to the theatre, as I say, except, occasionally, to something local: I remember my brother taking me to a production of *The Tempest* at a community hall in Kilburn, and we thought both Caliban and Prospero were badly handled. The Music Hall was my Friday night treat; but in your heart of hearts you felt you were slumming it.[6]

Notes.

1. He did, in fact, get an Open University degree, in Sociology.
2. Some time later, the daytime Latin class was restored, and I rejoined it. The things you remember. The things about the Latin class that stand out, in my memory, had little to do with Latin. In one session, for some reason, the master asked if we knew what Ku Klux Klan meant, and one quiet English boy came up with the answer. I was embarrassed not to have known. Embarrassed, also, that *he* knew. But it was good to learn that the great Roman general Scipio was pleased to be known by his African name, Scipio Africanus; it seemed an acknowledgement of Africa. Only later, talking with boys from the Polytechnic, whom you didn't realize knew about these things, they said the play I should be thinking of writing shouldn't be about Scipio, but about Hannibal, the greatest of all African generals, never defeated by Rome, and took poison rather than be captured, when his friends sold him out.

There *was* a play that I was thinking of writing, and it seems utterly trivial by comparison. The play was about 'The Jugarthine War, of which I knew nothing. But there was a sketch of Jugurtha, (king of Numidia, 1st century BC) in the notes of the *Caesar's Gallic Wars* textbook. I registered nothing of the story, except that Jugurtha's sketch made it difficult to determine whether he was a man or a woman. So how about a play about a man/woman warrior, set in those times, and build the Jugurtha story around it. Needless to say, that didn't even get to a first draft.

3. *On George Lamming's Couch*

> So, she comes down in a nightie revealing
> more than she intended: something has disturbed
> the Sunday-morning snooze: *what are you doing here?*
> she asks the stranger on the couch. She has seen him
> in the street, one of his colour: does he speak
> her language through those lips? Can they spirit
> themselves through the keyhole: *what are you doing here?*
> Though the house won't be paid for, it seems, in this lifetime
> she holds the key to the door: what hill did he climb
> to breach these walls; there are no weapons on him
> that she can see, and his body in repose reminds her
> they are said to be cunning. *So much black skin*

on her couch: is it hot to the touch? That's right, two men
in the house, before breakfast. Last time the government
promised an end to rationing: will every home now have one
of these for Christmas? Luck of the draw, maybe;
she has been warned what happens to a girl
with a will of her own: did peeing on the rubble with her friend
lead to this? His eyes seem to see her crouching
on the site, and here she is naked in a nightie. He's up
on two legs, reading her thoughts. He speaks through a mouth
of uncovered sex. And she will stand her ground
checking he's left nothing on the couch. *I live here.*
His voice close enough to trip her over: the curtains
are his; does he know curtains from nightie? She won't
call for help till she's ready and dressing-gowned. Standards:
I am English and this is my castle. She will banish
fear and do the normal thing; ask for evidence
of his claim to the couch. You get away with things
when your nerve holds: will he touch her before
she can wake the house? And through those lips, yes, he asks
to go to the bathroom. So he can't live here, after all.

4. The *Windrush* 'Jamaicans' included a scattering of passengers from other
   islands, including the Trinidadian calypsonian, Lord Kitchener (Aldwyn
   Roberts). On board there were 492 paying passengers and six stowaways.
   The fare was £28. 10s.
5. My friend, Judy, kept my feet firmly on the ground. 'Of course,' she said,
   people will think, looking at us, that I'm going out with you because I
   can't get a white boyfriend. Or that I'm a tart.' She affected to find that
   amusing. I didn't know if I wanted someone, who was seventeen or eighteen
   years old, to be thinking like that.
6. It was reading a biography, in university, that brought me round to full
   appreciation of the of the social art of acting. Nancy Mitford's account
   of the education of Madame de Pompadour (later to be mistress of Louis
   XV) seemed enviable. She sang and danced and played a musical instrument.
   She painted and drew and knew about natural history. But what caught
   my imagination was that she was able to memorize and recite complete
   plays in an invited audience. That won me over to the art of acting. Yes,
   give them the prizes.

CHAPTER ELEVEN
REMEMBERING LONDON

There were times when you felt it to be the right age: sixteen, in London, in 1956. Behind you were the terrors of growing up (God and church and family respectability); before you, something unknown but not unappealing. You liked living in a flat in a house joined to other houses; it was the opposite of the isolation of inhabiting that big old house in Harris' with your grandmother. You liked it that there seemed a sense of order in the street; streets regularly swept (the pavement, even, swept by some of the tenants or owners), the milkman leaving pints of milk on the doorstep, and no one stealing them. Riding the huge trolley-buses that hurtled down the Harrow Road towards Royal Oak seemed wonderfully risky and daring as they sent out blue sparks overhead, where their attachments slid along the electric cables high above the street. And there was the cinema, less than five minutes walk away, showing westerns, Alan Ladd, in *Shane*; all sorts.

Queuing was an interesting social activity. We admired the orderliness of the English, the fact that everyone seemed to recognize precedence and no one pushed ahead. Even if one person was busy and another idle, the busy person was still prepared to wait in the queue behind the one who might have nothing much to do. We admired this; but was it right? Was the valuable time of the busy to be wasted by the person in front who might have nothing pressing to occupy himself, herself? I remembered 'at home' in Harris' the procedure when letters came for the house. Teacher Kitty, across the way, was the Post Mistress, and at five o'clock in the afternoon she started distributing letters for the village. Well before five, people expecting letters would gather in Teacher Kitty's yard next to the playing field, waiting in expectation, their backs to the garage. And then at five o'clock Teacher Kitty would come to the door of her dining room facing the yard, with a pile of letters in her hand. The door was made of two halves, and the bottom half would be locked, so what you saw would be Teacher Kitty – fairly large was Teacher Kitty – from the waist up holding up the pile of letters preparing to call out the names.

Of course this didn't apply to us. I, or whoever went to collect the mail never stood with the crowd because Teacher Kitty put our (pre-sorted) letters aside on her large dining table, and whenever one of us arrived she broke off from what she was doing and handed over the letters. In England though you missed that sense of special treatment, queuing was a fairly painless lesson in democracy. (But others had to play the game; you heard mutterings – you sometimes read it in the papers – that some English people had reservations about standing in the queue behind the 'coloured immigrants'. One unintended consequence of this was having on occasion to minister to a white friend who got upset over having witnessed unfair treatment to a 'coloured' person.)

In our second (temporary) house – in Goldney Road, just round the corner from Sutherland Avenue – the house beside it gone, a bombed site that children sometimes played in, despite the warning that there might be an unexploded German bomb concealed there: you were, you thought with some sense of daring, in pioneer country. There was a feeling of release, also, that rationing had ended only three or so years back. Two or three years later, at school, we would discuss, in the common room, new buildings going up on the bombed sites: there was a sense, as a schoolboy, in being engaged in a discussion of how the new London should look. You disapproved of many of the new buildings going up, the flats off the Harrow Road that you had to witness on your way to school, the large church being rebuilt on the other side of Kilburn, in Quex Road, the West Hampstead end, put together by Irish volunteers: we, Londoners, deserve better, you thought.

At night you were watchful; you took the **KEEP BRITAIN WHITE** stickers more seriously; you avoided walking through certain areas that might be problematic. (Often, on your wanderings, an unknown man from the Caribbean would cross the road to tell you that there was trouble at such and such a place ahead, and suggest that you took another route to wherever you were heading.) But London seemed very *big*, avoiding trouble relatively easy; you were obviously perceived to be at greater risk if your partner was white-skinned. In those days my partner was white-skinned. That was, in fact, the real front line.

At some point – into the '60s – down from university and at home in Kilburn, I used regularly to visit my friend, Chinque in Hendon, just up from the tube station, Hendon Central. We would perhaps see a film at the *Classic* cinema, where Chinque's mother worked in the box office; and then repair to the Chinque household where Mrs. Chinque, back home again and the proud housewife, would produce one of her tasty snacks; then there might be a bit of talk, a bit of television. Afterwards I would set out to walk back to Kilburn. The journey took about an hour. The problematic bit was Cricklewood: there was a club on the main road where there was often a fight – West Indians and Irishmen, apparently, the worse for drink, settling their differences. You could tell well in advance whether it was safe to walk past the club. One option was to circle it and go round the back streets. But you'd do that only if you were sure it wasn't safe to go along the main road, which was well-lit. The side streets, being dark, felt less safe. You got home feeling a sense of relief; but you got home feeling that you were exploring London, with a view, ultimately, of possessing it.

The sense of belonging/not belonging never left you because to assume that you belonged in this or that group and to discover that you didn't would destroy your confidence and make you wonder if you were making a fool of yourself. At Kilburn, for instance, at school, one of our friends in the GCE class, E.C. (I must use his initials), admitted to me that he would not go out with a Jewish girl. Now, E.C. was as close as anyone to many of the Jewish girls (and lads) from Edgware and Golders Green, and I'm sure none of them knew that this was his feeling. (The boys, in particular, tended to think (or pretend) that there was no anti-Semitism in the school. But of course, the message to *me* was that E.C. would be even less likely to go out with a black girl. Could I, I asked myself, be as sanguine as the Jewish boys, thinking that their friends weren't prejudiced, because it suited their view of themselves? It gets more problematic when someone confides (another boy at Kilburn) to not having liked black people until he ran into me. What are the conversations, you ask yourself (endlessly) taking place in those homes (including those you visited) between family members on the issue of black people residing in Britain? When I look back now at the literature of the time, that type of family discourse seems, more or less, edited out. But London was bigger than its spoilers – even those at Notting Hill in '58. That was what you affected to believe. Indeed, that was what you believed.

And yet there are times when you think that the right age has passed. What is it? Is it the endless reports of stabbings, casual murder on the streets that make you fear for a hapless Little Nell's grandfather prowling the streets of London after dark? Of course, you know that London is safer now than it was then. But was it safer than in 1959 (or '65) when you ventured out at night and feared running into Irishmen and West Indians with voices and fists raised in Cricklewood? And then there are the terrorists who are no longer Irish, of a different kind; and no longer give a warning. And everyone you knew then is fifty years older, or dead. It's amazing to the visitor I am now, to someone who no longer lives in the capital, that whenever you contact anyone from that time the conversation runs to a funeral, just attended. If enough black people are buried or cremated in a place (And, please, children of Geoffrey Hamm, don't take this the wrong way) does that strengthen the claim of ownership of those of the 'clan' who are alive?

On the other side of the funeral there is carnival. The Caribbean's splash of colour to liven up the scene for a couple of days each year. It's made its mark. It's had policemen dancing in the streets; the research invested in the costumes is commendable. Would this were a transferable skill.

★ ★ ★

I remember reading Virginia Woolf's sketches about London, done in 1931-32 for *Good Housekeeping* magazine. (I scanned the *Diaries* for any barbed references to her writing for *Good Housekeeping*, but couldn't find any.) Woolf's perspective is of someone travelling on the river, with appalled fascination of the London Docks, the squalor, her delight at coming unexpectedly on a splendid building (Greenwich Hospital), etc. But really, what intrigued me was Virginia Woolf's view of the ocean liners come to anchor in the Port of London. There is romance, there is a sense of these disparate, floating 'palaces' from all over the world coming to pay homage, here, at the centre.

Well, it was and wasn't like that for those of us who might have come here on one of those boats. In my case, the three-week boat trip ended in Genoa, from there by train to Paris, and London. But London was for us, also, the centre of something long imagined, and my own family still think it odd that I have chosen to spend so much of my life outside London. (Outside England.) The difference between Virginia Woolf's view of London and mine wasn't, I imagine, the difference between Bloomsbury and the Maida Vale/Ladbroke Grove/Kilburn perspectives of my first few years in the capital. (We never accepted that we were contemporary versions of Woolf's shop-assistants living in 'little villas at Croydon and Surbiton'): the difference with Woolf was nearer to a view of the ships that came to the London docks.

Boarding the ship in Montserrat in 1956 we knew that we were setting out on a journey far beyond Antigua, thirty miles away; further, even, than to America or to Canada, where our family who went to those places hadn't returned, except for a couple of elderly great aunts, and great uncles, all fairly remote figures. And what of the boat? Cousin Gen (the most prominent of the Osborne clan) had bought a big boat, in Bermuda, a short time before, and it had sunk. It was a liner, large enough to sail up the islands to America, and it had been sunk on its maiden voyage home to Montserrat. Foul play, they whispered. Whatever word we used for 'racism' then, was whispered.

Cousin Gen, our family, was a black man; and the captain and crew of his new ship were white; and it was whispered on the island that a white captain and crew were not happy about a man who was black owning such a big boat. So the boat sank, and the captain and crew survived. (Of course, boats had sunk before, including three or four of 'Wally' Wade's, but these were smaller craft.) And now we were about to board an Italian boat for England: if we came across rough seas, who would be put into the lifeboats? Some said lifeboats were for tourists and we didn't know if we were tourists. Though if anything happened we would pretend to be tourists and head for the lifeboats.

No one knew for certain if it was better to sail in an Italian rather than an English boat (which would have been preferred); but speculation was soon given up as almost at the start of this three weeks of frightening water, with nearly everyone below deck sick, and with a differently sick smell coming from the kitchens as you struggled up to dinner. Fewer made it to dinner each day; in the end there was no one to drink the wine which kept being put on the table. *Dear Virginia.*

Casting her patrician eye on the 'dismal' dockyard, past the 'sinister' dwarf city of workmen's houses and warehouses, Woolf notes the gasometer – a word I associate so firmly with cricket commentary and John Arlott and Brian Johnston that I'm impressed that Virginia Woolf knew the term: surely, it has everything to do with Hall and Griffith coming in to bowl at that particular end of the Oval, and nothing to do with Bloomsbury and rural Sussex.

What was romantic about London in those days? they ask me. Oh, start with the bombed sites round the corner, which gave you a new view of England, less perfect, breachable, less intact, more manageable than you feared, a place you might now explore without having to adopt the posture of a supplicant. It encouraged you to see yourself as something of a pioneer, not an immigrant: as there were bits of London unbuilt (almost, you could pretend, for your benefit) you could somehow be part of the refashioning.

Come to think of it, the real different between Virginia Woolf's portrait of London and mine was less to do with the image of ships and more to do with the magic of prose: when she talks of the oddities that turn up, inadvertently, at the warehouses in those sacks of cinnamon, 'a snake, a scorpion, a beetle, a lump of amber, a diseased tooth of an elephant, a basin of quicksilver...' we are prepared for the delights of her later flights of fancy as she goes on to distinguish between an elephant's tusk and the tusk of a mammoth: the mammoth's ivory, you see, tending to warp, so no good for billiard balls, only good for umbrella handles, etc. The conceit is humbling.

The difference, too, is the sense of ownership exhibited by Woolf

171

over the place called London, the Houses of Parliament, the Tower and Westminster Abbey, the casual observation that 'It was always February' in the house of the puritan Carlyles (in Chelsea) whereas Keats's house in Hampstead was suggestive of Spring etc. When Woolf drops in on the house where Carlyle once lived, it isn't to learn something about how prominent lives were arranged, but with the confidence of someone, long grounded in this place, all critical features intact. (She notes that there was no water laid on in the house, water having to be pumped from a well in the kitchen – Carlyle's biographers not having noted this detail. From that observation Virginia Woolf sketches out the 'battlefield' that was Carlyle's fight against dirt, cold and termites; and senses again the 'oppression' which the women – mistress and maid – endured to make life bearable. And her wicked wit: her call for a house to have 'bath, h & c., gas fires in the bedrooms, all modern conveniences and indoor sanitation' which, she knows, would not have made the 'Scottish' Carlyles different from the people they were.

So, *here* was a writer.

★ ★ ★

We had been strangely relaxed, in 1956, in leaving behind all that could not be fitted into my mother's famous trunk. I have been prompted, over the years, to recall some of the things left out of the trunk. It makes predictable reading. Now, if I were a surrealist writer, I would pack so much more into that trunk. I would fit the whole house, really, into it; and that would include Nellie and Sarah. It would include our horse, Ruby, as well as the splendid views from the verandah in Harris': the trunk, opened in Sutherland Avenue, the eye would soar over the playing fields up towards the mountains shrouded in mist. That's in one direction. In the other, a couple of miles down beyond Farms village and Bethel to the sea – one would release that view, too, from the trunk.

One night I dreamt of Pilate, our barber; I suppose we would have had to pack him, too, in the trunk. Pilate was dumb and followed my mother's instructions (rather than mine) to cut my hair: did my mother have special skills, I now wonder, in talking to the deaf and dumb? I recall the scene of sitting in the yard of the little house in the village that Pilate rented from us. (One half of the house, rented from us.) I expect the barbering was in part payment. I would be sitting on a chair under a tree, partly draped in a white sheet, with Pilate standing over me with his scissors poised, and whatever the close-shaving implement was called. Passers-by would pause to comment, sometimes engage in a lengthy chat with the dumb man, and no one seemed to doubt that he understood what was being said. (Sign language was, of course, unknown to us.) Is it, I wonder, more difficult to write dialogue for a dumb man than for a stranger coming towards you, in London?

Talking of the trunk, it being a magic thing, I would pack the entire island into it, for it was a small island. And this being 1956, it would have escaped the hurricane, and the volcano.

This is probably the place to move a footnote up into the text, a thing that early feminists of the 1960s and other readers who felt themselves to be marginalized, urged us to do. The intended footnote is about a lost picture, a photograph lost in transition. It is of my mother, brothers, sister and myself taken sometime in the mid-1940s, much about the same time as the photograph included in this book, but very different in tone. Whereas this one is semiformal, the one lost is ultra-formal. In it my mother is wearing a polka-dot dress; she is sitting on the chair surrounded by her children (as in the present photograph, all in the same positions, but differently-dressed). The elder brothers are in sharp, white (churchgoing) suits, long-trousered, and my sister's dress is more elegant, right for someone slim and long-legged.

The photo, unlike the present one, has a context. It is taken at the bottom of the front steps – the broad, penultimate step – with that corner of the house in view, in the background; the sweep of steps behind, bits of the verandah (back and right), my mother's bedroom door, open (straight behind), the drawing-room door (left). Also on the left, the wall of the dining (below) and boys' room (above), with some shingles coming down the side of the boys' room, visible. The little dining-room window that opened out on to the front steps, is visible, open.

I've guarded this picture since my mother gave it to me in the early 1980s. I had it with me in Papua New Guinea (1983-'85) where it caused amazement among the Highlanders to see a black family, so far back in time, so securely dressed. A couple of years ago I discovered it in a safe place in Sheffield (where I still had a flat) and, thinking it would make an ideal cover for this book, put it in a special place for transportation to Paris, where I also lived. I have been looking for that photograph for over a year now, without luck; it's held up publication of this book by about eight months – not in itself a matter of great import – but the time comes when you accept that something else of the family is lost – and you move on. Yet, you do so with a sense of accepting the inevitable when, as in the case of the lost photo, other members of the family seem to have been unaware of its existence.

I have always, in a sense, lived in a third house, a house not associated with family. The first identifiable 'third house' was the one mentioned in the Preface, that of John Elsom and Sally Mays' in Shepherds Bush, this being after university in the mid-to-late 1960s. John was, as we said, a theatre critic and Sally a concert pianist; and it was in that house, at 69 Elsham Road (rather than at university, I suspect) that my artistic prejudices were developed. Through John one felt very close to the professional theatre; through Sally, one was exposed to the atonal (classical) music of the time. If there was a certain sense of 'the author as centre' in John's groups, the opposite emanated from the musicians surrounding Sally's quartet, the Mouth of Hermes. Hermes, in Greek myth, son of Zeus and Maia, inventor of the lyre (the day he was born) was, among other things, the messenger of the gods. The musicians saw themselves very much as messengers, as a conduit of the music: in that house in Elsham Road I oscillated between those two views of creativity.

It was out of that tension that I started to publish my first poems and to be relaxed about not being theatrically fashionable. The house was a centre of artistic activity (writers, musicians, actors, singers everywhere) with the large space downstairs converted, from time to time, for performance to an invited audience. There were recitals, poetry and short story readings (with paintings of contemporary artists hung for the occasion) and, from time to time, a play.

Other houses, some less conspicuously art-driven provided a home from home where so much of my thinking/writing took shape: friends' homes in Highgate, (a partner's home in Highgate and, again, in Stoke Newington); the homes of friends in Edinburgh, in Stockholm, in the South of France (and Boston & Toronto and Sydney & Maputo and Montserrat; and Mauritius ..) – all helped to contribute something towards that 'third house' never quite achieved. And of course there were my own homes, which always seemed to have something missing. This peripatetic nature of my life has led to comment: lack of continuity, lack of grounding, lack of *family*. At its least judgemental: is it right, they ask, to have spent so much of your life in the house of strangers? Playing the sophist I throw that question to someone from Montserrat (before or after volcano) and I hope to come up with an answer that, though unconvincing, might be divertingly ingenious. (Ingeniously diverting?)

★ ★ ★

It is undignified, when you are a certain age, to talk about regrets, and, on the whole, the god of biology has been kind to the family; and, if I'm allowed a cliché, the glass of ambition is half-full rather than half-empty. There are so many houses owned by the family, in so many places, it would be churlish to complain about the loss (or lack) of

174

home. When, occasionally, I walk past a house we once inhabited, and imagine the new owners secure in possession, I think of my mother, coming like a ghost in the night and giving them a turn: it would be good for them to know that she had resided there before them, and that the walls of their castle are breachable. It is a sadness, though, that she hasn't yet found her way to my modest abode, in Paris.

Sheffield, 2002 – Paris, 2007

AFTERWORD

FOR A BROTHER
(Joe: W.S.G. Markham, BA, 1932-2007)

i:

A man is dying in a hospice; this unknown part of town is now the focus of attention of those close to him.

But before we get ahead of ourself, the man is in bed, in his own room, glazing at the television; he is said by those who visit to want the television on, perhaps – this is speculation – perhaps to exert a little control over the bedside conversation where reference to the familiar daytime quiz might be less taxing than other types of mental probing. If the man in bed can't summon the energy to respond to these feelers it doesn't matter much; all can agree that the TV-induced subject is trivial.

Is his voice clear; is he still speaking in sentences?

The answers are contradictory.

Someone comes in to prove a point; there is some conversation; it is better than no conversation.

He is comfortable; he is not complaining about not being comfortable; the tension in his face mustn't be over-interpreted.

It must be good to have a familiar voice (familiar voices) around you; and he appreciates having his feet massaged. By a concerned niece.

It is confirmed: he likes to have his feet massaged.

Someone else, a brother, is on the way to the hospice. Like everyone else, he has forebodings about the term. 'Hospice' has never formed a sentence-structure with 'family' before. So this is a challenge larger than an individual's fate, this is a greyness signalling that something like summer is over. And yet, don't play to the mood, try to be specific and not be emotionally lazy: is this an endgame, an end-of-line time, a terminus where the buses and trains stop their journey? This brother is threatening to become something beyond that, like a parent you hadn't yet prepared yourself for being without.

This is, literally, beyond where the train terminates. End of the Northern Line. Morden. First time this far out. After the train there is a bus,

179

and fringes of unfamiliar country that is London: it is this sense of being ushered out of the city, past where the train stops, that most unsettles the visiting brother, confirming the superstition of 'hospice' as a point of no return.

The prospect of an elder brother dying before you is unsettling in a subtle way, for though it's more or less expected, that is a security not to be trusted. And this elder brother has lived an altogether safer life than the other has. The elder brother's going first assumes a logic of something somewhat more mysterious and arbitrary than reason: only the childlike or unimaginative welcome life's tidiness in these areas. So the predictability of this must have been a small weight for the elder brother to bear, not consciously, of course, not something pressing enough to warrant articulation, but something that might have appeared from time to time, a shadow at the edge of vision, before vanishing. (He must have defeated death on occasion, glancingly, unheroically, in the lottery of his own living; and that, too, must have communicated a sense of … journeys not cut short. If so, how to repay the thoughtfulness not to remind others of it. The brothers have never discussed this, of course: so is this the time for the younger to show appreciation that the other is prepared to play this old-fashioned ritual that makes no real sense any more?) Enough. Enough of this bus-passenger talk

He's got the daily paper, the younger brother. (There are some papers his brother will not read; he likes that.) He will go through items of interest in a paper that his brother reads. Then, perhaps, turn to the sport. (News on the radio is altogether too heavy, nothing but disorder in the world; and obscenity. They've had fifty years of railing against it and no one has listened. Now, a man of calm and benign temper would not want to go out to a world still given over to prejudice and violence and genocide. So, it'll be better to talk about sport. (Though not of the interview with Clive Lloyd, recently heard on the World Service, of West Indies touring Zimbabwe. The great man seemed curiously uncensorious of the Mugabe government: would he be comparing Mugabe's stewardship favourably with Ian Smith's, say; or with the earlier rapacious brother, Leopold of the Belgians, in another Africa?) So, an upbeat and heartyish review of the Sports comedy on the back pages might be the right tone for the hospice.

In a room at the hospice – the visitors' holding room, so to speak – family and friends gather, get updates, review the situation and visit the sickroom in rota, so as not to crowd the sick-bed. It is a Sunday; there is a whiff of church in the air.

The patient's wife and daughter have pride of place. Their body-language, their attentiveness to guests, etc. indicate that this is already home from home; they are in residence. The wife, too, is not well, her medical history recounted in some detail shows her as being stubbornly heroic; the daughter is, understandably, suffering. The obsessive reference to 'the silent killer' strikes a note of acceptance.

A young priest comes to pay respects; and someone – two people – from the Lodge, to which the man in question belongs. Friends and relatives from far away make light of their journeyings. The priest is female and pretty; she talks of dignity, of how difficult to be deprived of it, particularly when one is as dignified as the patient in question, his name on everyone's lips, surprisingly, a diminutive not used by the family: this then, this church, this Lodge, these friends constitute another family. Affection and warmth emanate from this family. Later, in the sickroom, the nurse, too, is warm and tactile. The visiting brother's prepared reservations begin to fall away and yes, in an ideal life he could commend both nurse and priest to his brother's service; they are unselfishly on the case.

He has an odd conversation with a man from the church whom he tries not to place in other – more theatrical – company. They disagree on the meaning of life and death, but with politeness and courtesy. They probe each other with light name-dropping. They share a joke about CREATION – a trade name stencilled on the metal frame of the patient's hospital bed. They end, like wary boxers, circling each other with a Bishop Berkeley reference and commentary; they end by being quietly pleased with themselves.

Waking up. Waking up in the middle of the night without a brother. Waking up in a strange flat in the south of London in the middle of the night without a brother. This is a first. You have woken in panic before, in consternation, but the loss of a manuscript, or of a partner has proved, in reflection, to be something in which you were complicit. You could resolve, in time, to play a better hand; to play the hand differently. But to wake up to the loss of a brother strikes at something elemental. Making yourself a cup of tea won't do it. Scribbling a few lines on your notepad won't do it. Resolving to be a better listener/correspondent/ linguist, etc. won't do it; it's not in your hands.

So you reach for foolish analogies. Like waking up with one leg missing. Like... In the end you settle for being in a country where you don't speak the language. This has happened to you, often. Recently, even. The humiliations at this or that national bank of language where you are overdrawn and the Manager pitiless – most recently at *Alliance Francaise* – is instructive. The brother is a source of that bank of language.

But there's the night to think it through, to mull things over, in a strange house, in an unaccustomed part of London. A small accident occurs here, in Balham; but it's not significant. And, of course, he has a dream which makes him uneasy.

★ ★ ★

The next day the brother repeats the journey; gets the train from Balham to Morden and then the 93 bus to the hospice. It's the bus ride that disconcerts him today, as it moves out of the city, London being left behind again. St. Pancras, where he came in yesterday is already a distant place. Theatre-land with lights and crowds and buzz – the river. Arsenal – these have to be abandoned like tittle-tattle among the healthy; this is the suburb of a city in the process of disowning you.

Another thing – this is what happens when, despite yourself, the gloom sets in. Another thing: this 93 bus is going to North Cheam. Is this real? In the 1950s, on a Sunday afternoon, the brothers, back in Ladbroke Grove, would listen to *Hancock's Half Hour* on the radio, the references to East Cheam making the programme slightly amusing, as it was assumed East Cheam to be a made-up name. A no-place. And now, fifty years later, this 93 bus to the hospice is heading for North Cheam. There is a feeling of light mockery in the air. This seems the opposite of dignity that the clergyperson spoke about yesterday.

Talking of dignity: does the brother know where he is? (Kidnapped prisoners in shuttered rooms come to mind. The visiting brother has been reading Alan Johnston's book describing the experience of being abducted in Gaza.) The elder brother's road-map of London, so laboriously set out in fifty years, has been snatched away, crumpled and binned; he's set down in a foreign place with only churchpersons and Lodge-members for guide. Members of the family had inspected the hospice prior to the residence, but *he* would not have done so: do the family have the strength to creolize this new part of London? Yesterday, the nurse had asked if the patient had anything specific on his mind that he would like to discuss. Or any questions he wanted to ask; and he had apparently said no. Which was not surprising as there were about six people crowded in the room at the time. And an appropriate answer to that sort of question needed, if not to be scripted, if not some preparation, at least some privacy. (Though, it could be argued that he had had preparation: something the brother and the churchman had put a different construction on the day before, and then called a truce, shaking hands on it.)

So the visiting brother had made a halfhearted attempt, overnight, to 'script' some possible 'issues' on the patient's mind, if for nothing else, not to cede the terms of the 'debate' to others. This sadly had nothing to do with the patient.

So of the hundred or so things that seemed relevant last night to ask when someone next invited questions from the deathbed, he had mentally crossed them out by the morning, along with the old favourites like 'Why me?' He must get closer to the brother's temperament, to his spirit. What was 'bothering/puzzling/baffling' him might be nothing new or different: *What's a Black Hole? Is Saturn nearer to the earth than, say, Jupiter...?* Or, stepping out of that play, 'Will I now never get to do this thing that I've never spelt out, even to the most intimate among friends?'

Surely, there's a better thought forming as he lies there listening to the recording of a Cornish choir rendering what were said to be his favourite hymns, as he appears to sing along; and then accepts the prayer that visitors bring as a gift.

There is mild controversy in the holding space, the visitors anteroom, as a niece holds the hospital treatment of her uncle (not the hospice's) up for scrutiny. But other visitors preach acceptance. In the sickroom the church members, the Lodge members call both for a miracle, and for acceptance.

In truth, the patient *had* said something in answer to the nurse. He had always been polite. Also, not to answer would indicate that you were more ill than you would like others to realize. And what he said was interpreted by those who heard it, in ways to reassure themselves. So there was no point in the supplementary list of questions. Or, *was* there an urgent need for a supplementary list of questions?

The brother, who lived abroad, was conscious that he shouldn't muscle past the guard of others who were near at hand, in case his concern might seem proprietorial. Among other things he was late on the scene.

Family and friends fully understood that he had had a cold ('French Flu') – a cough and a cold – and it would have been thoughtless to come sooner and bring a cough and cold to the sickroom. But he is welcomed to the gathering, adopted, even, by more than one person, as someone who sounds like his brother, a form of welcome. He is mildly surprised at this, but not unhappy. Maybe, at an opportune moment, he might risk ventriloquizing the odd saying or two, *a la* brother.

In the anteroom the talk is of miracles, miracles symbolized by present company cheating death. Just about everyone, over a certain age, seems to have survived despite the logic of science and the prediction of doctors. So who knows? The visiting brother is both uncomfortable and reassured by this elastic stretch of the term 'miracle'.

On the phone, later, to a more secular friend, he is able to agree that someone dying in this undramatic way is, perhaps, not the worst. The melodrama of deaths on the TV., say, or in the theatre, invite the audience to pose more credible alternatives. The pornography of death (mass death) on the evening news, or that encountered, violently, alone, in the street from a thug with an attitude would rightly be the spur to rage and anger. So the tone of death in the hospice showing respect for the living as well as to the dying, is perhaps right.

★ ★ ★

ii: *The Life & the Art of it*

There has to be a personal note, between brother and brother, a special look, correctly interpreted. If not it would have to be invented. *I missed a few of your birthdays: do I make up for it now with a dozen birthday cards, all at once, in compensation? I imagine the Hospice festooned with gifts that the neglectful feel they can unload onto the sick. But that's to assume that acts of omission can be righted by a last-minute rush of contrition.* Like a deathbed confession of the not-yet dying.

MAKE ME WELL, *the note will say.*

He's ill, but he hasn't lost his mind; he knows I'm not a doctor.

The note slipped under the bed-sheet while no one is looking will say something else.

Neither brother is able to devise that text at the moment.

The visiting, younger brother, long thought to be ambitious, secretly feared for because of that ambition, always in need of a steadying hand, still needs what you might call parenting. His brother, in bed, prone, is trying to transmit some thoughts that might help. *I will soon vacate that place at the edge of the precipice that prevents you hurtling over. Think of your books toppling off the shelf, without a book-stop. I drive within the speed limits to prevent you crashing, or to minimize the effects of the crash. I know you understand me. I am from a small island and know the lack of hinterland and know that the border of the land is sea: you're no swimmer, where are your Olympic medals for swimming? … I taught you to swim, remember! And you didn't learn to swim; not in the sea; you feared the sea. You learnt to swim, much later, in a pool at the Swiss Cottage library: funny that a library should have a swimming-pool. None of us can explore land that isn't there. We are not God. None of us can swim seas that are built for boats, that are crossed by aircraft. And they crash. Boats sink and aeroplanes crash. Accept your limitations, my brother, and live within the resources of the family.*

Or – to use another analogy, as you would say: *That picture, that landscape that you paint, with the family, of the family at its most ambitious, of possible imagined families, it needs a frame. We are lost in the vastness of that landscape, we don't recognize it as our own. You must start reminding yourself now that there are limits to ambition. You must understand the foolishness of vanity; you must not fear death.*

The visiting brother is thinking: It may be time to swap cosmologies: If the Elder has pencilled in heaven and Hosannas; the Younger could offer a more earthly road-map. 'This is where I find myself today,' sort of thing; my compass, my point of orientation. Here is my *Atlantic Monthly*, there is *The Paris Review*; it's taken, I don't know how many journeys, to get here. Now I'm preparing to meet my *New Yorker*. Which journey will lead to a fool's paradise need not be openly discussed; the brothers will have communicated. Other things can be brought up to pass the time.

What other things might be discussed?

Their long residence in this country might be discussed; they are not *new* Londoners. Did you know, for instance that Bethnal Green railway station in the East End and Bethnal Green Underground are different stations, maybe ten minutes walk apart? Well, then, that wouldn't be in a book for visitors to London. Even the new Londoners, from Poland and elsewhere, wouldn't know that. The brothers have a lived life in London in common, even though one of them no longer lives there. They have close to a hundred years of *knowledge* of London-living, in common. *And we're not even taxi-drivers!* Add the rest of the family, and they go back into history; they have provenance. They are good wine.

But he won't pursue the conceit.

A picture of the family comes to mind. Literally, that picture of the family; now lost. One that the older brother claims not to know. In it the older brothers are wearing sharp suits. (They'd be about thirteen and fourteen.) White suits as for church. They are standing on either side of their mother, seated on a chair at the bottom of the front steps of the family home. The two younger children are in front. The mother is wearing a polka-dot dress, and has on her rings, her bracelet, her earrings, and a broach. Just a few months ago the not-yet-diagnosed brother contested this; thought it historically incorrect that the brothers would be wearing jackets at that age. The younger brother had the photo in his possession, courtesy of his mother. Twenty years ago he had given lectures on it, on its circumstances, in the highlands of New Guinea, largely to demonstrate to folk there, how this family, on the other side of the world, dressed in the mid-1940s. This part of the family history is stored in the younger brother's archive; the history doesn't seem worth arguing about.

★ ★ ★

iii: *Preparing for the Eulogy.*

Back home in Paris after the second trip to London in two weeks. (Eurostar is thriving at his expense.) Important to be grounded, to sleep in your own bed. It's Sunday. Back in London on Thursday for the funeral. Must write the Eulogy tomorrow and then check with people giving Tributes that there's no unnecessary doubling-up. There's a time-limit on the proceedings.

Up very early in the morning, Monday, knowing that something is required, but not yet ready to attack the Eulogy. Did the washing yesterday, went to the launderette; if not would have used this, today, as an acceptable displacement activity. So, better have some breakfast; it's still only seven o'clock.

The obvious thing is to start rearranging the library, the bookshelves. The library is not a fixed thing, the books have never been placed in alphabetical order; more in terms of *genre*. Poetry and France in the sitting room. Art, drama and short stories pride of place in the entrance passage, the wide corridor – along with biography and Africa. Everything else – the bulk of the library – in the bedroom. This is the Writer's Room, should *The Guardian* choose to call; the writing desk and computer and everything else effectively here where this writer lives.

So – at seven o'clock in the morning – books are being quietly pulled off shelves. Big art books taken down from a top shelf, making use of the stepladder, *l' escabeau* (masculine). They'll be put on a large bottom shelf below the short stories. He recently came across a man, a writer, who boasted about the number of short story collections on his shelf. Slightly depressed by this form of vulgarity he is seeking ways to limit his short story selection, not to get rid of the books, but to make them less visible, less *countable*. So he'll keep the four corridor shelves of short stories for quality collections, and stock the other stories elsewhere, in an old bookcase at the opposite end of the corridor. (That means displacing military history (mainly Napoleon) and language texts from that bookcase; these can go in the large overflow cupboard, to join books parked there four years ago. In the end – after two hours – the reassembled library gives one a feeling of – not quite lift, but – of resettling.

Books are possessions, of course, to be left behind, unless some university could be persuaded to take them. But this act of reshuffling makes them still seem like part of the living experience – you can't just reach for a book on the shelf knowing that it is always in the same place – and that makes them seem less crudely, possessions; trophies. (Of course there's the famous Foyles post card produced during the war, a huge pile of sandbags outside the store, being added to by a couple of middle-aged Foyles' workers. The caption: "Books made good filling for sandbags during the war. Meanwhile, up on the roof copies of *Mein Kampf* were protecting the building against German bombs." He'd settle for that image: an irony of books, both English and German.)

The Eulogy must strike a balance between respect for the memory of the dead and care for the feelings (and prejudices) of the living – each member of the family expecting a different emphasis.

There's also the thing of acknowledging the reality of the majority (the family, who are staunchly Christian, the Church, who gave impressive support, the Lodge – all the things inimical to the person giving the Eulogy. So, some balance must be struck there. *Must check on the real meaning of 'staunch'.*)

But, the thing must be done; and done today.

How trivial to think that a missed conversation with a brother is the old one of what to do with the books after you're gone. Not even rising to the interesting level of the debate now being conducted between librarians and the illiberal Right in America. The militants of the Patriot Act (passed after 9/11) against those representing the Office of Intellectual Freedom. The order sent out to librarians demanding what certain 'suspects' are reading; the Gagging Order on librarians accompanying this, is an issue this brother will have to shelve till he has occasion to talk to someone available about 'democracy'.

So, he will recall talk about libraries in the old way. The fact that universities don't want them. That the children (assuming you have children) don't want them. A pathetic display of human vanity would be burying them with you, Pharaoh-like, and have later generations – who can no longer be relied on to read – puzzling over the gesture.

★ ★ ★

iv: *Eulogy*

(Delivered at Upper Tooting Methodist Church,
Balham High Road, 13th. December, 2007)

'I have an image of one brother holding his brother's hand, as they crossed the road on their way to school. These are my brothers, Joe and Norman, nearly seventy years ago, in far away Aruba, where the parents lived for a time. The one who held the other's hand, who guided him safely across the road, was Joe – William, better known to some of you here as Bill.

It's true to say that a few days ago, in Paris, where I live, on my way over to London to give what support I could to the family, I

187

had a curious sensation of needing that guiding hand. As I went out of the front door, into the main street I had a strange feeling of being newly-exposed, of needing that protective hand that the loss of a brother had removed from us.

Joe-Bill... had always been that protective presence. It wasn't a smothering or oppressive kind of protection, it was one that you might expect of a caring parent; indeed, of an older brother; a big brother.

But we're here today – I remind myself – to celebrate the life of someone who was important to us – important in some of the ways I'll try to articulate.

While we acknowledge that all life is important, in all its forms, from the least evolved, to its most complex, which is, as far as we know, human, it's a special privilege to be able to celebrate the life of someone in whom those special human qualities of tolerance and gentleness, of selflessness and modesty, predominated – qualities that earned my brother the love and respect of family, of extended family, of friends and neighbours, of fellow members of the church and Lodge, of people at his various places of work, over the years – many of whom are happily (unhappily) here today. To the above qualities we must add a Sense of Duty.

For the record; and to remind us of the reality behind the sentiment: Joe was born, William Sylvester Gurney Markham on the 20th of June, 1932, in Harris' Montserrat, an outpost of the British Empire. His parents were Linda Anne Eliza Markham (nee Lee) and Alexander Sylvester Markham of Bethel, later to be a Very Reverend, in Canada. Joe was the eldest of four children, Norman, Julie and my humble self.

Joe attended the Montserrat Secondary School, and is still remembered by contemporaries as a fine Grammar School athlete. He came to England in 1954, at the age of 21; and, nine years later, in 1963 (the 2nd of May) married Lydia Humphrey, from a Montserrat family, like the Markhams, long prominent in the Methodist church. Lydia played the organ at church. (She had been a school teacher and also cashier in the Royal Bank of Canada, on the island.) Later in life, as a mature student in England, Joe attended the Open University, and gained himself a degree in Sociology.

Of the marriage it was said – with Lydia's facility at the organ, and with Joe's fine tenor singing voice – that there was every prospect of musical harmony in the new Markham household. Their daughter, Glenda Elise, born in 1964 (on the 2nd of May) has inherited something of her mother's musical gifts. Joe's earlier daughter, Gloria Miriam Herbert, has been a valued addition to the family.

But back to the text. Joe was, for me, something of a role-model, against which I measured some of the qualities that I personally lack. Modestly, he would emphasize my own achievements instead of his own, and never take credit for the part he played in them. Modestly, he was quick to accept his limitations, and not fret about disappointment. He was not self-obsessed; he was not a prima donna; he did not rail against destiny; he was of a most equable temper, of a mature wisdom. (It pains me to speak of him in the past tense.)

Resolute & Selfless: an interesting combination. As a boy, just out of his teens, Joe was dispatched on that long sea-voyage to England that some of us remember with unease: did the fact that his father, and before that, a cousin on his mother's side, Reggie Osborne, had volunteered to fight in Europe's two Great Wars in the first half of the last century, make the welcome in postwar England easier? Don't bet on it. Nevertheless, Joe succeeded in creating for us (with the help of his mother and his mother's family) the conditions where the family could resettle in a spirit of dignity, without ever having to accept the hosts' careless valuation of us.

My niece recently said to me – I have four nieces and they're all wonderful. I have a nephew, Jimmy, and he's wonderful: My niece, Gwen, has just played an important part in this celebration. Gwen strives hard to educate us into more healthy eating (and we try to do what Gwen says, because she's a solicitor by profession, and we can't afford litigation). My niece, Glenda, has been, as you would expect, her mother's support, at this time. My niece, Yvette, was being kind when she said she thought of me as a free spirit. It is an ambition, certainly. Yet, we know, don't we, that some spirits are allowed to be free only because others put in the work on their behalf. In contemplating the loss of something nebulous in our translation from Montserrat to England in the mid 1950s I later wrote a story entitled, 'Taking the Drawing-Room Through Customs', hoping to suggest that this family was part of the nuance and texture of sophisticated living, before England. That was the free spirit approach. Meanwhile, my brother Joe and his brother Norman, and my sister Julie – and, yes, my mother – played their part in establishing that physical space – that emotional hinterland – to make the *idea* of taking the drawing-room through customs real. Joe was instrumental in producing that labour, in the process putting his own ambitions on hold. For that, my brother, much thanks.

I underline his selflessness. To the end he refused to take credit for the lifeline that he threw to us all when we needed it. I mentioned his sense of Duty. This went beyond the familial to the civic. For decades he was a member of the TA (the Territorial Army.) He wished to play his part in the wider community.

I've mentioned his modesty. To the end he persisted in thinking that my going to university at the right time, with family support, was a more significant achievement than his own long-striven for, hard-fought-for, well-earned Open University degree when he was of more mature years. I wish more of us had had his modesty.

And he was tolerant. We had a different world view: well – *he lived in South London, innit; I lived for years north of the river.* But no, we had sometimes different views of how the world works; we had different views, even, of how life ends. While disagreeing he was always tolerant of mine. For that grace; for that lack of dogmatism, I thank you, my brother.

So this is a life that it honours me to celebrate; and though my brother left us in a frame of mind that was positive, I have to admit that one of our last conversations was bordering on the gloomy. It had to do with some young people not fully respecting themselves. Eleven young people in particular. They sometimes dress up in white clothing and take to a field and pretend to be West Indian cricketers. Need I say more? But the point I wish to make is this. Even then, with that extreme form of provocation, reducing the rest of us to anger and despair, my brother found it in his heart to be generous. No, he said to me, the boys should not be punished in the mediaeval ways I suggested, for dishonouring us; instead, they should be pitied. Even at that late stage in his life Joe found it in his heart to be generous.

So, I still see a man with his family, a man and his extended family; a man and his friends; a man and his church; a man whose life has made a difference; a man who urged us not to bear ill-will; an exemplary son brother husband father uncle, friend; a role-model that I, as a writer, would have invented if he hadn't existed. Joe-Bill – William Sylvester Gurney – will surely live on in our hearts as a good, as a very good thing; as a part of our lives that will endure. Amen.'

★ ★ ★

v

The crisp December day, sharp but bright, seemed right for the occasion. Thoughts about the statement being made, the responses provoked on this busy early afternoon as the too-smart cars nose their way through streets of shoppers who try not to stare, must be put aside. The packed church was an answer to your own private anxieties. The tributes told you things about your brother you didn't know, all of which gave greater social depth to his life than you knew. The Reverend's 'Address' was well-crafted, well-balanced and devoid of private coding. (Reverends work harder than you realize. The emotional range to the job must make it strangely-fulfilling; like being a nurse or a doctor; or maybe like the challenge of writing poems and stories for a living.) So why carp at the sentiments in some of the hymns, at the invitation to 'join our friends above'; at all this 'crossing' to … 'the heavenly land.' This is part of the ritual, the imagery, however unpalatable, of the brother's world; and in 'Amazing Grace', sung at the graveyard, the resonance of 'grace' serves, as ever, to free us from a too narrow interpretation of the lines.

Why is the cemetery so large, you ask – beautiful in its spaciousness; tasteful in its layout, tidy clusters of gravestones in white and black marble. A hint of something ethnic – the Jews to one side, the Poles over here. The Jewish dead in raised tombs. The brother's body placed in a spot that might make it hard, later, to find without help of the caretakers. (A clump of trees here, a low building a couple of hundred yards outside the fence, to the left: neighbours are SYDNEY J. WATSON & GLADYS WATSON.) The ritual seems at its most appropriate here, a large group of well-dressed people facing the direction of the coffin, people wrapped up against the cold, not minding the mud on best shoes, singing in memory, in respect, for someone soon to be buried. (A tiny flare of rage escapes at those brutes in power in countries all over the world, disposing of humans without ceremony and respect.)

★ ★ ★

vi: *Another Earth*

The hymns, the givers of tributes, the clergyperson all promise a place beyond this earth. A brother would certainly have bought this. And a response that is not self-centred needs to be found to engage with this.

So you start by saying that we are all reasonable people, not extremists, not fanatics, you can come to maybe a compromise, certainly an accommodation. Recently, listening to the radio, following the talks in Bali on climate change, a useful image cropped up. In order to dramatize the issue one delegate (from England) said that we were using up the world's resources with a wantonness and at a pace as if we had another 'two worlds' standing by to supply us when this one was depleted. A useful image.

The image of parallel worlds seemed altogether more *sane* than a world down here and another world *Up There*. That's where the brothers' cosmologies could meet. In a parallel earth. A parallel world. It's largely fanciful, and yet, the little we know of Astronomy doesn't rule it out. (*Star Wars* seems as interesting a point of reference, in this context, as a Bible or a Koran.)

Already there are worlds – constituencies – familiar to one brother that the other would know little about.

The worlds of church and Lodge on this side; the library added to on that side....

The Gospels taken literally on this side; the Gospels as imaginative literature on that side...

Charles Wesley, missing the poetry, and of the Methodist Hymnal *here*; Shakespeare, etc. and the aesthetic of language *there* (And remember, no heavy statements about religion in Shakespeare anywhere.)

London and Paris, two big cities in common. But London and Paris, worlds apart, etc.

And back to earth. South London, with its new mix of population – a babel of Eastern Europe and the Middle East – seems full of new possibility. That Italian restaurant on Balham High Road was excellent, the young waitress respectful of an older man. The Afghan minicab driver to St. Pancras knew the way. He probably knows already that Bethnal Green railway and underground stations are a little way apart, and no problem in getting you to either.

E.A. Markham
December 2007

ABOUT THE AUTHOR

Born in Harris, Montserrat, West Indies in 1939, E.A. (Archie) Markham's large, cultivated, extended family continues to provide him with much material for his fiction and poetry. He began a classical education at Montserrat's only grammar school, but left the island in his youth to complete his education in Britain, studying at the University of Wales, and at the Universities of East Anglia and London. Nevertheless, he has remained closely concerned with the fortunes of Montserrat, particularly after the devastating hurricane Hugo of 1989 and the volcanic eruption of a few years later that continues to threaten Montserrat's very existence as a society. With Howard Fergus he edited the book, *Hugo versus Montserrat* (1989) produced to raise money for the relief effort.

He has lived in the UK since 1956, though he is an inveterate traveller, living for extended periods in Germany and France (involved with a house-building co-operative) and for two years was a Media Co-ordinator in Papua New Guinea, an experience he records in *A Papua New Guinea Sojourn: More Pleasures of Exile*. Since 2005 Markham has lived in Paris.

He has worked in the theatre, in the media, as a university lecturer and is a literary editor. From 1970-71, he was director of the Caribbean Theatre Workshop in the Eastern Caribbean. He has been writer-in-residence at the Universities of Humberside and Ulster, has taught at the University of Newcastle and has been a Visiting Writing Fellow at Trinity College, Dublin, and, for fourteen years was Professor of Creative Writing at Sheffield Hallam University. He has edited *Artrage*, *Writing Ulster* and *Sheffield Thursday*, and two important collections of Caribbean writing, *Hinterland: Caribbean Poetry from the West Indies and Britain* (1989) and *The Penguin Book of Caribbean Short Stories* (1996).

His own poems first appeared in literary journals and pamphlets in the 1970s. During that period he began to experiment with various personae. He wrote as E.A. Markham, but also as Paul St. Vincent, who is given the biography of a St. Vincentian of working class origins, and an angry inner-city voice quite distinct from that of E.A. Markham. Paul St. Vincent even invented a further persona who speaks in his verse, the anti-hero Lambchops. Markham then went one further by publishing poems in the persona/voice of Sally Goodman, a young, feminist Welsh woman. Later, in his short stories and in his novel, *Marking Time* Markham creates a regular alter ego, the shrewd but comically bumbling figure of Pewter Stapleton. All this is evidence of Markham's refusal to be defined by the kind of stereotypes which he felt dominated too much of the discourse of the 1970s and 80s concerning Black writing in the UK. He has always demanded the freedom to go where he pleased. But it was also a profoundly Caribbean position: to play with masks, to engage in the trickster posture of Anancy, to speak with a voice in dialogue and contradiction with itself.

E.A. Markham
Marking Time
ISBN: 9781900715294; pp. 262; 1999; £8.99

Pewter Stapleton is drowning under a pile of marking. He teaches creative writing at a university in Sheffield, a campus peopled with malign cost-cutting accountants, baffled security staff and colleagues cloning themselves.

Pewter is a brilliant comic creation, an endless lister of tasks which are never quite completed, who is strung forever between seriousness and send-up, a commitment to his writing and boundless cynicism about writers and the arts industry. From his desk, the novel radiates backwards and forwards in time, to his childhood in the small volcanic Caribbean island of St. Caesare and memories of his headmaster, the libidinous Professeur Croissant and Horace his half-mad cousin, and to his relationships with Carrington, a highly successful Caribbean writer whose plays Pewter is editing, to Balham, a professional of the race industry (where Pewter is a self-admitted slow learner in blackness) and to Lee, the woman he loves, but who despairs of him as 'sporadic'.

Jim Hannan writes in *World Literature Today*: 'Markham demonstrates a laudable wider range of talents, and shows himself to possess an inquisitive, keenly perceptive, and jocular mind. *Marking Time* succeeds in part because of its broad perspective not only on Caribbean affairs but on contemporary English manners and society. Readers of this book will undoubtedly hope that Markham will publish another novel soon.'

Taking the Drawing Room Through Customs: Selected Stories 1972-2002
ISBN: 9781900715690; pp. 332; 2002; £9.99

Boyd Tonkin writes in *The Independent*:

'*Taking the Drawing Room Through Customs* collects 33 droll and charming stories written over the past two decades. Many of them feature Markham's celebrated alter ego 'Pewter Stapleton': a double who cunningly permits his creator to transform biographical experience into properly detached art...

Markham's deadpan wit and self-protective irony never desert him. He's never less than funny, and never less than moving. The English-speaking Caribbean has bred some wonderful wanderers from his generation, but none (certainly not Walcott or Naipaul) can boast a literary voice as wryly companionable as this. Read the poetry and prose back-to-back, and you'll feel you have made a friend: learned, intimate, sometimes angry at injustice, delighted by his wayward family amazed by how far this clan has come but always sensitive to 'that vague threat in the air' posed by racial bigotry, illness or misfortune.'

All Peepal Tree titles available from: peepaltreepress.com
or from 17, King's Avenue, Leeds LS6 1QS, UK